A HISTORY OF BRITAIN BEFORE 1066

VOLUME 1

The Roman Invasion
55 B.C.–410 A.D.

BRITANNIA

English Miles

■ Legionary Fortresses
□ Forts
◪ Forts certainly or probably established before A.D 110
◉ Large Towns
○ Small Towns (and modern names)

A HISTORY OF BRITAIN BEFORE 1066

VOLUME 1

The Roman Invasion
55 B.C.-410 A.D.

Charles Oman

LEONAUR

A HISTORY OF BRITAIN BEFORE 1066
VOLUME 1
The Roman Invasion 55 B.C.-410 A.D.
by Charles Oman

FIRST EDITION

Leonaur is an imprint of Oakpast Ltd

ISBN: 978-1-78282-962-1 (hardcover)
ISBN: 978-1-78282-963-8 (softcover)

http://www.leonaur.com

Publisher's Notes

Contents

CHAPTER 1

Prehistoric Britain

Geology is not history in any proper sense of the word, nor is prehistoric anthropology, though both of these sciences may prove useful handmaids to their greater sister. It is therefore unnecessary to follow the successive changes in the contour of North-Western Europe, or the character of its climate, and its fauna and flora, in the days when there was as yet nothing that could be called Britain. So long as the land of which some remnant now forms the British Isles was a part of a great European continent, not yet cut up by the existence of the North Sea or the Channel, we have no concern with it, or with its successive rises and fallings in level, or its alternations between a glacial and a tropical climate. They may be very interesting to the student of geology at large, but they are not British history.

Nor need much more attention be paid to these regions, which had not yet settled down into their final geographical shape, when the first faint traces of man begin to be found in them. For there seems to be in Britain a break between the days of the "Palaeolithic period" as it is called, when the first human beings, provided with nothing but the simplest stone implements, are found existing in this remote corner of North-Western Europe, and the more definitely known period of "Neolithic man that was to follow." (So Boyd Dawkins and Sir John Evans.) There were still no Straits of Dover when these earliest aborigines appeared, presumably drifting (like all their successors) in a westerly direction.

The greater part of the North Sea seems to have been a marshy plain, over which the Thames meandered to join the lower course of a greater Rhine, which discharged itself into the distant Arctic Ocean. The worst of the ice age—or rather of the ice ages—which had made North-Western Europe a desert, had passed away, and animals suited to a more temperate climate, the woolly rhinoceros, the hippopotamus, the mammoth, the grizzly and brown bear, the lion, and the hyena, were roaming over the land, when man first appeared as a hunting

7

and fishing savage. His rude weapons, of flint or other stone, have been found in river drift, or in the caves which were his habitual dwelling-places. He was certainly contemporary with all the formidable beasts mentioned above: apparently he even dared to contend with them, trusting to the cunning of his human brain—little developed though it may have been—and to the advantage which the hand that can wield a weapon has over the paw or the tusk of the animal.

Probably he acquired the art of making fire from the flints that were his favourite weapons, or from the friction of sticks, such as is still practised by savage tribes: he may have used it not only for cooking his food, but as a formidable weapon of offence or defence against the beasts with which he contended. He was not destitute, strange as it may appear, of artistic instincts; numerous carvings on bone found on the Continent, and a single solitary instance from Britain, show that it sometimes pleased him to make reproductions of the animals that surrounded him, from the mammoth that may have been the supreme terror of his life—though he perhaps plotted against it by pitfalls and suchlike devices—to the horse, which was still nothing more than an eligible source of food.

But between Palaeolithic man and his more advanced successors there seems to be, in Britain at least, a distinct break, corresponding to a contemporary change in the geological conditions of North-Western Europe. (Not, however, in France and other continental regions. See Rice Holmes, *Ancient Britain*.) The Channel had broken in between England and France, the North Sea had overflowed the plain of the lower Thames and the lower Rhine, seventeen of the forty-eight various species of mammals which were contemporary with Palaeolithic man had disappeared, when the later race came upon the scene; there is often a thick deposit, implying a gap of many centuries, between the strata in which the remains of the earliest aborigines are found and those in which the better-finished Neolithic tools and weapons occur.

Did the older race die out from some change of climatic conditions, or retire before them to more southern regions—or was there some cataclysmic disaster to account for their disappearance? Or did some of them survive to be conquered or exterminated by their successors? None can say; but whatever may have been the case farther south and east, there seem to be few or no remains that link Palaeolithic and Neolithic man in Britain.

The land had become an island, the greater part of the terrible beasts of old had disappeared, and conditions of climate and geography had apparently come to be not very different from what they are at present, when Neolithic man begins to be discernible. Whether the gap that divided him from those who went before is to be numbered by thousands of years, or was comparatively short, in would be dangerous to say. The evidence is as yet insufficient to enable us to speak with certainty. But since his first arrival there has been no cataclysmic break in the occupation of Britain, even though race after race may have pressed forward into its borders.

His occupation of the island must have lasted for many ages, since the first relics show tools not very much advanced beyond those of the Palaeolithic people, and imply a life of hunting and fishing under squalid conditions, while the later ones show something that might almost be called without exaggeration an early civilisation. Enough of bones and skeletons of this age have been found to prove that the Neolithic people were a race of moderate stature and slender proportions, with skulls that were markedly long in shape, whence they have often been called simply the Early Dolichocephalous people, in order to avoid the use of misleading national names.

The archaeologists who have called them "Iberians" seem to imply that they had some special connection with the well-known people of later Spain who bore that name. But all that it is safe to say is that they were kin to the similar races that occupied in the same age all the territory in the basin of the Mediterranean, of which Iberia is but a small part. Another name for this race that is often used is the "people of the Long Barrows," for, in contradistinction to their successors of the next age, their characteristic form of tomb was an oval mound, which sometimes did and sometimes did not include an elaborate central core of stones. (The Long Barrow, it must be remembered, is not the sole type. The Neolithic people, at least in their latest period, sometimes used a round barrow.)

The most typical form of their sepulchre was a "*dolmen*" or chamber of large stones set on their ends or their sides, and roofed in on top by other large stones placed horizontally, after which the whole was covered in by an immense heap of earth. There were, however, districts where large stones were not easily to be found, and where burial, for want of them, merely consisted in the placing of the body of the defunct under a long mound of earth. Where the stone sepulchre had been prepared in the normal fashion described above, it was sometimes single-chambered, but often consisted of a more or less complicated system of recesses or compartments, each containing its one or more corpses according to the needs of the family. In the earlier days of the Neolithic age simple inhumation seems to have been universally prevalent, but before it was over cremation had begun to be practised, though it would still seem to have been comparatively unusual.

Whether or no the change in the method of sepulchre had any relation to the changing conceptions entertained by man as to the fate of the soul after death, it would be profitless to inquire. Burning and burying were practised simultaneously and in the same districts, so that any generalisation is dangerous. There seems to be clear proof, from the bones found in certain barrows, that in some cases the slaves or concubines of a dead chief were slaughtered at his graveside, in order that their spirits might follow him and minister to him in another world. The same belief is indicated when we find animals buried at their master's side, or tools, weapons and drinking cups, broken or intact, left within his reach.

The Neolithic man was still a hunter and a fisher like his Palaeolithic predecessor, but he was also a herdsman. He had domesticated the dog, the ox, the sheep, and the hog, and lived largely on the produce of his folds and stalls, so that he was not dependent on the chances of the chase. He had an ample provision of pottery, though it was still extremely rude. His tools and weapons, however, were often elaborate, and sometimes shaped with an evident regard to ornament, though the material was only flint or other hard stone. But the practice of ages gave men marvellous skill in the trimming of the flint, or the cutting and polishing of the lump of rock, so that a wonderful symmetry was attained from very unpromising material.

Spear and arrow heads, scrapers, knives, and even saws were made, but the most typical instrument of the age was the Celt or stone hatchet, which could be used equally as a tool of carpentry or as a weapon of war. Bone, as in older days, supplied the rest of the instruments of mankind, and especially the needles which served to sew, with threads of fine sinew, the garments of skin which were the universal wear. Apparently weaving and the cultivation of cereals by agriculture were unknown; for vegetable food the Neolithic man evidently depended on the fruits, berries, and roots supplied to him by nature: in winter he must have fallen back almost entirely on to an animal diet.

At the very end of the Neolithic age a new race of invaders came upon the scene, intruding among the older people whose graves and tools are found everywhere, from Syria and North Africa to Scandinavia and the remotest British Islands, for even in the Shetlands Neolithic remains are found in profusion. The newcomers were two races of a new physical type, the Brachycephalous or round-headed peoples, who were about to introduce the bronze age, though the first few traces found of them in North-Western Europe show them armed with stone implements only. They were equally well distinguished from the tribes whose lands they invaded by the fact that they generally buried their dead in round, and not in long, barrows. Very soon after their first appearance they are found in possession of bronze tools and weapons, so that by the discovery of the use of metal the whole face of human life was changed.

The majority of the Brachycephalous invaders of Britain belonged to a race far larger and more powerful than the Neolithic men; their average height, as deduced from their skeletons, must have been as much as five feet eight inches. But in a few districts the first round-skulled immigrants seem to have been of a shorter type, not exceeding in stature the Dolichocephalous people whom they superseded. Whether by superior vigour or by reason of their knowledge of the use of metal, the Brachycephalous races evidently got the better of the older inhabitants: but that they did not wholly exterminate them, but retained many of them as serfs or tributaries, is shown by the fact that skulls of mixed type, evidently those of people in whom the blood of the long-headed and the short-headed races was mingled, are frequently to be found in interments of the bronze age.

In a few regions the elder people seem to have retained their independence for a considerable time. There is no reason to doubt that a strain derived from the Neolithic man not only diversified the race of the metal-users, but persisted on from these again to the later coming Celts, and from the Celts to the inhabitants of Britain in our own day. On the whole, however, it would be true to say that the Brachycephalous invaders absorbed the race that went before them.

The age of metal, in Britain at least, starts at once with the use of bronze, there being little or no trace that unmixed copper was used, before the method of hardening and alloying it with tin became known. This is not the case in certain other countries, and even in Ireland there is some trace of a copper age: but the copper of Britain was found where tin, its invaluable corrective, was also easily to be won.

Copper from the outcrops or boulders, found on the surface in many parts of Wales, could be mixed with the tin that came easily enough from very light working in Cornwall, so there was no need for any further importation from the Continent, from which (no doubt) the first bronze tools had been brought over. (But certain types of bronze implements continued to be imported nevertheless. See Rice Holmes.)

The general shape of these implements does not seem traceable to direct copying from the old flint implements which they superseded, but rather to have been thought out on new principles, which could only be used in melted metal, and would not have been possible with stone. These tools are very varied in size and design, and, in their later stages at least, very ornamental. It is curious to find that two classes of implements alone continued to be made from stone, when all the rest were now designed in metal. These were hammers, which very seldom occur in bronze, and arrow-heads, which (whether for war or for hunting) still continued to be made of flint, even by tribes whose other tools, even the smallest, were now of metal. Early bronze arrow-heads seem hardly to be known at all in Britain.

The brachycephalic people used other metals besides bronze, though this formed the main staple of their manufactures. They had gold, sometimes in considerable quantities, which was made into torques, bracelets, pins, breast ornaments, and other jewellery in great profusion. They had also lead, to be used for metal work that required neither a cutting edge nor a strong resisting power.

From the enormous number of camps of the Bronze Age found in Britain, it is clear that the tribes of that time were very small in numbers, and always were liable to plunge into internecine war with each other. Otherwise there would be no need for the tribal strongholds to be so numerous, and (for the most part) so small. Most of them are found enclosed by one or more concentric lines of ditch and palisade on isolated hills; but a few are constructed on the edge of the sea, or with their backs to a sheer precipice, so that only their front side required the artificial protection of a stone or earthen wall.

But, despite their wars, it is clear that the bronze-age folk were not so continually engaged in strife as to render commerce impossible. Many of their luxuries must have been brought from very far afield, such for example as the amber with which they decorated their persons; much of their pottery and metal utensils seems to have been introduced from Gaul and the Rhineland, and there is every reason to think that they may have communicated with Scandinavia also.

They were dispersed over the whole of the British Isles from Shetland to Cornwall, but the distribution of population was very different from that which obtained in later ages, since they seem to have sought not the most fertile ground but that which was most open and easy to clear. Hence they were found very thickly on poor soils, like the chalk downs of Wiltshire and the Wolds of Eastern Yorkshire, while in some of the richest river valleys there is little trace of them, since such tracts were originally covered by woods and morasses, into which they had no wish to break so long as more easily cleared ground was available.

But swamps were not always considered impracticable, as is shown by the interesting lake village on piles, belonging to the later Bronze Age, which was discovered half a generation ago in Holderness. This was a settlement very similar to the larger establishments which have often been found on the Swiss lakes, but by no means so rich as its continental prototypes. The larger and more interesting lake village near Glastonbury belonged to the iron age, and probably to the Celts.

The men of the Bronze Age not only possessed flocks and herds like their Neolithic predecessors, but cultivated the soil for several sorts of grain. Wheat was grown as far north as Yorkshire; other cereals were known all over Scotland. Weaving was also generally practised; spindle-whorls are among the commonest finds in sites of this age. Man was not, therefore, any longer dependent on skins alone for his clothing. Pottery was elaborate, highly decorated, and differentiated into many shapes, according to the purpose for which it was required. There seems even to have been a special manufacture for funeral purposes—many of the typical vessels which occur in graves being hardly found in any other conjunction.

The typical decoration was in stripes, chevrons, and angular geometrical figures, the curves which were to be the special mark of the iron age and the incoming Celt being not at all usual. Dwellings were usually round huts, which stood together in villages, but pit-dwellings were well known, and even caves seem occasionally still to have been inhabited. (The most fruitful excavation of bronze age objects in Britain was in a cave, that of Heathery Burn in the county of Durham.)

In the extreme north the curious subterranean chambered borrowings called "weems," which persisted into historic days, seem already to have been in existence, though they were still being used long after the Christian era began.

Cremation had already, as we have seen, begun to be practised in Neolithic times, and it grew steadily more usual as the Bronze Age wore on. In many districts it was universal. The custom was of course not calculated to preserve for the archaeologist of the future nearly so many relics as were left by the earlier practice of inhumation; it also rendered the calculations of anthropometry impossible, since burnt bodies cannot be measured. Thus, in some ways less is known of the physical type of the later Bronze Age men than of their Neolithic predecessors.

The most notable monuments of the period are its great circles of standing stones, of which Stonehenge is the best known, but not the largest, example. They are very widely spread, from the islands of the extreme north down to Cornwall. They are of various designs and sizes, some more and some less complicated, but they all seem to have been associated with burials. Some of them are the centimes of such immense numbers of " round-barrow" *tumuli*—there are three hundred close around Stonehenge—that it has been suggested that bodies or burnt bones were brought even from distant places, in order to be deposited in the neighbourhood of some spot considered sacred. The theory of the seventeenth and eighteenth century antiquarians that stone-circles were "Druidical Temples" has long been discredited; but some measure of truth may lie beneath it.

It is even possible that the enormous wrought-stone temple to Apollo in "the Hyperborean Island" mentioned by Hecataeus of Abdera, the Greek geographer, from whom we get one of our earliest notices of the extreme north, may refer to Stonehenge, or to the still larger, though not so elaborate, stone-circles of Avebury, not far from the better-known monument. The endeavour to work out Stonehenge and certain of the other circles as astronomical monuments, intended to point out the rising of the midsummer sun by their Orientation, need not, however, be taken seriously. (See Rice Holmes's *Ancient Britain*.)

Nor need any attention be attached to the various dates, 1680 B.C. or 1460 B.C., deduced by very hypothetical and dangerous astronomical calculations for the erection of these strange works. It is safer to hold with Dr. Arthur Evans that "Stonehenge was built comparatively late, that its connection with sun-worship, if any existed, was at most a secondary object in its structure," and "that it is one of the large series of primitive religious monuments that grew out of purely sepulchral architecture".

Its late date is proved by the facts that two ordinary barrows of the round type, such as are typical of the Bronze Age, are encroached upon and partly cut through by its containing rampart, and that chippings from the two sorts of stone employed for the structure, "sarsens" and "blue-stone," were found in one of the closely-neighbouring barrows along with bronze objects, a dagger and a pin; the debris of the stones therefore was being shovelled about by Bronze Age grave-diggers. But the most conclusive discovery was that of clear stains of bronze or copper on one of the great sarsen-stones, seven feet below the surface.

With the end of the Bronze Age we are at last approaching the commencement of true British History, which for us begins with the arrival of the Celts, the people who were found there by Pytheas of Massilia, the first visitor from the civilised, recordkeeping, peoples of the Mediterranean who wrote a full account of his travels in the extreme North-West. He was a contemporary of Alexander the Great, a man of the end of the fourth century before Christ. There is no reason whatever to doubt that, when he landed on the shores of what he called the "Pretanic Isle," the same people were in possession of it of whom Posidonius, five generations later, and Caesar, six generations later, have left us more elaborate accounts.

But it is a more difficult thing to settle how long before Pytheas the Celts had crossed the Channel and subdued the Bronze Age people, with whom they afterwards intermingled, much in the same way as the Bronze Age men had mixed their blood with that of the earlier Neolithic races. The Celts seem to represent for us the triumph of iron over bronze, and for North-Western and North-Central Europe that triumph seems to have taken place between 600 and 450 B.C., if deductions may be generalised from the great excavation at Hallstatt in the Tyrol, the only place in barbarian Europe where the transition from bronze to iron can be followed in detail It is not impossible that the first Celts may have come hither before the Bronze Age was over, but it is clear that the greater part of their invasions must have taken place after iron was thoroughly well known.

Roughly speaking, therefore, we should be inclined to place their appearance in Britain somewhere about 600, and to allow another couple of centuries, if that is not too much, for their establishment of a complete domination in the land. The invasion period may perhaps have fallen a little later, but at any rate it was well over before Pytheas landed on the coast of Cornwall, and circumnavigated the whole island, in the end of the fourth century. The mere fact that he gives a purely Celtic name to the land is conclusive, not to speak of other evidence to be deduced from the fragments of his work that survive.

CHAPTER 2

The Celts in Britain, Down to the Invasions of Julius Caesar (600?-55 B.C.)

The entire history of Europe, from days long before written history begins, is occupied with the southward and westward movements of a series of races who start from the unknown darkness of the North and East—from Scandinavia or Central Asia or regions yet more remote. These movements did not entirely come to an end till the tenth century of the Christian era, when the Magyars, the last to arrive of the nations of modern Europe, conquered their position on the Middle Danube. It would be wrong however, to count the still later establishment of the Ottoman Turks in the Balkan Peninsula as part of the same story of the "Folk Wanderings": it belongs to a different category of invasions.

The Celts in successive waves were moving westward when first we get a glimpse of them. Already in Herodotus' day (440-30 B.C.), they had got so far, that the "father of history" reckons them, with the Cynetes, as the farthest of mankind in the direction of the Atlantic. But the head of the column had reached the Western Sea, thrusting aside Ligurian and Iberian and many a primitive tribe more, long before the bulk of the army had reached its ultimate home. The main body of the Celts were not only in the Black Forest or the Alps, but far back by the Danube, or even farther off, when their forerunners were occupying Gaul and Spain and Britain.

Of the movements of their southern wing we have a fair, if intermittent, knowledge, because it came into collision with the literary peoples of the Mediterranean. It is clear that the main movement was *north* of the main chain of the Alps, because it was not from Dalmatia or Pannonia but from Gaul, and by way of the Western Alps, that the Celts, somewhere about the end of the sixth century swarmed down into the plain of the Po, and all Northern Italy, driving out the Etruscans who had previously occupied in force the modern Lombardy, and confining them to Etruria alone. (This statement would not be altogether admitted by all French scholars. See Rice Holmes's *Caesar in Gaul*, and Camille Jullian's, *Hist. de la Gaule*.)

★★★★★★

Roman tradition, as given by Livy, places the Gallic passing of the Alps in the time of the Tarquins, or a generation before the ending of the Roman Kingship in 510 B.C.—or whatever the

16

real date may be.

★★★★★★

At the same time, or a little earlier, they had pushed the Ligurians, who had shared with the Etruscans the control of the lands between the Rhone and the Mincio, into the Maritime Alps and the Provençal and Genoese Rivieras. The high-water mark of this southern line of Celtic invasion is, for us, the sack of Rome by the Gauls, in 387 according to the accepted chronology: but it must not be forgotten that their armies were seen in Central Italy for many generations later, indeed it was not till after the Battle of Telamon (225 B.C.) in the period between the two Punic wars, that the Gaulish danger may be counted to have wholly come to an end. Nor was it till Hannibal had been finally crushed, twenty years later, that the Romans made an end of the Celts of Italy as an independent power.

It was more than two centuries after the time when the South-Western wing of the Gauls entered Italy, and cut short the Etruscan power, that their South-Eastern wing, descending from the middle Danube, the land afterwards called Pannonia, overran Thrace and Macedonia in the days of the Diadochi, and pushed as far as Delphi and Thermopylae. A section of this same Gaulish swarm even crossed the Bosphorus into Asia Minor, set the whole of that peninsula aflame, and finally settled down as permanent inhabitants in the old Phrygian region around Ancyra, whose name was consequently changed to Galatia.

Pannonia was still half Celtic in the days of Julius Caesar and Augustus, and Celtic elements were to be traced among the peoples of the northern part of the Balkan peninsula down to the moment of its conquest by the Romans. The great tribe of the Boii, one section of which had occupied the lands between Po and Metaurus in the fourth century before Christ, had a greater establishment in the quadrangular plain of the Upper Elbe and Moldau, where the name of Bohemia still preserves their memory, though the German Marcomanni crushed them in the days of Augustus. Meanwhile the forefront of the southern Celtic column of advance had entered Spain, subdued much of it, and finally coalesced with some of the earlier inhabitants into the tribes that were known as Celtiberians.

All this is clear enough: the movement took place between the sixth and the third centuries before Christ, in lands that were within the ken of the Greek and the Italian; sometimes it actually penetrated into Greece and Italy. But at the same time a similar advance was tak-

17

ing place along a northern line of progress, in lands absolutely hidden by the mist of a past without records, such as Northern Germany, the Netherlands, and the British Isles. All that we can know of this advance is that it was in successive waves of tribe behind tribe, each impelling the other westward, while at the back of the whole Celtic flood there was another oncoming tide of nations, that of the Germans, who only reached the Rhine and the Alps at the end of the first century before Christ, when they forced themselves on the notice of the civilised world by their irruption into Celtic Gaul and the northern frontiers of the Roman Republic. But the Teutons and their kinsmen were still far out of sight when the Celts came to the Rhine and the British Channel.

There seems no reason to doubt that the three Celtic swarms which successively crossed into the islands of the remote North-West all came originally by the obvious route across the Netherlands and the narrow seas, between the mouths of the Rhine and the Seine on one side and Southampton Water and the Humber on the other. Legends that bring some of them from Spain to Ireland or South-West Britain, or which land others directly upon the north-east coast of Scotland are late and literary, not genuine survivals of the prehistoric memory of the tribe. Such long navigations seem incredible, when the passage from the Rhine mouth to the Thames, or from Picardy to Kent, is so easy and obvious.

Be this as it may, the three Celtic waves of population in the British Isles seem clearly marked by geographical position, by linguistic differences, and (in the end) by definite historical statements. The first wave must have been that of the various tribes whom historians have called the Goidels, the ancestors of the races which in the British Isles afterwards spoke the kindred dialects of Erse in Ireland, Gaelic in the Scottish Highlands, and Manx. On the Continent the descendants of the similar tribes were to be found among the Pictones and certain other septs of Western Gaul, whose tongue (from the small traces of it that survive) is held to have been very similar to that of the Goidels of the British Isles.

The second wave was that composed of the vast majority of the tribes of Central and Eastern Gaul, those whom Caesar calls the Celts proper; in Britain it was represented by the peoples who overran the central and western parts of the island, as far as the Firths of Forth and Clyde and the Irish Sea, from whose language descended the Welsh that is still spoken today, the Breton that still survives in the extreme west of France, and the now extinct tongue of the Cornish people. Lastly the third wave, which had only reached Britain in the second century before Christ, and probably about the middle of that century, was that of the Belgae, the race whom Caesar found in occupation of Northern Gaul and Belgium on the hither side of the Channel, and of South-Eastern Britain from Somersetshire to Kent, and as far north as the farther edge of the Valley of the Thames. We incline to place the commencement of the Celtic invasion of Britain about 600 B.C. or a little later, because the parallel irruption into the slightly more remote Italy is recorded to have begun about 540 B.C.

The language-division between the early coming Goidels and the later-coming Britons and Belgae has many marks, but the clearest of them is that which has caused the former to be known as the Q Celts and the latter as the P Celts. That is to say that whenever in Irish, Gaelic or Manx a Q sound is to be found, the corresponding word in Welsh, Breton or Cornish would be spelt with a P. Celtic philology is a mysterious science, because the written records from which it has to be deduced are extremely late.

Putting aside a few coins and inscriptions, they all belong to centuries long after the Christian era had begun. These coins and inscriptions, supplemented by a modicum of Celtic names and words preserved in classical authors, are all that we possess to enable us to deduce the early history of the language. Their evidence is so scanty, and so liable to diverse interpretations, that even to the present day the wildest divergencies of opinion prevail among linguistic specialists as to the early history of its various dialects. All will agree that Celtic is one of the great family of Aryan tongues, and that of all its sisters the one to which it has the greatest affinity is the Primitive Italian—from the Hellenic, German, or Slavonic groups it differs in a much greater degree.

But whether we are to consider that the Goidelic dialect of the Western Celts is nearer the original language of the whole race than is the "Brythonic" dialect of the later comers, or whether both are parallel developments of equal antiquity, who shall say, when the few skilled philologists who are entitled to an opinion differ hopelessly among themselves? The greatest continental Celtic scholar will have it that when the first invaders reached Britain the difference between Goidelic and Brythonic was not yet developed, so that it is an anachronism to call the early comers Goidels—though their descendants might correctly bear the name. The majority of authorities, on the other hand, see no reason to doubt that the tongues were thoroughly

19

disassociated before we can get the earliest glimpse of the tribes that used them.

The all-important point for the chronology of the successive Celtic invasions is that if we take the dialectic differences between the families who preferred the Q and those who preferred the P to have been in existence in the fourth century before Christ, then the Goidels had long been in Britain and the Brythons had already followed them to its southern parts, when Pytheas made his great voyage somewhere about the year For the Massiliot explorer calls the land "the Pretanic Isle," a form which shows that he got its name from P-using Brythons and not from Q-using Goidels, unless indeed he learned the name in Gaul, and not in Britain itself.

This all-important name, which has stuck to us to the present day, and has spread to so many Britains beyond the seas, simply means the land of the painted or tattooed men. In Irish, which preserves the Goidelic form of the word, these folks, the "Picts" of the Roman, the Pechts of the Anglo-Saxon, are called Cruithni or Cruthni. The archaic form, if writing had existed among the Celts six centuries before Christ, would have been Qurtani. The corresponding form used by the Brythonic "P Celts" would be Priten, or in later shape Pridein, Prydyn, or Pryden.

Since therefore Pytheas called the land that he visited the Pretanic and not the Kuertanic Isle, (Greek having no Q, he would have called it so, I suppose), he must have heard its name, when he visited its southern shores, from Brythonic and not from Goidelic inhabitants. The various spellings of the name which prevailed in later days, when B was substituted for P as the initial letter, has been attributed to a bad Latin pronunciation of the forms Pretanic, and Pretani, and Pretannia, which the Romans first heard from their allies the Greeks of Massilia a century after the time of Pytheas. (Though the change of a Greek n into a Latin B is to say the least unusual.)

This seems preferable to the other view which has been put forward by some Celtic scholars, to the effect that, entirely independent of the word Priten, the painted, there was another Celtic word Brittõnes (from an archaic form of the Welsh word Breithyn, cloth) meaning " the clothed people," which was applied to themselves by the inhabitants of the southern parts of the island to distinguish them from the more scantily garbed aborigines whom they had been driving out. This seems unlikely, considering that archaeological evidence seems to show that the Brachycephalous men of the round barrows, whom the Celts conquered, wore just as much clothing of both woven woollen material and of dressed skins as did their successors—so that the name would be entirely inappropriate.

The story therefore of the invasion of Britain by the Celts would seem to be that somewhere about the year 600 B.C. Goidelic tribes, the forerunners of the whole race, began to cross into the island, and to subdue or intermingle with the men of the short skulls and round barrows who had been dominant in the Bronze Age. The earlier people were mainly thrust North and West into the Scottish Highlands and Ireland, where they were ultimately followed by their conqueror's. But enough of them always remained, mingled among the Goidels, to influence the physical form and perhaps also the customs or even the language and religion of the victors.

Then, some considerable time after 600, but also some considerable time before 325 B.C., the second Celtic waves of Brythons crossed the Channel, and treated the Goidels just as the latter had treated the Brachycephalous races. This second invasion, which forced the Goidels into the North and West, completely swamped the last remains of the pre-Celtic population, who were absorbed by the tribes driven in upon, and over, them. The Brythons occupied the whole land from the Channel, as far as Forth and Clyde, absorbing, in their turn, so many of the Goidels as were not content to flee to Ireland, the Highlands, or the remoter isles of North and West.

Thus, in the Goidelic lands the governing classes would be Celtic, the servile classes largely non-Celtic, while in the Brythonic lands the dominant aristocracy would be Brythonic, the serfs Goidelic, with a surviving dash of blood from the earlier people whom the Goidels had subdued a couple of centuries before. Both Britain and Ireland, in short, would be Celtic lands, but in both there would be a percentage of the blood of the older non-Aryan aborigines. But this percentage would be much smaller in the South than in the North and West.

There is no clear proof that in any part of either island a non-Celtic speech survived a century or two after the Brythonic invasion, *e.g.,* in the time of Julius Caesar. The whole population of both islands may be treated as Celtic, though the proportion of non-Celtic blood in the remoter Goidelic districts may have been considerable.

The survival of this blood is marked by the existence of a dark-haired race of shorter stature among the conquering Celts who, as all authorities, both Roman and Greek, assure us, were a tall race with red or fair hair. That this was the characteristic appearance of the Celtic chiefs and their warriors cannot be doubted, but even before arriving in Britain both Goidels and Brythons may have already mixed their race somewhat on the continent, by conquering and absorbing other shorter and darker peoples, of race similar to that of their later victims in the island. In their progress by Danube and Rhine they must surely have picked up some serfs and dependants, or ever they crossed the Channel.

Be this as it may, the comparatively few remains of bodies of the Celtic period in Britain, the relics of the Iron Age men, are by no means all of the large stature that we should have expected, though they define themselves clearly enough from the skeletons of the Bronze Age, through the fact that their skulls are more or less dolichocephalous. It must be remembered, however, that the Celts were addicted to cremation, and that their kings and chiefs and warriors were very often burnt, so that there is small chance of systematically inspecting or measuring the bones of the ruling class. Still, the bodies discovered are often those of men of moderate stature, even those of persons who had been buried along with their chariots, and who must therefore have been of some importance. Yet the whole number discovered is so small, owing to the preference for cremation, that all inductions are dangerous.

The third Celtic wave of invasion in Britain was that of the Belgae, whose settlements, as Caesar informs us, took place only a comparatively short time before his own visits to Britain, perhaps as late as 180 or even 150 B.C. They were apparently akin to the Brython rather than the Goidel, (but see objections to this statement in E. B. Nicholson's *Celtic Studies*), but had evidently no mercy on their relatives, whom they conquered or drove northward or westward in the usual style. Caesar remarks that the Belgae beyond the Channel still showed their ancestry in his day by the fact that they preserved in Britain the tribal names which they had borne on the continent.

From this we may deduce that the Atrebates of Berkshire and Surrey, whose name is identical with that of the Atrebates of Artois, the Catuvellauni of Hertfordshire, Bedfordshire and Oxfordshire, whose fathers were the Catuvellauni or Catalauni of Chalons, as well as the confederacy of small communities in Hampshire, Wiltshire, and Somersetshire, who called themselves by the racial rather than tribal name of Belgae, were in Caesar's mind. But to the same Belgic race must also have belonged the tribes of Kent, who simply bore the local name of Cantii, taken from the word Caint, and also the men of Sussex (Regni)

22

and Essex (Trinovantes), for it is inconceivable that Belgae should have occupied the basin of the middle Thames and the whole of the downs of Hants and Wilts, unless they were already in possession of the estuary of the great river and the Kentish promontory, through which lay the easiest entry from their original continental seats.

These, to the best of our knowledge, were the Belgic tribes: beyond them to the North and West were their Brythonic kinsmen— the Eceni (or Iceni) in the eastern counties, (but some will have it that the Iceni were Belgic), the Durotriges and Dumnonii in the South-West (Dorset, Devon, and Cornwall), the Dobuni of the lower Severn Valley, the widely spread but apparently thinly scattered Coritani and Cornavii of the woodland district of the North Midlands, the Silurians, Demetae, and Ordovices of the modern Wales.

Then, from sea to sea, came the Brigantes, most numerous of all the Brythonic tribes, who held the six northern counties entire, save the district round the Humber-mouth belonging to the Parisii, and the part of Northumberland beyond the line of the later Roman Wall, where the Otadini dwelt. Lastly, in the Lowlands along the Solway and the Irish Sea were the Novantae and Selgovae. The second section of the Dumnonii, a name identical with the distant Cornish tribe of the South, lying northernmost of all the Brythons, on the spot where the island is narrowest, and the two firths of Clyde and Forth almost meet, ends the roll. Beyond them the Goidelic races began.

It has been sometimes alleged that several of this list of tribes were Goidelic, or had a preponderant Goidelic element in them, such as the Dumnonii of the extreme South-West, the Demetae and Silurians of South Wales, and the Novantae and Selgovae of the Lowlands. The evidence alleged for this statement seems insufficient, as it is all drawn from facts of too late a date, mainly inscriptions of Roman or post-Roman date found in the territories of some of these tribes. (Especially an Ogham inscription at Silchester, and three or four South Welsh tombstones of post-Roman date which show names of a Goidelic cast.)

Since it is acknowledged that there was in the fourth century after Christ, and later, a Goidelic immigration from Ireland into South Wales, and possibly into Devonshire also, any dialectic traces of that race in fifth or sixth century inscriptions may be ascribed to late-coming visitors, without it being necessary to suppose that the whole region was originally Goidelic.

The place-names of these districts which are to be found in Ptole-

23

my and other classical authors seem mainly Brythonic: the Celtic tongues which survived in them into post-Roman days was most certainly Brythonic, not Goidelic, *viz.*, Welsh and Cornish. So was the other dialect which was borne into Gaul in the fifth century by exiles from Britain, who carried with them not only the racial denomination of Bretons, but local names like Cornouailles and Domnonie, showing the exact district from which they had come.

The same seems the case in the western Lowlands of Scotland, where the tribes of historic days, with the exception of the intruding Picts of Galloway, were reckoned "Welsh," and not "Picts," by their Anglian neighbours, and were, according to their own legends, connected with kinsfolk to the south, in Wales proper, while they held the Goidels north of them, whether Picts or Scots, to be alien. Indeed, all that can be said in favour of the theory that the Dumnonians or the Silurians and other tribes along the western shore of Britain were Goidels, is that there probably was a larger proportion of men with Goidelic (and we must add pre-Goidelic) blood in their veins among the servile classes of this region, than there was among the other Brythonic peoples of Britain, and specially more than among the south-eastern tribes, which were not only Brythonic but Belgic, and had the least percentage of non-Celts in their ranks.

The survival of the pre-Celtic and pre-Aryan blood is marked by low stature and dark complexion, of which one or both may be found clearly prevalent in some parts of Brythonic South Wales and Damnonia, no less than in many districts of the Goidelic Scottish Highlands, where the typical conquering Celt, the tall red-haired man described by the classical authors, is less numerous than the small black-haired man. But there is no reason to suppose that anywhere in Britain did the pre-Celtic population maintain itself independent, or succeed in swamping and denationalising its conquerors. The Goidel-Picts, Caledonians, or whatever we choose to call them, are to be reckoned predominantly Celtic like their southern neighbours, though the predominance of the Celtic element in their blood was less marked than among the Brythons and Belgae.

Pytheas, whom we already have had occasion to mention so often, gives us the first definite literary picture of Britain, though he does not help us, except indirectly, with its ethnology: probably one sort of Celt seemed to him much the same as another. He was a younger contemporary of Aristotle, and his journals are said to have been published after the death of that philosopher, so that no information from them got into the encyclopaedic works of the greater man. He was a professional explorer, mathematician and astronomer, who was employed by the government of Massilia, or perhaps by a syndicate of Massiliot merchants, to head an expedition into the Atlantic waters, in order to see whether anything could be done in the way of developing trade in that direction, where only the Phoenicians of Carthage had yet ventured to advance.

But being a scientist by nature, and a commercial explorer only by force of circumstances, he evidently put more of geography than of trade information into his works. Perhaps his employers directed him to keep the practical information for traders dark, that they might have the monopoly of it, while permitting him to say as much as he pleased about tides, climate, solar equinoxes, longitude and latitude and such like things. It is sad that Pytheas's work (or two works) has perished, and is only known to us by copious extracts in Polybius, Strabo, Diodorus Siculus, Pliny, and other later writers, of whom Strabo and Polybius were bitterly hostile to the earlier geographer, and mentioned him in a carping way, disputing many of his statements which there is no real need to reject.

Pytheas sailed through the Straits of Gibraltar and up the coast of Spain, being fortunate enough to escape the notice of the Carthaginians, who would have stopped his voyage if they had been able. He then felt his way all along the Bay of Biscay to Corbilo, a great port at the mouth of the Loire, where in this age the British tin was wont to come ashore, in order to be taken overland all over Gaul and as far as Marseilles. He next rounded Cape Ushant, where he reports the existence of the Osismii, the same tribe who were there three hundred years later, in Caesar's day. From Uxisama, as he calls this cape, he struck across the mouth of the Channel, and in one day's sail reached Belerium, the Cornish Land's End, where he found the people comparatively civilised and ready to trade for their tin.

He then pushed right along the south coast of Britain to Cantium, or Kent, for a distance which he calculated at 833 miles, the voyage not being very much more than half that number of miles in reality. But calculations made (like those of Herodotus in an earlier day) by the day's journey of a ship, are notoriously untrustworthy. In Kent and the neighbouring regions, he noticed that corn was produced in abundance, but that owing to the damp and gloomy climate it could not be thrashed on open floors, as in the Mediterranean lands, but had to be dealt with in covered barns.

Wheat was common in the South, but the more northern tribes had to be content with oats, which suited better their still more inclement climate. The national drink was a sort of beer, or rather mead, prepared from grain fermented with honey: this remained the favourite beverage of the Celts right down into the post-Christian Middle Ages. He reports that the tides were portentous, as indeed they must have appeared to a navigator from the tideless Mediterranean, but states their maximum at eighty cubits, which exceeds by the proportion of two to one even the bore of the Bristol Channel, the greatest tidal wave of the British Isles.

After visiting Kent, Pytheas went into the North Sea, in search of the sources of the amber trade: for amber was much esteemed by the Greeks, who had, however, been compelled to depend for it on overland trade from the Baltic through Central Europe. How far in this region the explorer made his way is difficult to determine, it is pretty certain, however, that he did not round Denmark, or get to the real amber-coast of Pomerania and Prussia, though he reached the district east of the Helder, where tide-washed amber is thrown ashore, then inhabited by the "Ostiones" and Cimbri.

Apparently, he returned round the north of Britain, where he gives curious notes about Thule, which he calls a great island under the Arctic Circle and near the Frozen Ocean, six days' voyage from the northernmost of the British Isles. In the last point that he visited himself, the Shetlands probably, the shortest midsummer night was only four or five hours long, but farther off, in Thule, there was no night at midsummer, and no day at midwinter. This would seem to show that Thule must be Norway, wrongly conceived of as an island, where the midnight sun is a reality which could not fail to strike any observer. There seems no reason to think that Pytheas visited Thule himself; he had to rely on reports from Britons who had been in more or less direct touch with the inhabitants of Scandinavia, where (as we have already mentioned) there was a well-developed Bronze Age, and considerable trade, long before the Celts came to Britain.

Finally, Pytheas came back to the Channel, apparently without having seen Ireland. For this the carping Strabo calls his veracity into account, saying that, if he had really rounded the extremity of Britain, he must have been close to Ireland, which Strabo wrongly conceived to be north of Cape Wrath, instead of west of Galloway and Wales. He finally concluded his voyage by going overland from Gaul to Marseilles, probably from Corbilo. Presumably his report must have been that the sea-voyage to the extreme North-West was so long that it had no preference for practical purposes over the land route across Gaul, which the Massiliots were already wont to use for their tin trade.

Poseidonius, more than year's after Pytheas, gives us much more information about that trade: we have from him a long account of the region of "Belerium," of the working of the tin in superficial veins near the surface and from streams, how it was cast into ingots of astragalus shape, of which two were the proper load for a beast of burden, and taken by the natives to the island of Ictis, where they sold it to merchants, who carried it to Gaul, and sent it overland on pack horses to Marseilles and the mouths of the Rhone.

★★★★★★

It is curious to note that an ingot of astragalus shape, fitted with straps for carrying it, was the coin-type of the remote Illyrian mining town of Damasstium. No doubt the form was convenient for transport, as the splaying out at the corners prevented the straps from slipping.

★★★★★★

This Ictis, which is described as an isle at high water and a peninsula at low water, must evidently be St. Michael's Mount, the only place in the tin-producing district which answers the description. It is useless to think of the Isle of Wight (Vectis), for not only is there no certainty that in historical days this island was connected with Hampshire at low tide, but also it is absurd to suppose that the Cornish tribes, well provided with harbours, would have sent their tin two hundred miles eastward to be shipped.

The best proof of the mercantile habits of the Celts of Southern Britain is that they adopted a coinage at least one hundred and fifty, and more probably two hundred, years before the Christian era. Their earliest coins are of gold—silver, bronze, and tin were not coined till much later—and are copied in a barbarous fashion from the well-known gold *staters* of Philip of Macedon, the first gold coinage which spread far into Europe. Since the money of the Southern Gauls and the Celtiberians imitated not this model but the coins of Marseilles and the other Greek colonies of the shore of the Gulf of Lyons, or else the *denarii* of the later Roman Republic, it is clear that the Britons must have got the originals which they imitated from another direction, and this direction was undoubtedly the course of the Rhine and Danube.

Imitations of the money of the Macedonian kings, Philip, Alexander, and Lysimachus, were common among the barbarians of Thrace and Pannonia, and it must have been from thence that the models of the first British coinage came. When it is remembered that in the early years of the third century the south-eastern wing of the Celtic race was occupying the middle Danube, and devastating Macedon and Greece, we can easily see how the gold *stater* of Philip made its way in such quantities to their kinsmen of the North-West, that it became the most convenient unit of value for them to copy.

It must have taken some generations, however, for the Philippic *staters* to travel to Britain, as is shown by the fact that even the earliest of them are from fifteen to twenty grains less in weight than the original Macedonian coin.

The first British pieces show a clear imitation of the head of Apollo, and the chariot and driver, which formed the types of King Philip, but in the course of ages the copy became more and more barbarous, till of the face on the obverse only the laurel-wreath and some meaningless lines survived, while of the chariot only one horse remained: the charioteer and his vehicle had become a hopeless confusion of dots and curves. By Caesar's time this typical British degeneration of the Macedonian type had become more or less fixed, with varieties of execution between the money of different tribes. Soon after his day inscriptions giving the names of kings begin to appear, and a whole new series of types, borrowed from the Roman contemporary coinage, was introduced into the island in rapid succession. Of these pieces and the valuable historic evidence to be deduced from them we shall have more to say in the proper place.

As might have been expected from a people advanced enough to adopt a coinage, the Celts of Britain had attained to a very considerable degree of culture and civilisation. Their bronze, iron, and gold work was extremely artistic, in a style differing widely from that of their predecessors of the Bronze Age. (Gold ornaments of the early Iron Age are, however, rare both in Gaul and Britain.) While chevrons and other geometrical patterns, chiefly of straight lines, were the main types of decoration alike of pottery and of metal-work in the earlier time, Celtic art was distinguished by its preference for graceful curves, and for patterns derived more or less closely from foliage.

Animal subjects were not unknown, though less common, but scroll work inspired by vegetable forms was the typical ornament. Circles filled up with smaller curved designs, and branching out into meandering patterns of all kinds, were also frequent. The whole effect was usually very artistic. Enamelling with red inlay was frequently used in metal work, and studs of coral and other bright-coloured material were used to diversify the surface both of small decorative ornaments and of larger objects, such as shields or helmets.

Yet primitive barbarism lingered; the practice of tattooing was almost universally prevalent in Britain, as Caesar had occasion to remark; it survived among the remoter Goidelic tribes for centuries after the first Roman invasion, and so caused the Romans to call them the *"Picti,"* in contradistinction to the conquered Britons, who had dropped the custom when they were taken into the pale of the general civilisation of the Roman world.

A more horrid mark of barbarism was the survival of human sacrifices, which (as we have already seen) had certainly been practised by the remote forerunners of the Celt. The custom was to immolate victims to the gods, or to the shades of the dead, by burning them alive in large wicker cages or frames, sometimes apparently as part of funeral ceremonies, sometimes as thank-offerings in the day of victory, or as propitiatory offerings in the day of distress.

★★★★★★

Boadicea in her day of victory over the Romans is recorded to have offered many human sacrifices to Andate, the goddess of victory in battle, with horrible details of torture. See Dio Cassius, epitomised by Xiphilinus, lxii. §4.

★★★★★★

This brings us to the religion of the Celts, and to their famous priesthood, the Druids, whose central focus of power is said by Caesar to have been established in Britain. The Celts were polytheists of the usual Aryan type, with a pantheon which seems to have differed much between tribe and tribe. This was the case with many another Aryan race—with the Greeks, for example, till the day when Homer and Hesiod popularised the system which was afterwards generally accepted, "and made regular the attributes and functions of the various divinities," as Herodotus remarks.

This much is clear, that some of the deities most worshipped by the Celts of Gaul cannot be traced in Britain, while many gods made known to us by British inscriptions cannot be traced in Gaul. Caesar says that the Celts specially honoured a divinity whom he identified with the Roman Mercury, the inventor of arts, as well as Mars, Apollo, Minerva, and Dis Pater, the god of the shades, from whom, according to their Druids, they themselves were descended.

It is not exactly easy to reconcile this short notice with the glimpses that we get of British deities from the dedications made to them in Roman times, or the scanty hints that can be gathered from early Celtic tradition preserved into Christian times. The British provincials, after the Roman conquest, behaved like most other barbarian subjects of the empire, and roughly identified their own local gods with members of the Olympian family worshipped by their conquerors. The most frequent of all such dedications are those of altars to a war-god, whose usual names or epithets were Belutucadras, Camulus, or Coccidius, and who was equated with the Roman Mars. Then comes Sulis, a goddess to whom the medicinal waters of Bath were sacred: she was usually, we know not why, identified with Minerva.

The Apollo of Caesar seems in Britain to be represented by Mabon, a young god who was connected with the sun, or perhaps was actually the sun. Dedications to Mercury, who, according to Caesar, was so prominent in the Gallic pantheon, are not at all common in Britain, nor can we even be sure of his local name—possibly he was the Lug who in Irish mythology was the patron of smithcraft, music, and poetry, and whose name seems to be compounded in some British local and personal names, such as Luguvallium (Carlisle) and Lugotorix.

We see no signs of his having been one of the greatest gods on this side of the water, whatever may have been the case beyond the Channel, Jupiter, on the other hand, was very largely worshipped in Roman Britain, but apparently he was the Roman Jove, "*Optimus Maximus*"; only one inscription among many scores in Britain equates him with the Celtic Tanarus, a thunder-god who was well known in Gaul.

But there seems to be connection in ideas between the two deities by means of the thunder alone—Tanarus does not appear to have been the king and father of the gods, like Jupiter. There was another British deity whose altars have been found without any classical name added to his Celtic title, Nodons or Nudens, whose temple overlooked the Severn Estuary near Lydney. He seems to have been the lord of the sea or the abyss, something between Neptune and Jupiter. To the proper god of the lower world, whom Caesar calls Dis Pater, and for whom, according to him, the Gauls had much reverence, there are only two doubtful allusions in the epigraphy of Celtic Britain, epitaphs in which Dis is mentioned in such purely classical connection that we feel no certainty that the erector of the monument was thinking of the native god at all.

Many other deities are known to us by name alone, such as Andate

(Andaste), of whom we know no more than that she was identified with Bellona or Victory, and was a war-goddess. (Is this a misreading in Dio Cassius for Ancaste, a goddess to whom an altar was discovered at Bitterne near Southampton; C. I. L., vii. 4?) In many parts of the country the local deities of rivers, springs, and forests were worshipped—we know that this was the case with the goddesses of the Dee and the Mersey (Deva and Belisama), and of the spring on the Northumbrian wall called, after the nymph, Coventina.

All the knowledge that we possess of the British gods, as will be obvious, is woefully lacking in precision but it may be pleaded that the actual beliefs of the Britons were equally vague, and that the character of the deities varied indefinitely from tribe to tribe. It is more important, perhaps, to know of their curious and well-organised priesthood than of themselves. Among the Celts, says Caesar:

> There are only two classes which are held in consideration and honour, the Knights (*equites*) and the Druids. The latter are concerned with all things divine, manage the public and private sacrifices, and interpret sacred omens and religious scruples. Great throngs of young men come to them to be trained, and they are held in much awe by their pupils. For they make decisions on almost all disputes, both private and public, and if a crime is committed, a murder, or if a lawsuit arises concerning heritages or disputed boundaries, it is they who give the judgment. They name the compensation or assess the penalty: and if any private person, or even any community, will not accept their award, they interdict them from taking part in the sacrifices.
>
> This is the heaviest punishment that they can impose. Persons thus placed under interdict are held impious and accursed, men quit their company and avoid meeting them or speaking to them, lest they may come to harm from the contagion of the wicked; nor can the excommunicated plead in any lawsuit, or share in any public office. All the Druids are under one arch-priest, who has the highest authority among them. When he dies the man of most dignity among the rest succeeds him: if several seem of equal worthiness the dispute is settled either by the votes of the whole Druidical body, or (not infrequently) by force of arms. At a certain season of the year they hold a solemn synod at a consecrated place in the land of the Carnutes (about

31

Dreux) which is held to be the middle spot of Gaul. Hither come from every side all who have controversies, and submit them to the decrees and judgment of the Druids.

The system was invented in Britain, and from thence brought over to Gaul, as is generally believed; and even still those who wish to get the deepest possible knowledge of the Druidical training go to Britain to seek it. The Druids are free of military duties, and pay no taxes, having immunity from all service both in war and elsewhere. Attracted by these privileges, many young men come of their own accord to be trained by them, and many are sent by their parents and relatives. They are said to learn by heart enormous quantities of sacred poetry: some spend as much as twenty years in this training. None of their lore is permitted to be put down in writing, though in other matters public and private the Gauls are accustomed to use the Greek script.

This prohibition seems to me to have two causes—first that the Druids do not wish their knowledge to be published to the common herd, and second that they imagine that those who trust to writing pay less attention to memory—as indeed may commonly be seen—so that, when they have got a thing committed to paper, they neglect the practice of learning by heart, and allow their memories to grow slack. The chief doctrine of the Druids is that the soul does not perish, but at death passes from one body to another, and this belief they consider a great incentive to courage, since the fear of annihilation may be put aside.

★★★★★★

Note: Two interpretations of this statement are possible: the one that the Gauls held the Pythagorean belief that the immortal soul went round many bodies—perhaps of beasts as well as of men, if there is an echo of Druidism in the strange passage concerning the transmigration of the soul of Taliessin in the early Welsh poem. The other is not that the soul of the dead man went into the body of some other person, but that it acquired a new spiritual body, in that land of happiness beyond the Western Ocean (Tier-nan-Oge in the Irish tradition) in which the Celts seem generally to have believed. The latter interpretation seems more likely.

★★★★★★

They hold many discussions concerning the stars and their movements, about the size of the world and the universe, about nature, and about the power and attributes of the immortal gods.... The whole nation of the Gauls is much given to superstition, for which reason those who are afflicted by a dangerous disease, and those who are involved in wars and dangers, either make human sacrifices, or vow that they will do so, and use the Druids as their agents at these ceremonies; for they think that the divine power cannot be conciliated unless a human life is paid for by a human life. They have public sacrifices ordained in this same fashion.

Some tribes make great images, whose limbs, woven of wickerwork, they cram with live human victims, and then place fire below and slay them by the flames. They consider that thieves and highwaymen and other criminals are the sacrifices most pleasing to the gods; but when the supply of such victims has failed, they have been known to lay hands even on wholly innocent persons. . . . The Germans are entirely different from the Gauls in these customs. For they neither have any Druids to take charge of their religious business, nor do they pay any attention to sacrifice.

From other authorities than Caesar we add to our knowledge concerning the Druids the fact that they were given to augury and to the choosing of lucky and unlucky days—a Gaulish bronze calendar of this sort has actually been found. (At Coligny in the Department of the Ain, but made after the Roman Conquest, probably in the time of Augustus. See Sir John Rhys, *Celtas and Galli*, i.) Also that they reverenced the mistletoe growing upon the oak (not a very common vegetable combination), and that when it was found, the chief Druid would sacrifice a white bull below the tree, before he ascended to cut the mistletoe with a golden sickle. (Pliny Senior, *Natural History*.) Apparently the bush was considered mysterious and divine because of its obscure origin and growth.

What are we to make of Caesar's surprising statement that the Druidical lore had its origin in Britain, and that the deepest knowledge of it was in his day possessed by those who dwelt in the island? Some modern historians have argued that if there was anything specially strong and peculiar in the religious organisation of the British Celts, as compared with that of their Continental kinsmen, it must have owed its source to that racial element which was stronger among the insular people than among the Gauls. They explain that this element is the infusion of pre-Celtic blood, and with to regard the Druids as survivors of the medicine men or wizards of the Bronze Age people, (perhaps even of the Neolithic people, see Rice Holmes's *Ancient Britain*), who had somehow contrived not only to continue their existence but to impose their power on the conquerors.

This is not absolutely impossible: the sacerdotal caste of conquered races has sometimes obtained an influence over their victors, like the Canaanite priests of Baal among the Jews, or—a more striking instance—the Christian priesthood who tamed the Frank, Goth, and Burgundian in the fifth century of our own era. It may also be conceded that the Druids, as remembered in Irish and Welsh traditions of post-Christian date, are often represented as *magi* wonder-working wizards, who used marvels against St. Patrick and his followers, as Jannes and Jambres did against Moses.

Nevertheless we have no sufficient evidence to link the Druids with the pre-Celtic element in the population of Britain, and certainly the classical authors who touch upon the subject were convinced that Druidism was a typically Celtic institution, that it prevailed everywhere from the Rhine and the Garonne to the farthest coast of Britain. Some of them thought that the conception of the transmigration of souls, which evidently formed an important part of the Druidical teaching, had been learnt first by the Gauls of the South from Pythagorean philosophers, with whom they had come into contact at Massilia or some other Greek colony of the West.

Possibly Caesar argued wrongly that Druidism originated in Britain, merely because he saw that in his own day it was more severely dominant in the Island than on the Continent, whereas the fact may have been merely that the Celts of Britain had been less influenced by external influences—Roman, Greek, or German, or Ligurian—than their continental kinsmen, and so may have preserved in a more intact shape a religion that had been somewhat modified in the South. How dangerous it would be to argue that the place where any lore is most thoroughly studied at a certain time is the place where it originated, may be exemplified by an instance taken from an age seven centuries after Caesar's time.

If a Chinese or an Arabian traveller or statesman had visited Western Europe anywhere between 650 and 7.50, he would have found Ireland the centre of Christian learning, and its monasteries frequented by Frankish and English novices; it would have been easy to deduce that Christian lore must have had its origin there.

In Tacitus's time the island of Mona (Anglesey) was the religious centre of British Druidism; whether this had always been the case, or whether the cult had shifted its centre westward because of the oncoming Roman invasion, no man can say. But clearly Britain must always have had some central focus, corresponding to that for Gaul which Caesar noted as existing in the territory of the Carnutes. Very possibly it may have been among the prehistoric monuments of Salisbury Plain.

If arguments may be drawn from one branch of human activity to another, it is certainly probable that British Druidism may represent a survival of an original Celtic institution rather than a new discovery. Caesar notes that the Britons were a stage behind their continental kinsmen in general development, with the exception of the newly arrived Belgic tribes on the south coast, who differed little from their neighbours beyond the Dover Straits. The difference was specially marked in military usages; while the continental Gauls had entirely abandoned the use of the war-chariot, it survived everywhere in Britain. The Romans of the third century before Christ had been well acquainted with the cars of the Gaulish chiefs, and triumphal monuments still recalled their shape.

But since the days of Bituitus and Viridomarus the Gauls had abandoned the device, probably (as has been remarked) because they became acquainted with better breeds of horses in the South. In the northern island, where the undersized Celtic pony was still prevalent, the chariot remained, because the horses available were not fit to carry the fully armed warrior with ease. Even among the newly arrived Belgae chariots were still employed, and Caesar found that the flower of the host of Britain came out to battle like the chiefs who fought before Troy. Their tactics we shall have to describe when we are dealing with the campaigns of the first Roman invader.

This survival of primitive customs in Britain remains all the more striking because we know that the intercourse between the continental and the insular Celts was close and continuous. As we shall have occasion to note, when dealing with Britain at the time of Caesar's invasion, the two were so closely connected that the great pro-consul found the attack upon Britain a necessary corollary to the attack upon Gaul.

CHAPTER 3
Caesar in Britain (B.C. 56-54)

A very cursory exploration of Caesar's account of his earlier Gallic campaigns suffices to show the close connection of the Britons of the South and their relatives beyond the Straits of Dover—a connection that was both political, commercial and religious. Within human memory Divitiacus, King of the Suessiones, and for a time suzerain over most of the continental Belgians—had extended his power over some of the British states. (Caesar, *B. G.*, ii.) This empire, like all Gaulish hegemonies, had been short and fleeting. But there were still close personal connections between the Island and the Continent. Commius, whom Caesar had made king of the Atrebates, the tribe between Somme and Lys, had great authority, as we are assured, in certain British regions—presumably among others in that occupied by the insular Atrebates along the south bank of the middle Thames.

★★★★★★

Caesar, *B. G.* iv. It would be invaluable to us to know whether other tribes kept up the same touch as the Atrebates: *e.g.*, were the Menapii of South-Eastern Ireland (a Belgic colony sent out to Wexford by the Menapii of Picardy), in similar correspondence with the mother state: or the Parish of the Humber with the older Parish of the Seine, from whom we cannot doubt that they originally came? Unfortunately, surmise is all that is left to us: no evidence is forthcoming.

★★★★★★

Gaulish exiles, who had made their own countryside too hot for them, were wont to take refuge in Britain. (Caesar, *B. G.* ii.) British adventurers used to cross over in a similar fashion to Gaul: Caesar remarks that in nearly every Gallic campaign he had found Britons fighting among the ranks of his Celtic enemies. (Caesar, *B. G.* iv.) How close was the religious tie between the continental and the insular Celts, we have already seen, when dealing with the vexed question of the Druids. Gallic merchants and shipmen were well acquainted with the southern coast of Britain, and we can hardly doubt that Britain, too, had its seafarers, who were equally conversant with the shores of Northern Gaul.

Yet though in Caesar's war against the Veneti in 56 B.C. that tribe is said to have sent for aid from Britain, we cannot believe that the Britons had any fighting ships to lend: the succour must have been given in men. This Venetian war, however, had, if we may trust Strabo, its origin and root in British commerce. He asserts that the Veneti resolved to withstand Caesar because they were, before the appearance of the Roman galleys in the Atlantic, the main holders of the cross-Channel trade, and were set on keeping off a new claimant for maritime supremacy in those waters. It was not therefore mere jealousy of the growing power of Caesar in Central Gaul which led them to risk and lose their national existence by an attack upon him, but a commercial motive.

That same motive was also at the bottom of Caesar's attack upon Britain. It was not merely to punish the British tribes who had sent auxiliaries to join the Veneti or the Belgae, nor to show the Gauls that no enemy was safe from his sword, nor again to dazzle the Romans by the report of victories over foes as remote as those Iberians and Albanians whom Pompey had defeated in the Caucasus, that Caesar first conceived the idea of crossing the British Channel. All these ideas were present in his mind, but he had also a notion that profit might be made out of the subjection of Britain. It was believed to be fertile in gold, and Caesar must undoubtedly have seen many a British gold piece among the treasures taken from conquered Belgae and other Celts, for (as numerous finds show) *staters* from across the water were circulating freely in North Gaul. There was also the report of its tin trade to attract him; he knew that tin was produced in Britain, though he wrongly thought that it came from the inland parts of the island.

<hr>

★★★★★★

In mediterraneis regionibus, B. G., v., 12. This curious blunder can only arise from his having discovered, when he was in Britain, that it was not found in those southern and eastern coast tracts which he himself visited; apparently he argued that, if it came from a distance, it must have been from the inland.

★★★★★★

He also mentions the iron that was produced in regions nearer the coast, no doubt the shallow mines of the Sussex Weald, which from the beginning of the Iron Age to the eighteenth century were the best-known British iron-field. It is curious to find him adding that for bronze the islanders depended on the Continent, for the copper mines of Wales and Cornwall were worked as early as the tin mines; perhaps he was misled by finding that southern articles of luxury in bronze were eagerly sought by the Britons. It is certain that they made their own ordinary bronze implements in enormous quantities and with no small degree of art. Perhaps Caesar may also have heard of the British pearls, which later Romans found so disappointing from their bad colour—so that the British oyster was of better repute than the gems which it sometimes sheltered. It is significant to find that the only definite article of spoil which he is recorded to have earned home from Britain was a breastplate adorned with pearls, which he dedicated in the temple of Victory at Rome.

In dealing with all Caesar's wars of conquest, it is well to remember that there were two very different classes of motive governing his actions. On the one hand he was a great statesman and strategist, who was extending the Roman Empire to its natural geographical limits, and providing against further dangers, alike from Gallic turbulence, and from the more perilous invaders from beyond the Rhine, of whom Ariovistus was to be the last example for some 400 years. On the other hand, he was a Roman faction leader, at the head of a most miscellaneous and unscrupulous following, who disguised themselves under the name of the "*Populares,*" the democratic party. The chiefs of that party, with few exceptions, were greedy, self-seeking men, who had to be kept loyal by continual payment.

Caesar had to make money by his campaigns, or he could not have kept his followers in good temper, or have continued his policy of buying up the services of every young man of promise who was for sale. It was necessary for him not only to make war support war, but to have a surplus, with which he could continue his purchases in the market where politicians were to be bought. Hence he was anxious for plunder of all sorts, whether it took the form of tribal hoards of gold and silver or of prisoners of war: the most productive of all his sources of revenue was the sale of captured slaves: it was probably this prosaic and cruel motive which lay at the back of his frequent orders for the demolition of whole clans and nations.

A general sale of the population, male and female, of a tribe which had proved obstinate or treacherous, enabled him to find the money both for shows which amused the whole Roman populace, and for the purchase of individuals whose brains and activity were likely to be profitable to him. We may be tolerably certain that the British expeditions of 55 and 54 B.C. were not undertaken merely because the adventurers of Britain had helped the Gauls, nor because the news of British triumphs would have an imposing sound at Rome, nor because the subjection of the insular Celts seemed a logical sequence to the subjection of their continental relatives, but also because Caesar believed that there was tangible profit to be got out of the expedition—a belief in which (as we shall see) he was woefully deceived.

The *proconsul's* first venture was on a small scale and in a tentative style. The summer of 55 B.C. was already far spent, operations near the Rhine having extended over many months, when he made up his mind to cross the Channel, as he writes:

> Thinking that it would be very useful to him merely to visit the island, to get a thorough knowledge of the character of its people, and become acquainted with its topography, ports and landing-places.

He began by collecting Gallic merchants and cross-questioning them as to the nature and resources of Britain: they apparently told him as little as they dared: such strange statements as that quoted above, concerning the production of tin in the Midlands, must have been false, to the clear knowledge of any far-travelled trader. The Gauls had no interest in seeing the Roman intervene in a region where they themselves had till now enjoyed a monopoly of trade. It is possible that some of the other improbable notes in Caesar may have been part of a set of tales told him by these untrustworthy informants, in order that he might be put off from his design by an exaggerated account of the savage nature of the islanders. Such, for example, is that which tells that some of the British tribes were still in the horde stage, that:

> Ten or a dozen men would have wives in common, often brothers with brothers or fathers with sons.

This was certainly not possible with the Celts, whether Brythons or Goidels, and we can hardly believe that there still survived in the remoter corners of the isle remnants of some pre-Celtic people still sunk in such barbarism, or that, if there had been, the merchants of the South would have had any knowledge of them. Equally untrue was the statement that most of the people of the inland parts of the isle had no knowledge of cereals, and lived wholly on flesh and milk, as also that they dressed in skins for want of linen or wool. Considering that we have ample proof that corn was cultivated not only in the Midlands but far in the North, even beyond Forth and Tay, and that all the Britons were skilful weavers, we are driven to suppose that some of Caesar's informants were trying to convince him that nothing profitable could be got out of the degraded savages whom they described to him.

If this was so, they were unsuccessful. Caesar had made up his mind to try the experiment. He collected two legions, the Seventh and the famous Tenth, in the territory of the Morini (Picardy), from which he had heard that the voyage to Britain was shortest. He brought up ships, both galleys and transports, to the Dover Straits, and arranged, as it seems, that the legions should embark at Boulogne, (Gessoriacum), while the cavalry were to go on board eighteen horse-transports, at a harbour a little farther up the coast (probably Ambleteuse). A preliminary exploration of the shore of Kent was made by a tribune named Volusenus, who coasted for five days along the land opposite those ports, in search of spots suitable for a landing.

The Britons had been warned by Gaulish traders of Caesar's designs, and were already under arms; Volusenus could land nowhere, and had to content himself with such reconnoitring as could be done from a safe distance. It was apparently during the short time of his absence at sea that Caesar was visited by envoys from several British communities, who announced that their tribesmen were prepared to submit to the Roman people, and to send over hostages. If this was done with the object of turning Caesar from his design the plan failed: he merely commended their friendly intentions, told them that he should be among them in a few days, and sent them away, and in their company his dependent Commius, the king of the Atrebates, who was to use his well-known influence in Britain for the purpose of inducing his friends to make their submission to the pro-consul. It was afterwards discovered that this emissary was thrown into chains, and put in ward, the moment that he had landed. The Britons had no intention of giving up their independence without a blow.

Soon before midnight on the 25th of August a fleet of some eighty transports and a few war-galleys put out from Boulogne, carrying the two legions and a certain number of light troops—archers and slingers. The eighteen ships from the neighbouring harbour to the north were to bring over 500 Gallic cavalry. The whole expeditionary force must have been under 10,000 strong, as the legions had seen much service and had not been recruited up to full strength. Supplies for only a few days were taken, as Caesar intended to live on the country, whether he was received in a friendly or a hostile fashion. The wind apparently was favourable at first, but it very soon began to shift, and the cavalry transports never got out to sea. The rest of the armament was off the cliffs of Dover by nine o'clock in the morning, the galleys close inshore, the heavy transports straggling behind. The spot cannot be mistaken: Caesar describes it as:

A place where the sea is so closely shut in by abrupt hills that a dart can easily be cast from the summit above on to the fore-shore.

Numerous armed natives could be seen on the heights. This was not the locality at which the expeditionary force could be safely landed, nor had Caesar any intention of doing so, as he knew from Volusenus's report that there was shelving beach instead of rugged chalk cliffs only a few miles away to the north. He waited till his slow-sailing transports had come up, and till the tide had begun to run eastward, and then in the afternoon bade the whole armament steer along shore in the direction of Deal and Walmer. The moment that his intention was visible the Britons on the cliffs above were seen streaming off for the same goal.

With the tide in their favour the Roman ships could sail faster than the British levies could march, and when Caesar bade his captains turn their prows shoreward to a point some seven miles north of Dover, only the chariots and horsemen of the Cantii were in sight, the tribal levies on foot were panting far behind. Still a fierce resistance was made to the landing; the transports had run aground some way from the shore, since the beach was gently shelving. The *legionaries*, when invited by their officers to leap into water from four or five feet deep, and to wade up for many yards to the land, hung back, daunted by the shower of missiles already playing upon them, and by the sight of hundreds of wild charioteers careering along the shingle and shouting their discordant war-cries.

Caesar was obliged to order his war-galleys, on which the archers and slingers were serving, to push as near the shore as possible, and to cover the disembarkation by their shooting. Many of the Britons fell, and others drew back, so that the Romans were emboldened to plunge into the water and push forward. We are told that the standard-bearer of the Tenth legion showed them the way, by pushing far ahead and challenging his fellow-soldiers to desert their eagle and betray their general if they dared. But when the *legionaries* began to wade up the watery slope in disordered groups, the boldest of the Britons came down to meet them, riding or even driving into the waves, and coming to hand-strokes with the invaders.

Now that both were mixed together, the Roman archers and slingers could no longer let fly, for fear of harming their friends, so that

41

they ceased to be of any assistance. But chariots are poor devices on a shingly beach, and when the British chiefs leaped down and fought on foot, knee-deep in the water, they were no better off than their opponents. Gradually the Romans formed into solid clumps and fought their way up the beach. When they felt firm ground under their feet, and could close up in some sort of regular array, the Britons began to draw off, and presently the whole band gave way, and rode, drove, or ran off towards the interior.

There was no pursuit, because the Romans were utterly destitute of cavalry: the eighteen horse-transports had never come up. Whether the tribal infantry of the Britons arrived in time to take any serious part in the fighting is uncertain: they had seven miles to run, and must have arrived dead beat, long after the battle had begun. Caesar makes no mention of them, dwelling on the audacity and courage of the charioteers and horsemen alone.

That night Caesar entrenched a camp close to the beach, and hauled his galleys ashore: the heavy transports were anchored where they had run aground, the labour of hauling them up beyond high-water mark seeming to the proconsul excessive and unnecessary. On the following day he was delighted to receive a deputation from the enemy: the men of Kent, on whom all the fighting had fallen, for no one had yet come to their aid, were disheartened. They gave up their prisoner Commius, apologised for their resistance, which they ascribed to the hot-headedness of their young men, and offered to submit and give hostages. Caesar accepted their excuses, received their submission, and chose a certain number of hostages; the rest were to be sent in within a few days.

It is probable that the Britons might have kept the terms if the powers of nature had not intervened. But on the morning of August 30, just as the belated horse-transports came in sight, a terrible north-easterly gale arose. The approaching ships were swept down channel, and ultimately came ashore after many perils, at various points on the coast of Gaul. As night came on the weather grew worse: many of the anchored transports were driven ashore, while the galleys which had been dragged up to the line of the ordinary high-water mark, were not beyond the reach of the specially high tide accompanying the time of full moon.

The sea, helped by the wind, washed over them and did them much harm. When the morning light came it was seen that many vessels of both classes had been broken up, and that most of the remainder had lost oars, spars, and tackle, and were in an unseaworthy condition. The Britons noting the effects of the gale, a line of wrecks and stranded vessels, thought that the powers of the air had come to their aid, and resolved to try once more the chance of war. No more hostages came in, and it was clear that trouble was impending. Caesar turned all hands to work to repair his fleet: twelve ships were given up as hopeless wrecks, and with their timber, metal fittings, and surviving tackle, he began to patch up the rest. Meanwhile the stores brought from Gaul were exhausted, and the *legionaries* had to forage for food, which they got by cutting all the standing corn for some miles inland from the camp.

Some few days later the Britons made an attempt to cut off the large foraging parties, supplied on this occasion by the Seventh Legion, which were abroad, hard at work with the reaping hook, at a long distance from the shore. They had a special good chance given them by the fact that the *tribune* in command had posted no outlying pickets to guard his fatigue parties, and had allowed the men to stack their shields and armour while they were at work. Suddenly a mass of British charioteers and horsemen swept down upon the reapers from under the cover of the surrounding woods, taking them wholly by surprise. Something like a panic took place, while the Romans were collecting in groups and running to their arms.

Caesar is at some pains to explain the terrifying effect of a charge of chariots. The mere clatter and rush of wheels counted for something, even with veterans who were accustomed to face with serene confidence ordinary charges of infantry or cavalry. The agility of the British chariot-fighters was as great as their courage.

> They could drive and turn their teams over ground of even the most steep and precipitous contours. They might be seen to run, balancing themselves, forward along the pole, and to stand on the yoke, and then to spring back into the chariot with ease.
>
> ★★★★★★
>
> Note: Apparently, the object of this acrobatic feat was to get a good cast with the spear over the heads of the galloping horses. A Gallic chief (Bituitus) casting a javelin, with one foot standing on the pole of his chariot, seems to be represented on the coins of the Roman moneyers Aurelius Scaurus and Domitius Ahenobarbus (see *Babelon's Monnaies de la Republique Romaine*, i.).
>
> ★★★★★★

Their tactics were:

First to gallop round the enemy and hurl darts at him, which often put his line in disorder, and then to fall in among the intervals of their cavalry, when they leap down and fight on foot.

★★★★★★

Note: I take it that the *equites* of Caesar's sentence, "*quum se inter equitum turmas insinuaverunt*" means the British cavalry, because during this expedition Caesar had no horsemen at all. The meaning must be that the charioteers first made a demonstration, and then charged in company with their own horse, dismounting just before contact with the enemy's line, and running in on foot against foes who were expecting to meet only mounted men.

★★★★★★

The charioteers meanwhile retire a little way from the battlefront, and draw up the cars in such a position that, if the warriors are oppressed by the superior numbers of the enemy, they can have a quick line of retreat to their vehicles. Thus, they combine the mobility of cavalry with the stability of infantry.

No doubt the Britons could have found no more favourable opportunity for a sudden terrifying swoop than that given them by the scattered half-armed soldiers of the Seventh Legion, surprised in the midst of their harvesting. They would probably have been cut to pieces if Caesar, on hearing a report that great clouds of dust were visible in the direction where the Seventh were foraging, had not hurried out with the two *cohorts* which were under arms as camp-guard, and ordered the rest of the Tenth to follow in haste. He arrived in time to rescue his endangered troops, and then retreated with them to his camp, "thinking that the conjuncture was inopportune for attacking the enemy and courting a pitched battle."

There followed, after this narrowly escaped disaster, several days of heavy rain, which fixed the Romans to their camp, and deterred the Britons from making any further attacks. But auxiliaries from some of the remoter tribes joined the local levies during this interval, and their spirits grew so high that they were eager for another fight When, on the first fine day, Caesar filed his legions out of his gates, and drew them up in battle order in the open, his challenge was at once accepted. The Britons charged in with vigour, but were repulsed after a sharp struggle, and fled in such disorder that a mere thirty mounted men under the Atrebatian Commius, all the cavalry that Caesar could produce, were able to cut down a considerable number of them—straggling footmen, it is to be presumed.

On the same evening envoys appeared again to ask for terms of peace. Caesar amused them with a discussion of details, announced that he should demand double the number of hostages that he had asked before, and said that they should be sent over to Gaul. But that same night he quietly embarked his whole force on his fleet, which was now in fair order, and set sail for Boulogne, which he reached after an uneventful voyage. It is clear that the expedition had been a failure: the army had not moved ten miles inland, it must have suffered appreciable losses in men, as it had in ships, and it had brought back no trophies—indeed it had absconded from Britain in a surreptitious fashion, which must have done much to destroy the effect of its victories in the three combats in which it had been engaged.

The sole advantages to Caesar were that he had discovered a good landing-place, that he had learned the tactics of the Britons, and that he had found that they could be defeated, even if they were a more formidable foe than he had suspected when he first crossed the straits. One thing was clear—their celerity of movement made it useless to attack them with infantry alone: if the 500 horse, which had never got to Britain, had only come ashore with the rest of the army, something more considerable might have been accomplished. Nevertheless, Caesar wrote a despatch to the Senate representing the campaign in such a brilliant light, that a "*supplicatio*" of twenty days was voted to commemorate his exploits. Of tangible result there was none, save that two solitary Kentish tribes, out of all who negotiated for peace, sent hostages over to Gaul in the winter, as they had undertaken to do.

But Caesar was not the man to accept a defeat: he was determined to repeat his invasion with a more formidable army and at a more favourable season of the year. He retired, as usual, to Cisalpine Gaul for the winter, to pick up the threads of his intrigues with his supporters and enemies at Rome. But his legions were left behind in Belgic Gaul, with orders to spend their time in stationary quarters, in building a new fleet and repairing the old one. The new vessels were specially designed for use as horse-transports, and were all fitted with oars, for Caesar had been discontented with the slowness of his sailing transports during his last voyage.

The general shape of the ships was somewhat lower and broader than had hitherto been customary, in order to facilitate embarkation and disembarkation of horses and stores, and also to permit of their running closer inshore, and being more easily hauled up above high-water mark than the old type of transport had been. The scale of the expedition was to be very large; as many as 600 ships had been collected; no less than 2,000 cavalry were to be taken over, and the preliminary expenses were very heavy. But everything was done to avert the chance of a second fiasco like that of 55 B.C.

Some troubles among the Treviri, on the Moselle, kept Caesar from commencing his second British expedition quite so soon as he had expected, but by the middle of June he had concentrated a very large army on the coast of the Channel, from which he selected five legions and 2,000 horse, leaving the rest to garrison Northern Gaul. The whole force that embarked must have been at least 25,000 men, when the light troops were counted in, or more than double that employed in the preceding year.

The Britons had long warning of Caesar's intentions, but made no good use of it: Cassivellaunus King of the Catuvellauni, the most powerful prince of the South, and the natural leader for a confederacy, had been engaged that spring in attacking his neighbours the Trinovantes of Essex: he had occupied much of their territory, and slain their king, whose son Mandubratius fled to Caesar, and promised to join him with the wrecks of his tribe. Thus, the invader was certain of at least some assistance on his landing. His starting point seems to have been Portus Itius (Wissant), the harbour of Boulogne (Gessoriacum) not being large enough to accommodate so large a fleet as that which had been collected for this expedition. (See Rice Holmes' *Caesar's Conquest of Gaul,* 2nd edition.)

On this occasion Caesar ran, once more, to the northward of the Dover cliffs, and being apparently earned by the tide a little farther than he intended, finally came ashore some five or six miles beyond the place of his former landing, not far from Sandwich (July 6-7, 54 B.C.). No resistance was offered, and he was able to build a base-camp without molestation, at which he landed a great store of provisions, for this time he was resolved not to trust entirely to the resources of the countryside. Not sufficiently warned by his former experience of the storms and tides of the Channel, he once more left most of his fleet at anchor, being apparently anxious to save the time which would have been required to drag the heavier ships ashore.

He then told off ten *cohorts*, under a *tribune* named Quintus Atrius, for the defence of his base, and advanced into the interior, taking, as it appears, the trackway in the direction of Canterbury, Rochester and London, which already existed, and along which population and food-resources lay thickest. The men of Kent, aware of the formidable numbers of the Roman Army, had no wish to engage in a pitched battle, till they had been joined by all the other tribes threatened by the invasion. But they made some attempt to defend the fords of the Stour, and had occupied and covered with abattis the line of woods which lay above them.

★★★★★★

Were the fords those of the Little Stour, three miles east of Canterbury, by Littlebourne and Bekesbourne, or those of the Great Stour, just beyond Canterbury, between Sturry and Thanington? The distance given by Caesar, twelve miles from the base-camp by the sea, is in favour of the former river. But the ground is better for defence on the Great Stour, and there seem to be some traces of entrenchments on the low hills above Thanington, which would form a very good position. This was probably the battle-spot, as Caesar's estimate may have been rough.

★★★★★★

Their cavalry and charioteers were driven from the river after a skirmish, and fell back to the entrenched wood side, where more serious resistance was made. But the Seventh Legion, advancing in column, and forming the *testudo* of locked shields to keep off the British darts, charged straight at the entanglements and cut their way through with no great loss. The Britons thereupon melted away among the trees, where it was useless to pursue them, and Caesar encamped for the night near the place of combat.

Next morning the Roman cavalry rode out in three directions, with infantry supports, to see whether the enemy was making preparations for further resistance. They had not returned when Caesar received an urgent message from Atrius at the base-camp. A storm, not unlike that of the previous August, had caught the ships at anchor: many had been driven on shore and damaged, some had been sunk by collisions with each other. The whole armament was disabled.

This was a hard but well-deserved penalty, to be paid for a neglect of the warning of the preceding year. Caesar, with a heavy heart, called back his cavalry and ordered the infantry to return to the coast. Inspection showed that forty ships had been destroyed, or damaged beyond possibility of repair. He was then forced to spend ten days in hauling up the uninjured vessels above high-water mark, a tedious business; while the military artificers of all the legions were turned to work on patching up the unseaworthy ones; messages were even sent across to Gaul, to direct Labienus, who was left in command in Belgica, to forward all available shipwrights to aid in the repairs.

On the eleventh day only could Caesar resume his march, after leaving the same force as before, under the same officer, to guard the camp and protect the artificers. This delay had given the Britons time to collect in full force, King Cassivellaunus had called upon all his tributary chiefs and neighbours to march to the aid of the Cantii, and his levies had reoccupied the positions beyond the Stour, which Caesar had stormed twelve days before. There was trouble, however, preparing behind Cassivellaunus, for Caesar had sent his *protegé* Mandubratius, the exiled Prince of the Trinovantes, to land in the territory of his tribesmen, and to incite them to rise against their oppressor's the Catuvellauni. But this diversion would only commence to affect the fate of the campaign after a space of some days.

Meanwhile Caesar found himself involved in a running fight, which seems to have lasted almost the whole way from the Stour to the Thames. On the first day the Gaulish cavalry, in advance of the legions, got involved in a long skirmish, and, pursuing too far after a small success, were charged again, when they were in disorder, and lost many men. On the same evening the enemy made an unexpected assault on the troops who were busy laying out and entrenching the usual camp. Their cavalry and charioteers drove in the outlying guard, and cut their way in a circle between the supports that came out successively to intervene in the fight, finally getting off with small loss after causing much confusion.

In this fight fell the *tribune* Q. Laberius Durus, the only officer of distinction whom Caesar lost during his British campaign.

On the next morning the proconsul, finding no great force of the Britons in sight, sent out three of his five legions and the whole of his cavalry, under his *legate* Trebonius (afterwards destined to be one of his murderers), to sweep the countryside for food. The enemy had only been waiting for the Romans to scatter, and at a well-chosen moment suddenly emerged from the woods on all sides, in the greatest numbers that they had yet shown. They drove in the foraging parties and then boldly attacked the embattled legions: but to break the Roman infantry, when it was not caught unprepared, was beyond the power of the Britons.

After a sharp fight they were repulsed with loss; Caesar then let loose his cavalry upon the routed mass, and bade his *legionaries* follow the horse as fast as they were able. The Britons, not daring to halt and turn upon the horsemen so long as the infantry was close behind them, were pursued and cut down for some distance—the loss, as we must suppose, falling rather on the tribal levies on foot, who could he easily overtaken, than on the swiftly moving charioteers. The chase was not pushed far enough to permit the enemy to turn and rend the cavalry, when they should have got out of touch of their supports.

This was a decisive defeat for Cassivellaunus, who made up his mind that it was useless to try another pitched battle at the head of the tribal foot-levies, who were hopelessly incapable of facing the legions. He sent them all home, and only retained the flower of his chiefs and their retainer's, 4,000 chariot-fighters in all. With these he dogged the steps of the Romans as they marched from the neighbourhood of Canterbury, with the forest to their south and the Thames estuary to their north. Whether Caesar's advance followed the line afterwards marked out by Watling Street, past Rochester, or whether it took the "Pilgrims' Way," along the slope of the chalk ridge of the North Downs, it is impossible to say with certainty. But since he lays stress on the fact that he was marching through a populous district, and that he did as much damage as possible, by burning and wasting on all sides, it seems more probable that he took the former route, and not that along the untilled downs.

The harm that he did, however, was limited by the fact that Cassivellaunus hung on to his flanks, and fell upon his raider's whenever they went far from the main body. The Gaulish cavalry could gain no mastery over the British charioteer's, and had to stick close to their infantry supports, so that the limit of ground overrun was bounded by the distance that the infantry could diverge from the line of march, in search of huts to burn or crops to carry off. As the Britons had sent all their women-folk and their cattle into the Weald, to be out of harm's way, the devastation cannot have been very effective.

Caesar's objective was the territory of the Catuvellauni, whose king was the head of the British confederacy, since he was convinced that if he could break the power of Cassivellaunus the other tribes would sue for peace. That territory lay entirely north of Thames, and seems (as we have already seen in a previous chapter) to have extended from the Lea on the East to the Cotswolds on the West, and from the Thames on the South to the Nen and the Warwickshire Avon. No serious pressure could be brought to bear on the Catuvellauni by ravaging the boundaries of the men of Kent: they must be sought in their own land.

It was therefore necessary to cross the Thames at the lowest possible point, and the nearest ford to the sea appears in those days to have lain somewhere in the neighbourhood of Kingston, possibly opposite Brentford, (though the name of that place refers to a ford on the little Brent, not on the Thames), possibly at Halliford, ten miles farther up the meandering river.

★★★★★★

There is a whole literature dealing with the question as to where Caesar crossed the Thames. The old view, from the time of Camden downward, was that the passage was at Coway Stakes, near Walton-on-Thames. The statements in the text above are those of the latest pronouncement on the subject, those of Mr. Rice Holmes's *Ancient Britain*.

★★★★★★

The depth of the Thames has been so much affected by the silting of twenty centuries, and the building of locks and weirs, that it is impossible to make any certain affirmation about its condition in Caesar's day. We only know that there was one obvious and well-known ford, which was pointed out by prisoners and deserters, and that Cassivellaunus had caused this passage to be obstructed with stakes, and entrenched his army in array behind it, so certain was he that this would be Caesar's point of attack. The remnants of a large and elaborate stockade are said to be found in the bed of the Thames opposite Brentford, and these may mark the precaution of the Catuvellaunian king.

The defence of the ford, however, was a complete failure. There must have been some miscalculation in the staking of the river bed, since Caesar merely tells us that his cavalry was sent first into the water, and that his infantry, following close by, plunged into the river, though it ran as high as their shoulders, and crossed it in column with little delay. Whether they pulled down some of the stakes, or whether they eluded them by passing just above or below, we are not told. Nor would the words forbid the idea that the cavalry may have swum the river at an unfordable point on the flank, while the legions went straight at the ford a little later, when the turning movement of the horse had already shaken the enemy. All that is definitely stated by Caesar is that the cavalry was sent in first, and the movement of the infantry came a little later. But considering the fact that he has, in the preceding paragraphs, told us that all through this campaign the horse were liable to be checked, and roughly handled, unless they were closely supported by the foot, it seems likely that the two arms worked together on this, as on other, occasions.

The retreat of Cassivellaunus was hasty, and can have been accompanied by little slaughter of his men, yet Caesar had won a great advantage by crossing the Thames. He was now only some fifteen or twenty miles from the boundary of the Trinovantes, among whom his emissary Mandubratius had already penetrated. The resentment of that tribe at their late conquest by the king of the Catuvellauni was so bitter that they had risen at the summons of their exiled prince, and were ready to join the Romans. Their ambassadors came at once to Caesar's camp, handed over to him as many hostages as he required, and began to send him in great stores of corn. Moving across the Lea into their land, he procured for himself a near and secure base in a friendly country.

A few days later other tribes made their submission—the Cenimagni, who seem to be the Iceni of later history, the inhabitants of East Anglia, together with the Segontiaci, Ancalites, Bibroci, and Cassi. These last four obscure septs, whose names never occur again in history, may have been sub-clans of the Belgic population between the Thames and the New Forest. Possibly the Bibroci and Segontiaci were sections of the Atrebates, who dwelt in Berks and Surrey, while the Cassi and Ancalites may represent fractions of the Belgae proper of Hants and Wilts. But this is wholly uncertain.

★★★★★★

On some of the British coins of the next generation, belonging to Tasciovanus' time, the inscriptions *sego* and *catti* occur. Are these the tribal names of the Atrebates people? or are they part of the names of kings, such as Segonax or Cattigern?

★★★★★★

Cassivellaunus had yet one card to play. While he himself hung about the line of Caesar's march, he sent messages to the kings of Kent, begging them to make a vigorous assault on the Roman base-camp near Sandwich, and so to call the invaders away from the Thames, to the rescue of their comrades and their fleet left behind on the shore. This plan met with the approval of the Cantii, who were more irritated by Caesar's late ravages in their land than tamed by their defeats. Under their four kings, Cingetorix, Carvilius, Segonax, and Taximagulus, they assembled round the basecamp and laid siege to it.

But they were unable to crush the moderate force of ten *cohorts* and 300 horse which Q. Atrius had at his disposal, and a sudden sally of the Romans scattered them with great loss. Caesar specially records the capture of a chief of high birth and importance, named Lugotorix, though he was not one of the kings.

Thus, since the diversion in Kent proved of no effect, Cassivellaunus had to face Caesar at the head of his own tribe alone, since his tributaries had dispersed or surrendered. He was finally reduced to despair by the capture of his chief stronghold, the "*Oppidum*" of Verulamium—for this seems undoubtedly to be the place whose storm is mentioned in the *De Bello Gallico*. A British "*oppidiim*," as we are here told, was simply a place of refuge for folk and cattle, protected by woods and fenced round by ditches and abattis. Though the fortress of the Catuvellauni was a formidable specimen of its class, it was taken with no great difficulty, by a simultaneous attack on two of its fronts. An immense amount of cattle and many prisoners were captured—no doubt the whole of the families of the southern section of Cassivellaunus's tribe had been stowed away for safety in Verulamium.

Alter this disaster the king sued for peace, being anxious to get rid of Caesar at all costs. He made his overtures through the Atrebatian Commius, and they were accepted. For the proconsul was anxious to leave Britain: not much of the summer remained, and the reports of trouble and disloyalty in Gaul were beginning to disturb him. Indeed, the great insurrection which broke out in the next year but one was already brewing, and if the five legions now in Britain had remained absent any longer, the revolt might have started in the autumn of 54. Accordingly, Caesar only insisted that Cassivellaunus, like the other tribal kings, should make over many hostages to him, and covenant that he would pay an annual tribute to the Roman people. He was specially ordered not to molest the Trinovantes and their newly chosen king Mandubratius.

Having received his hostages and an instalment of tribute, Caesar took his way back through Kent to his base-camp, and re-embarked for Gaul. He was obliged to make two trips, on account of the loss of ships and the number of slaves whom he was bringing back. For the surrender of the Britons had not secured them the restoration of their captives, from whose sale in Gaul and Italy Caesar hoped to make much more profit than was brought him by the moderate war-indemnity imposed upon the tribes. No attempt was made by the islanders to molest the second section of the army after the first had sailed; they were now thoroughly cowed.

Indeed, but for the great revolt of the Gauls under Vercingetorix in the year 52, it is probable that the Britons would have continued to pay their tribute, and to observe the terms imposed upon them, for some time. But when in 52 all Gaul was aflame, and Caesar was fighting for life rather than empire, he had no thought to spare for the Britons and they could do as they pleased without troubling themselves about his wrath. Following the two years of the Gallic revolt came the Roman Civil War after a short interval, and Caesar's insular conquests pass out of our ken. Twilight descends once more upon Britain for nearly a century.

Thus, Caesar's invasions, though fraught with important results for the future, had little importance for the present. He had shown the way to Britain, but had not left it open. On the whole the campaigns seem to have been considered rather disappointing by the practical mind of the average Roman. In one of Cicero's letters the matter is summed up by the prosaic reflection that there was practically no money to be got out of Britain, nothing but slaves; and these slaves were the roughest field hands for manual labour, "naturally there are not among them scholars or musicians," so that they were not valuable items in the Roman market.

And in the clash of the oncoming Civil Wars the memory of the projected conquest of the northern island passed out of the brains of the soldiers and statesmen of Rome. It was not till after Philippi and Actium, when the Mediterranean world had settled down under a single master, and internal wars had ceased, that the British Question began once more to flit at intervals before the imagination of the subjects of Augustus Caesar.

CHAPTER 4

Britain Between the Invasion of Julius Caesar and the Invasion of Claudius (B.C. 64–A.D. 43)

Though Caesar's projected conquest of Britain came to such an abrupt and unsuccessful conclusion, he did not leave the island as he had found it. When in 49 B.C. he crossed the Rubicon to engage in his great civil war with Pompey and the Optimates, he left Gaul behind him tamed, and organised into the shape of a Roman province. So thorough had been his work that the newly subdued tribes made no endeavour to assert their independence during the absence of their conqueror, or even during the chaos that followed his murder by Brutus and his fellows on the Ides of March, 44 B.C. There were one or two abortive Gallic risings during the long reign of Augustus, but they were so insignificant, and so promptly crushed, that it is clear that the nation as a whole had given up hope after the fall of Vercingetorix, and had fully accepted its new position as a part of the Roman Empire.

For the future, therefore, the neighbours of Britain across the Channel were no longer a weltering mass of Belgic and other tribes, sometimes united for a short moment in an uncertain league, or bowing before a common master (such as Divitiacus had once been), but more frequently engaged in unending civil wars. Belgica, like the rest of Gaul, had become an orderly Roman province, kept down by the strong hand of the conqueror, and engaged in assimilating with a marvellous rapidity Roman customs and Roman civilisation. The close touch between Gaul and Britain that had always prevailed did not cease for a moment, but Gaul having been transformed, Britain began to come under new influences.

The traders who came over to the island were in the new generation Gallo-Romans, and probably to a considerable extent Romans born, for no one was more daring than the Italian merchant in "pushing ahead of the flag". The frontier troubles of the Roman world, both under the republic and under the empire, were more frequently caused by merchants who got into trouble with barbarian peoples than by any other cause. The merchant question was to the Roman Government what the missionary question is to the British Government of today. Any exiles who now came over to Britain were fugitive rebels against the Roman Empire, not the mere tribal outcasts of old. Young Gauls who crossed the Channel to study in the schools of the British Druids were equally Roman subjects, engaged in keeping up a superstition on which the imperial authorities did not look with a favourable eye.

Similarly, the British trader who crossed to the Continent found himself no longer among kinsmen living under conditions similar to his own, but was forced to notice and to ponder on the manifold activities of the Romanised cities that were springing up all over Gaul. The British exile, too, if he fled abroad with some hopes of returning to take up an old quarrel, found that he had to make his petition for aid not to a medley of tribal chiefs, but to the great central power of a world-wide empire. Such exiles, as we shall see, fled to ask Roman aid, not once or twice; but a century was to elapse before it was granted. Several times, however, in the early years of Augustus's reign there seemed to be an imminent prospect of the third invasion of Britain coming to pass.

In the interval between Philippi and Actium, when he was still sharing the dominion of the world with Antony, he was in Northern Gaul with a considerable force, and intended, so it is said, to have turned it against Britain, if he had not been distracted by a rebellion in Dalmatia (34 B.C.). Then came the struggle with Antony, and it was not till some years later that the hands of Augustus were again free. The poetry of the post-Actian epoch is full of hints that the emperor may take up again his uncle's work—the best known of them is Horace's *Odes*, lines that would not have been written unless the poet had believed that there was a great probability that the invasion of Britain was at hand.

In 27 and 26 B.C., when Augustus was for some time in Gaul, it was once more believed that a British expedition might take place. The explanation that he deferred it because of a revolt of the Alpine Salassi, who were after all an unimportant race, does not seem adequate. Probably he had already in mind his great plan for giving the empire a scientific frontier along Rhine and Danube, which was to be the great work of his middle life, and saw that while this was unaccomplished the annexation of Britain would be a mistake, and a waste of power in the wrong direction. In his later years he had become too set on the principle "*coercendi inter terminus imperii*" to revive the scheme.

In Britain itself the old state of things continued: the tribal strife seems to have recommenced the moment that Caesar's back was turned. And we cannot doubt that the tribute which had been promised him ceased to be paid, either when the rebellion of Vercingetorix broke out in 52 B.C., or at least when the great proconsul went off to the civil wars in 49 B.C. The next development of local politics in Britain is to be traced from the evidence of coins alone—evidence very useful, but not always easy to interpret with certainty. But almost immediately after the time of Caesar's departure the coins of Britain begin to show inscriptions, which they had never borne before. Moreover, their types begin to change; new devices drawn from the money of the Roman Republic commence to appear among the distorted copies of the Philippic *stater*, which had hitherto been the only model for all the issues of the island.

What is more surprising is that the inscriptions seem all to be in Latin, not in Celtic—a fact which shows not only that new continental moneyers must have been imported, but that Latin must have been understood at the courts of the kinglets for whom the coins were struck.

The evidence of the coins of the period between Caesar's departure and the commencement of the Christian era seems clearly to show that the British states were coalescing into larger units, by reason of the conquest of the smaller by the more powerful tribes. At the head of one of these incipient empires appears no less a person than that Commius the Atrebate, of whom we have already had to discourse. Though he had been given his kingship by Caesar, he quarrelled with his benefactor and joined in the great rebellion of Vercingetorix. Conscious that he was likely to have little mercy from the Romans, he was one of the last chiefs to keep up the standard of revolt. But after some hairbreadth escapes, one of which is recorded at length by Frontlines in his *Stratagems*, he came to terms with Caesar's lieutenant, Mark Antony, by means of intermediaries, for he had sworn never to look on a Roman again. (*B. G.* viii.)

★★★★★★

Strategemata, ii 13. Commius being pursued shorewards by the Romans towards his ships, arrived to find them left grounded at low tide. Nevertheless, he ordered the sails to be hoisted, arguing that when his pursuers saw the canvas stretched, they would conclude that the vessels were afloat, and the escape complete. And this happened, for when it was seen that Commius was apparently safe, the Roman cavalry halted, and never came down to the beach. And so, the king got off. Frontinus plainly says that he was flying to Britain.

★★★★★★

He seems immediately after to have removed to a new land, where he need never be offended by such a sight (51 B.C.). This land of course was Britain, and he apparently retired, as was natural, to his kinsmen the Atrebates of Berkshire, for soon after we find gold coins struck in his name, which appear to come from the lands south of Thames and west of Kent. But there are far more numerous pieces issued by his sons, each of whom describes himself on his issues as "*Commii filius*". These princes were named Eppillus, Verica (or Virica) and Tincommius. Their coins are fairly common, and are found in Berkshire, Hampshire, Sussex, Kent, and Surrey. Apparently the three brothers reigned simultaneously over different portions of their father's realm, as the names of two of them are often found on the same coin.

Eppillus certainly held the Atrebatian territory proper, since some of his money bears, besides his own name, the mint mark *callev*, for Calleva (Silchester), the well-known capital of the Atrebates. It may be regarded as demonstrable to all probability that Tincommius must have been the British king who is recorded to have fled to Rome, and to have done homage to Augustus, on the famous "Ancyra Marble," the long inscription in which the emperor records the history of his reign. He claims to have sheltered two British exiles, Dubnovellaunus (of whom more hereafter) and Tim —, or Tin — (the name is broken across through its third letter). British proper names beginning with these letters are so uncommon that there is reasonable certainty that this must have been Tincommius, who may have been expelled either by his brothers or by some other foe.

The coins of the Commius dynasty appear to range over the last half of the first century B.C. No later prince calls himself the son of Eppillus or Verica, so presumably the line ended with them; it is probable that they or their sons were crushed by Cunobelinus, the Catuvellaunian high-king who subdued all Southern Britain in the later years of Augustus's reign.

Contemporary with Commius and his three sons was, on the north of the Thames, a prince called Tasciovanus, who was evidently the King of the Catuvellauni, and very possibly the son and heir of Caesar's enemy Cassivellaunus.

★★★★★★

This is suggested by the fact that in Tacitus. *Annals*, xii. 34, the Catuvellaunian King Caratacus says that his ancestors (*majores*) had repulsed Caesar. This ought to mean that his father, Cunobelinus, descended from Cassivellaunus.

★★★★★★

This is indicated by the fact that his money is found scattered widely over Herts, Bedfordshire, Oxfordshire, and the other regions held by that tribe, but still more clearly by the name of Verulamium, found as mint-place on the larger number of his coins. The quantity of gold pieces that he issued testifies to his wealth, and the fact that, while his early money continues to copy the barbarised Philippic *stater*, the later pieces bear types borrowed from contemporary Roman *denarii*, proves that art and civilisation were progressing under his rule among

57

the Catuvellauni. He had, however, a son much greater than himself, Cunobelinus, Shakespeare's Cymbeline, who ultimately became king of all South-Eastern Britain. There was another son named Epaticcus, whose comparatively rare coins come from the south side of Thames, Surrey and East Wilts, districts that he may perhaps have conquered from one of the sons of Commius. But he cannot have reigned long, and his dominions must have passed to his greater brother.

Cymbeline was the greatest prince of his time—in Roman authorities he is sometimes called simply *rex Brittonum*, as if he were supreme in the whole island. Certainly, he conquered the Trinovantes of Essex, for their chief town Camulodunum (Colchester) appears as his chief minting-place. It seems probable that he may have driven out from this region that Dubnovellaunus whom Augustus mentions as an exile on the Ancyra monument, since coins of that prince, a little earlier in appearance than Cymbeline's issues, are found in Essex, though they also appear in Kent.

Possibly Dubnovellaunus may have ruled on both sides of the Lower Thames before he was expelled by the Catuvellaunian conqueror. Cymbeline's money abounds all over Southern Britain from Kent to Gloucestershire, and seems to bear witness to the existence of a veritable empire, since no other coins which can be ascribed to the time contemporary with his later years are to be found anywhere on the South Coast, or the valley of the Thames.

The limits of this power northward seem to be indicated by the fact that we have money belonging to the Iceni, the tribe which occupied the modern Norfolk and Suffolk, which from style and appearance must belong to Cymbeline's epoch. Presumably, therefore, they were not annexed to his realm. Since his issues are seldom or never found west of Wiltshire and Gloucestershire, it would seem a reasonable deduction that the Dumnonii of Devonshire and Cornwall were not in his sphere of influence, nor the Silurians of South Wales. It is, however, a notable fact that Cymbeline's son Caratacus, in the next generation, took refuge with the Silures and apparently acted as their chief commander: this suggests that his father may have had some power over them, though his coins are not found in their borders. And since this South Welsh tribe appears not to have used coined money at all, the fact that Cymbeline's issues are not found in their territory is not conclusive one way or the other.

Cymbeline's reign was very long, it extended at least from 6 *A.D.* to 40 *A.D.*, and very probably may have begun somewhat earlier. It was clearly a time when wealth and civilisation were growing fast, as was but natural when the suzerainty of a single prince had put an end to the petty states and the constant tribal wars that went before. The wealth of Cymbeline is sufficiently vouched for by the enormous number of his gold coins that have been discovered, and which still continue to turn up every year. The growing culture of his court is indicated by the fact that, while his gold coins resemble those of his father Tasciovanus, and are still semi-barbarous, the silver and copper ones are beautifully struck, and bear a large variety of good classical types, evidently designed by competent moneyers from the Roman Empire.

On a few his own portrait appears—a head evidently imitated from that of Augustus, with the Latin inscription *cvnobelinvs rex*: more frequently we have mythological figures of the more fantastic sort, a centaur, a sphinx, a Pegasus, or occasionally the figure of a divinity which appeal's to be a classical Apollo, Hercules, or Mars, though the subjects of Cymbeline may have recognised in them representations of their own local Celtic gods. Oddly enough, the silver coins of this king are always more handsome and better executed than the gold.

The relations of Cymbeline with Augustus and Tiberius were evidently quite friendly—the imperial government made no attempt to restore by force of arms the princes who had fled to Rome from Britain—the Dubnovellaunus and Tincommius of the Ancyra Marble—and evidently recognised the accomplished fact, and left Cymbeline undisturbed. A curious note in Strabo referring to these times deserves a word of comment.

> In our own days certain of the princes of Britain by their embassies and polite attentions have secured the friendship of Caesar Augustus, they have even put up offerings in the Capitol, and have made the whole island almost as it were native soil to the Roman. They pay very moderate customs dues both on the goods which they export to Gaul, and on those which are sent to them from thence—which are mainly ivory, bracelets, necklaces, amber, glass vessels and such-like small merchandise. So, the Romans have no need to garrison the island, which would require at least one legion and some cavalry to enforce a tribute from them. For the cost of keeping troops there would be at least as much as the tribute received, and if tribute were imposed the customs dues would have to be lowered, and moreo-

ver there would be some military risks when forcible subjection was taken in hand.

Strabo notes in the same paragraph that the exports of Britain were gold, silver, iron, skins, slaves, hunting dogs, and (what is more surprising) corn and cattle. We should hardly have expected to hear of these two last staple commodities being imported into Roman Gaul from the still semi-barbarous island.

We should have deduced what Cymbeline made Britain, if Strabo had made no mention of the fact, from his coinage, with its Latin inscriptions and its neat classical devices. That he was doing wisely for himself in keeping on good terms with the great empire across the Channel was obvious. That he was doing ill for his successors in allowing the Romans free access to Britain, and permitting them to spy out all the resources of the island, was less visible at the time.

But nevertheless it is evident that the Roman conquest, when it at last came, in the next generation, was rendered easy by the fact that the geography of Britain was now well known, and that its political factions were well understood, so that the invaders knew perfectly well who would be their friends and who their enemies. There must also have been a nucleus of Roman subjects, Italians as well as Gauls, settled in every important town of South Britain, and perhaps, we may add, a native commercial class, which for reasons of trade would look upon the conquest with equanimity.

It would be interesting to know whether the great Gaulish revolt of Florus and Sacrovir in 21 *A.D.*, the eighth year of Tiberius, which was intended to be a national and religious protest against assimilation to Rome, got any support from Britain. On the one hand it seems to have been favoured by the Druids, and that priesthood, still all-powerful in Britain, must have resented the disabilities which Augustus had imposed upon it in Gaul. Naturally the Continental Druids would have asked for help from their more fortunate insular brethren. On the other hand, Cymbeline was set on keeping upon good terms with the Roman Government, and would be likely to do his best to keep his subjects from aiding the revolt. Unfortunately, we have no hint whatever in Tacitus's narrative to enable us to come to any conclusion on the subject.

The end of the reign of Cymbeline seems to have been disturbed by the family troubles that generally vex the old age of a king in semi-barbarous countries. Adminius, who is supposed to have been his eldest son, rebelled against him, and had to be expelled by force of arms. (This prince is probably *not* the Amminus or Amminius whose name is found on a few rare British coins. They seem from their style to be earlier than 35-40 *A.D.*)

The exile fled to the court of the Emperor Caius Caesar (Caligula), who had succeeded to the throne of Tiberius in 37 *A.D.*, and was now in the third year of his reign. That eccentric monarch, as Suetonius narrates, received him with gladness, and induced him to make a formal cession of his rights in Britain; after which he wrote a magniloquent letter to the Senate, stating that the whole island had become Roman soil. His messengers were told to drive straight to the Forum in their travelling car, as if bearing in haste despatches of the highest importance; but they were also directed to see that the consuls should have collected every available senator, and should have appointed the temple of Mars as the meeting-place—which argued preparations incompatible with the ostensible hurry of the proceedings.

Then follows a much stranger tale: Cymbeline having made no signs of taking his son's proceedings seriously, the emperor massed troops somewhere on the straits—apparently at Gessoriacum (Boulogne):

> And then, as if about to engage in warlike operations, drew up his force on the seashore, with a display of *balistae* and other military machines. No one could know, or even form a conjecture, as to what he intended to do: but suddenly he bade the soldiers to gather shells, and to fill their helmets and their laps with them. 'These,' he said, 'are the spoils of the Ocean, due to the Capitol and the *Palatine.*' And in testimony to this triumph he erected a high tower, on whose summit a fire was to be kept burning at night, by way of a lighthouse, to aid ships in the direction of their course.

These antics recall a much better remembered display on the same shore by a Gallic emperor in 1804, where once again an "Army of Britain" was reviewed in state, and then (instead of embarking) received a shower of crosses of the Legion of Honour. Napoleon's review, like Caligula's, was afterwards celebrated by the erection of a lofty column. Conceivably there was some political idea at the back of the earlier monarch's manoeuvres: but Suetonius will have it that mere insanity inspired them: the psychology of megalomania in all ages is difficult to interpret, especially if we have no sufficient details left us by the contemporary historians. Suetonius was writing three generations after the famous review, and evidently thought that madness explained all.

Caligula was assassinated in the following year (41 *A.D.*), to the relief of the whole civilised world, and his uncle, the learned and absent-minded Claudius, was forcibly extracted by the soldiery from his hiding-place, and invested with the unexpected purple. The new emperor was the James I. of Roman history, the wisest fool of his age. Despite of the greedy parasites who surrounded him, the Rochesters and Buckinghams of the *Palatine,* he made a much better ruler than might have been expected. His domestic infelicities and his frequent lapses into the grotesque only affected the court and the city: for the empire he was rather a successful and provident ruler.

It was not for nothing that he had devoted long study to Roman history and antiquities. He had a policy of his own, and could justify it by apposite, if pedantic, quotations from the past. He was a kindly creature at the bottom, though his morale had been ruined by a youth and middle age spent in constant terror, under the inquisitorial eye of the gloomy Tiberius and the freakish cruelty of the mad Caligula. His long weak neck, his shambling gait, his eccentricities of speech, made him appear much more contemptible than he really was to those who were in daily contact with him. From sheer want of nerve or love of quiet, he would allow himself on occasion to be bullied by his worthless wives and his impudent freed men. Yet he clearly had his views of imperial policy, and carried them out not without success.

One of them was that the provinces were becoming so rapidly Romanised that large extensions of the franchise were practicable, and ought to be begun without delay. He earned them out with the best results. Another was that the times were ripe for a large addition to the number of colonies. A third was that moral reforms were necessary to save the ruling classes, and he tried to do something to deliver corrupt Rome from herself—only to be laughed at because his own wives and favourites were the very centres of her corruption.

Among other humanitarian reforms he set himself to suppress Druidism in Gaul, because of the cruelty of its rites, which even after Augustus had discouraged them, continued to be practised in secret. It may be possible that his crusade against the Druids partly tempted him into making his attack on Britain, in which he broke with the non-annexation policy that have prevailed during the later years of Augustus and the whole of Tiberius's reign.

The priests of Gaul were encouraged and recruited by their insular brethren; it was necessary to strike at the central focus of the creed even if it lay beyond seas. No doubt there were other motives at the root of the invasion; from the mere political, as opposed to the religious, point of view it might seem anomalous to leave a section of the Celts in a state of liberty, in such close neighbourhood to their kinsmen who had become subjects of the empire. We know of no national Gaulish insurrection since that which had disturbed the commencement of Tiberius's reign, but it may be possible that subterranean heavings and convulsions were visible to the Roman government, and caused fear and suspicion.

That Northern Gaul was still capable of a great outburst was to be proved a quarter of a century later by the great rebellion of Civilis. Moreover, at this particular moment the peace which had long prevailed in Britain under Cymbeline's rule had been ended by the death of that great king (41 *A.D.*?). Civil war had broken out among his sons, and it would appear that several of the races subject to the Catuvellauni were either already in revolt against the suzerain tribe, or were at least ready for it. The intervention of the emperor was solicited by Bericus, who seems to have been a son of Cymbeline driven out by his brothers, and we cannot help suspecting that it may also have been secretly solicited by the tribes which were found submitting to Rome the moment that the legions landed—the Boduni and Regni in the South-East, the Iceni in the East, the two former subjects, the latter perhaps foes of the Catuvellauni.

An obscure sentence in Suetonius may perhaps mean that the victorious sons of Cymbeline, Togodumnus and Caratacus, had demanded, in terms that did not respect the dignity of Rome, the surrender of Bericus and other exiles. Nor can we doubt that a policy of annexation must have been demanded both by the merchants from the Continent already domiciled in Britain, who had everything to gain from the end of Celtic independence, and from the great speculators and financiers of Rome, who were eager, as always, to extend the sphere of their operations. The moment that the conquest began they fell upon the island like a brood of harpies.

In short, it is easy enough to find reasons why Claudius should have undertaken his expedition; his own general ideas on imperial policy must have fitted in with the private motives of his greedy advisers and favourites, who saw plunder everywhere, and with the ambitions of the whole mercantile class. Probably the wealth of the island, considerable as it was, was greatly overvalued, and the difficulty of its conquest minimised.

CHAPTER 5

The Roman Conquest of Britain. Claudius and Nero (43-69 *A.D.*)

The third year of his reign had begun when Claudius made up his mind to undertake the conquest of Britain, and commissioned Aulus Plautius, a veteran who had been consul fourteen years before, and was now far on in middle age, to concentrate the troops that had been designated to form the expeditionary corps. The old legate was to organise the force and to lead it across the Channel, while the emperor himself was to follow a little later, and only to join the army when it was already on the road to victory. Since Claudius's own person and good fortune were to be risked, it was necessary to make the expedition too strong to fear any possibility of disaster. Four legions had been told off, three drawn from the Rhine, one from Pannonia, (see note following); added to them was a body of auxiliaries, horse and foot, more than equal to the legionaries in number; the whole army of invasion probably counted over 60,000 men, or about one-eighth of the entire Roman regular forces then in existence.

★★★★★★

Their names are worth remembering, since two of them were destined to find a permanent home in Britain: These were the Rhine Legions, II. Augusta and XX. Valeria Victrix. The third Rhine Legion, XIV. Gemina Martia, went back to the continent after twenty-five years in Britain. The Pannonian Legion IX. Hispana was destined to perish in Britain, in the early years of the reign of Hadrian.

★★★★★★

It was a somewhat smaller host than that which Julius Caesar had taken over on his second expedition, but its task was not so hard as his, for he had been entering the unknown, while the troops of Aulus Plautius were seeking a country whose resources and geography had been thoroughly well explored by the all-pervading Roman mercantile adventurer.

The moving of a Roman legion was no light matter; ever since Augustus fixed the establishment and the cantonments of the regular army, its units had continued fixed down to the stations which he had appointed for them, with their dependants dwelling close by the camp in their "huts" (*cannabae*), and many time-expired veterans settled on allotments in the surrounding countryside. To disturb such a community was a serious matter, and one not to be undertaken without a clear necessity.

Tiberius only shifted one legion during the course of his long reign. Hence when Claudius ordered no less than four corps to hold themselves ready for a move to Britain there was much murmuring and almost a show of mutiny. The measure which the emperor took for dealing with it—the despatch of his hated favourite Narcissus as a special commissioner to argue with the troops—was ill-advised, since the soldiers despised him equally as a civilian, a Greek and a freedman. But after insulting Narcissus, and indulging in a general riot, the legions returned to their duty and consented to depart, mainly (it is said) owing to their love and respect for the veteran, Aulus Plautius, who had been placed at their head.

The army sailed in three divisions, presumably from Gessoriacum, and came ashore without any hindrance save that caused by the uncertainties of wind and tide, which are said to have given rise to much trouble and anxiety. The Britons had not come down to the shore to offer opposition, though they had received ample notice of the expedition, owing to the long naval and military preparations on the opposite shore. We are told that they had believed that the sailing of the troops had been postponed owing to the mutiny, and were caught unprepared by the sudden arrival of the Romans.

The defence of Britain lay in the hands of Togodumnus and Caratacus, the two sons of Cymbeline, who ruled jointly over their father's lands, and seem to have preserved to some extent his hegemony over the lesser kings—Kent at least, which was no integral part of the Catuvellaunian State, was under their suzerainty. When Plautius first came ashore he found that the local Britons had retired into the woods of the Weald, and seemed inclined to avoid battle, and to do no more than hover on the flanks of the army and harass its foragers—the tactics that Cassivellaunus had used against Caesar a century before.

There was no serious fighting till the Romans reached the line of the Medway, and before they got so far one local tribe had already made its submission. Where these Boduni dwelt we cannot say, but since Plautius left a garrison to protect them, it is clear that they were dwellers in Kent or East Sussex. They are not to be confused, despite of the similarity of name, with the Dobuni of Gloucestershire.

Presently the Romans, following the great track that in all ages has led from Dover and Canterbury towards London and the passages of the Thames, reached the Medway in its lower tidal reaches somewhere near the site of Rochester. Here at last serious opposition was offered to them; the two kings of the Catuvellauni had come out, with all their tributary princes, to defend the passage of the river, which seemed a formidable enough obstacle, with its great breadth at high tide, and its broad sheet of inaccessible mud flats, a still worse hindrance to crossing at low water. But Plautius had with him many auxiliaries from the army of Gaul, troops accustomed to operations in marshes; mainly, as we may suppose, Batavian and other auxiliaries from the mouths of the Rhine.

While Plautius made a demonstration with his main body against the front of the British position, a large force of these auxiliaries swam the river on his right flank, while the legate Vespasian—who was destined to become emperor a quarter of a century later—turned the other flank of the enemy by going far up stream with a second detachment. The Britons were driven away from the river, but rallied on the ground beyond, where they offered battle again on the following day, and maintained the contest for some time on equal terms They surrounded and nearly captured Hosidius Geta, the legate of one of Plautius's legions, but were finally defeated with loss and forced to fly. They then retired behind the marshes of the Thames estuary, being still bent on fighting for their liberty.

The second engagement must have taken place close to the site of London, since we find a bridge mentioned in the topography of the battle, and it is incredible that such a structure should have existed at any other point on the Thames estuary than that which was to bear the famous structure of later years. According to Dio's account the second combat bore much similarity to the first; once more the Gallic auxiliaries swam the estuary at a point lower than that which the natives were guarding, while some of the legionaries forced the passage of "the bridge that lies a little way up stream". The Britons were turned on both flanks and routed with heavy loss; but the Romans also suffered, for they pursued the fugitives into a morass whose paths were unknown to them, and many soldiers perished in it.

Togodumnus, one of the two kings of the Catuvellauni, had perished in battle—whether in the first or in the second fight we do not know. But his surviving brother, Caratacus, rallied his levies and kept at least part of the confederacy together, and it was clear that there would be more engagements before Camulodunum was reached. At this moment Plautius halted, and sent for his master Claudius to conclude the campaign. Dio states that he did so because the campaign had been so fierce that he required the reserves—the Praetorian Guards, no doubt—which the emperor would bring with him. But it is equally probable that he waited in order that Claudius might have the glory of concluding the war, by winning the last decisive battle.

At any rate, the emperor came up in due course, bringing with him both the reserves and a large train, which included even elephants. He picked up the army on the Lower Thames, and then advanced on Camulodunum. Caratacus gave him battle somewhere on the road between London and Colchester, but was completely defeated. Not only did he lose his capital, but all his dominions were overrun, and he himself was compelled to fly into the West, with the wrecks of his personal following. All the tribes of south-eastern Britain, the Catuvellauni, Trinovantes and Cantii, were subdued, while other and more remote peoples did homage in order to save their territory from invasion. Among these latter were the Iceni of the Eastern Counties and the Regni of Sussex, whose kings, Prasutagus and Cogidubnus, were allowed to become "allies of the Roman people," and kept their thrones as vassals of the Empire.

The province of Britain was formally constituted, and Camulodunum was fixed upon as its capital. Then Claudius returned to Italy, having, as we read with some surprise, remained no more than sixteen days in Britain—a time that seems hardly sufficient for the campaign in Essex, the capture of Camulodunum, and the submission of the British kings. He celebrated a triumph of great splendour on his return to Rome, and set up there an arch whose design is commemorated on many of his coins. The Senate voted the title of Britannicus both to Claudius and to his little son, the boy who was destined to be the victim of Nero twelve years later.

Aulus Plautius was left in command of the newly acquired province, and ruled there for the next four years (43-47) with great vigour and success. He seems to have established a military frontier of considerable strategical merits, by conquering all the country south and east of a line drawn from the mouth of the Severn to the Wash. This advance involved a triple conflict—with the tribes of the south-west, those of the Lower Severn valley, and those of the Eastern Midlands. We know that the campaigns in the south-west were earned out by the legate Vespasian, the future emperor: of him it is recorded that:

He fought thirteen battles with the natives, and added to the Roman Empire two powerful tribes, twenty towns (*oppida*) and the Isle of Wight, which lies near to the British coast. (Suetonius.)

The two tribes we may presume were the Belgae, whose territory extended from the Solent to Somersetshire, and the Durotriges of Dorset. The oppida would mean not so much towns as these fortified tribal camps to which Julius Caesar applied that designation. It may be taken as certain that the troops employed in these operations were the Second Legion and its auxiliaries, who always worked in Western Britain. (See Haverfield in *Arch, Journal* xlix.) The fighting may often have been heavy, as Dio records that on one occasion Vespasian was surrounded by the enemy, and would have been slain, if his son Titus had not rescued him by a vigorous charge, and broken the Britons. How rapid and thorough was the conquest of the south-west may be judged from the fact that the lead mines of Mendip were being regularly worked for the Roman Government within six years of Plautius's landing.

Two pigs of that metal, accidentally lost at the time of their casting, have been discovered, which bear the names of Claudius and his son Britannicus, and can be accurately dated to the year 49 *A.D.* On the other hand, there is no trace of the extension of the Roman power over the Dumnonians, the inhabitants of the peninsula of Devon and Cornwall. Since there is no mention of trouble in the extreme south-west, and since no legion was left on guard in this quarter, it is clear that they must have made some form of submission. But few traces of Roman occupation west of Exeter can be found in the first century after Christ, and for some generations these remote regions seem to have been practically left to themselves.

The great road system which was perfected in the second century stopped on the Exe, and it is not till the time of Constantine that signs of activity farther west become clear. Apparently, this had something to do with the decline of the old Cornish tin-trade, which was at a low ebb in the early empire, but revived in the third century. (See Haverfield on the Cornish tin-trade in *Mélanges Boissier.*)

When the land up to the line of the Exe had been subdued, the Second Legion seems to have been drawn up to the line of the Lower Severn. Its next regular station was to be to Isca (Caerleon) in the land of the Silures, beyond that river. But it is not probable that it reached that advanced point during the governorship of Plautius: Glevum (Gloucester) has been suggested by several specialists (Hübner, Furneaux, Panza) as a likely abiding place for the legion, when the first work of subduing the Belgae was over. There is, however, no proof whatever that it ever had its permanent camp at that place, and it moved on to Isca so early that, even if it was stationed for a few years at Glevum, it is unlikely that it would have left any memorials of itself behind.

Of the forward movement of the opposite, or eastern, wing of the Roman advance we have no record in the historians, and indeed we should have known nothing about the conquests of the southwest had not Vespasian, the man with a future, been in command in that direction. It seems, however, that Aulus Plautius, after subduing the Catuvellauni, probably advanced the Roman frontier to the Wash. The Iceni of the Eastern Counties having made an early and willing submission because of their dislike to their old enemies of the house of Tasciovanus, the natural front of the new province would be along the line of the rivers which cross England in a diagonal direction from south-west to north-east. The empire of the Catuvellaunian kings seems to have reached beyond the Ouse, but never to have touched the Trent.

The Nen or the Welland would have been natural boundaries at which to draw the line of occupation. But there is some reason to believe that Ratae (Leicester) found the extreme point of the advance, and that the Legion IX. Hispana was in garrison there very shortly after 43 *A.D.* (The only evidence, however, is tiles found there bearing the stamp of the IXth Legion, wrongly read as the VIIIth, *Journal Brit, Arch. Assoc.* 1863, p, 46.)

The locality is a very suitable one, since it covers the gap of plainland, between the marshy lower course of the rivers which flow into the Wash, and that central forest of Britain which divided the basin of the Severn and Avon from that of the streams falling into the North Sea. Its strategical importance was shown a little later by the fact that it became the only important town on the great Roman wad which crossed the Midlands from Cirencester to Lincoln.

As to the central space of Britain, between Leicester and the Lower Severn, it is obvious that it cannot have been left wholly unguarded. It seems pretty certain that one legion remained behind at Camulodunum, to hold down the Catuvellauni, the old rulers of Southern Britain, as long as Aulus Plautius was governor.

★★★★★★

I think that Hübner's view, is pretty certain and can only mean that Scapula wanted to move legions against the Silurians, and in order to get as many as possible available, collected a veteran colony at Camulodunum as a substitute for a legion up to that time quartered there. Probably this was Legion XX. of whom tombstones are found at Colchester.

✶✶✶✶✶✶

Where the other legion lay, we have no means of determining. But as the front of the province was now drawn in advance of the Fosse-Way, which probably represents an early Celtic track from Cirencester to Leicester, running along the line of easiest passage through the Midlands, and avoiding the forest regions of Arden and Cannock Chase, we should expect to find the central legion on or just behind it. Durocornovium (Cirencester), appears rather too near the region in which the Second Legion was operating, yet there seems reason to believe that it was a very early military centre.

✶✶✶✶✶✶

See Haverfield, *Archaeological Journal*, 1. Many military tombstones have been found at Bath, some very early, but these seem merely to prove that convalescents went to take the waters, and sometimes died there.

✶✶✶✶✶✶

On the other hand, on purely strategical principles we should expect to find a legion somewhere in support of the line of the Fosse, and for choice on Watling Street, the line by which London is (indirectly) connected with Leicester, at some such point as Lactodurum (Towcester) or Bannaventa near Daventry. But this is pure hypothesis.

Aulus Plautius came back to Rome in 47, and was duly commended by his master "for having conducted and concluded the British War with honour." He was granted a triumph, which ended with a great gladiatorial exhibition in the Amphitheatre, at which many unfortunate captives fought and fell. His appointed successor was Publius Ostorius Scapula, a governor of whom we know more than of his predecessor, because the gap in Tacitus's Annals which covers the early years of Claudius has now come to an end, and we have not any longer to depend solely on meagre scraps of Dio or Suetonius.

Plautius had finished the conquest of the plain-land of Southern Britain, where population was comparatively thick, and where communications were easy. Perhaps the Roman government would have been content to halt, when this paying part of the island had been subdued. But this was impossible: the untamed and warlike tribes in the hills of North and South Wales—the Ordovices and Silurians, and the still more powerful and restless Brigantes, who held the whole North, from Derbyshire to the Solway, persisted in ravaging the borders of the new province. Probably they had been wont to harry their tribal neighbours in the plain from time immemorial, and would not desist even when the legions came to protect them. But a political aspect was lent to the war by the fact that Caratacus, the exiled king of the Catuvellauni, had taken refuge among the Silurians, and was leading their forays, having apparently not only been granted shelter by the tribe but also some share of military authority. His hope was to keep the war afoot, and wear out the Romans, in the expectation that his former subjects might someday rise to aid him.

Ostorius, on his arrival in Britain, had to face a dangerous series of these incursions, which at the beginning of the winter season were specially difficult to resist. But knowing that impunity would render the enemy more daring, and probably lead to a revolt inside the province, he called out his cavalry and light-armed *cohorts*, and set to work at once to hunt down the raiders. He surprised many bands, and drove them back to their mountains with heavy loss. He then announced that he should disarm all the provincials, whose loyalty he suspected, and so pacify all the land that lies on this side of Severn and Trent.

★★★★★★

There is a disputed reading and a topographical difficulty here. Some editors have substituted Aufonam for Antonam, thinking that the Warwickshire Avon was a likely line for a series of camps. But fortifications along the Avon would have nothing to alarm the Iceni, and it seems better to take Antona for the Trent, not as Mommsen did for the Shropshire Tern, whose ancient name is unknown, as is also that of the Trent. The ingenious emendation of cis Trisantonam for castris Antonam is very attractive, but the name Trisantona is as unknown as that of Antona in British geography, save as that of a small river in Sussex, in Ptolemy's description of the South Coast. See Furneaux's Tacitus, xii.

★★★★★★

These precautions roused a general revolt in Eastern Britain, which was headed by the Iceni, who had been the allies of the Romans ever since their landing, and resented the proposed disarmament. They were joined by their neighbours, no doubt the Coritani between Wash and Humber, and the wrecks of the Catuvellauni, and offered battle to

Ostorius on ground chosen by themselves, difficult of approach and fortified with earthern ramparts. The governor risked an attack upon the position, though he had no single legion with him, but only a mass of auxiliaries. His boldness was rewarded by a complete victory, in spite of the desperate resistance of the rebels (48 *A.D.*).

The Iceni seem to have been granted easy terms, as their state still appears under a vassal king for some years after this revolt. But the crushing character of the defeat induced all the neighbouring tribes "who had been hesitating between peace and war," to proffer their submission. It was probably at this moment that Ostorius pushed forward the frontier of the province, annexing the territory of the Coritani and Cornavii, and sending on the Ninth Legion from Ratae to Lindum (Lincoln), while the Fourteenth and Twentieth may both have been moved to Viroconium (Wroxeter) on the Middle Severn. This arrangement would be intended not only to hold down the newly won districts, but to oppose a solid force to the powerful tribes to whose border the province had now advanced—the Yorkshire Brigantes and the Silures and Ordovices of Wales.

It was probably from the new base at Viroconium that Ostorius sent out in the following year (49 *A.D.*) an expedition against the Deceangi, who occupied the lands at the mouth of the Dee in Flintshire, Denbighshire and Western Cheshire, and possessed valuable lead mines. Probably they were a section of, or subject to, the powerful race of the Ordovices. While engaged in devastating their territory, and "not far from the Irish Sea," Ostorius was drawn back by the news that the Brigantes were on the move. But on his approach only a few of these enemies were met and routed—the bulk of the great Northern tribe had held back, and now offered or accepted terms of peace.

This left Ostorius free to continue the campaign against the tribes of the Welsh hills. He is said to have prepared for it by making sure of his base; the legions being now transferred westward, he thought well to establish a great colony of veterans at Camulodunum, to serve instead of a garrison for the provincial capital. The time-expired veterans of his legions were settled there, and given lands in the vicinity; this nucleus of war-tried soldiers was the first Roman city in Britain: it was named Colonia Claudia after the reigning emperor. It would seem that Ostorius, leaving Eastern Britain ungarrisoned save by the legion at Lincoln, took all the other three off to his Western campaign. The Second Legion was brought up to Isca Silurum (Caerleon) from Gloucester, or whatever other place was its original headquarters: the

Fourteenth and Twentieth operated from the newly occupied base at Viroconium on the Severn.

At the beginning of the ensuing aeries of campaigns, which lasted for three years, the Silurians, the southern enemy, seem to have taken the lead, with the untiring Caratacus at their head. But when the governor had turned his attention to them, the exiled king drew away into the territory of the Ordovices, and transferred the main seat of the lingering war northwards. Ostorius followed him, and after many 'vicissitudes of fortune, found him offering battle in a very strong position, whose flanks were covered by precipitous hills and its centre protected by an entrenchment of rough stones, while a river, hard to ford, ran along its front.

This was the last chance of Caratacus: we are told that he rode along the line reminding the Britons of how his ancestors had turned back Julius Caesar, pointing out to them the meaning of the Roman yoke to men who had hitherto lived in freedom, and urging them to save themselves and their families from tribute, slavery and dishonour. The warriors shouted their approval of his words, and the Ordovices and Silurians bound themselves, each swearing by the gods of their tribe, that they would conquer or die.

Nevertheless, the battle, after a very hard struggle, went in favour of the Romans, who forded the river and stormed the entrenchments after a desperate struggle and with heavy loss. Even when their line had been pierced, the Britons rallied at the top of the hill, but in a second combat they were again broken, and then dispersed in all directions. (Cefn Carnedd, near Llanidloes, and Coxall Knoll, near Lentwardine, have been suggested as probable sites for the battle. No certainty is possible.) The wife and daughter of Caratacus were captured in the British camp, and some of his male relatives, who had hitherto followed his fortunes, surrendered themselves.

But the king fled to the Brigantes, and tried to rouse them up to engage in the war. This tribe was at the moment ruled by a queen named Cartimandua—a strange phenomenon among a Celtic race. She had already resolved not to court war with the Romans, and instead of taking arms, seized Caratacus and handed him over in chains to the governor (50 *A.D.*).

Ostorius sent the captive and all his family to Home, where Claudius made a great public spectacle of their reception. They were led through the Forum under a military guard to a high tribunal, where Claudius sat to determine on their fate. Caratacus is said to have displayed an undaunted spirit, to have told the emperor that he considered himself justified in having defended himself and his possessions to the last gasp, and to have added that his long resistance had made the Roman triumph all the more conspicuous in the end:

> If I had been betrayed and captured when the war began, neither my fortune nor your glory would have been so notable: I might have been put to death without attracting much attention: but now, if you were to spare my life, I should be an example of Roman clemency for all ages.

Yielding, we may suspect, rather to his natural good nature than to this argument, Claudius granted Caratacus and his whole family their lives, and ordered their chains to be removed. Apparently, the king ended his days as a pensioned exile in Italy; history only preserves the anecdote that walking through Rome after his release and gazing at the splendour of its palaces, he exclaimed, (Dio Cassius, *Fragments*):

> And yet the owners of all this must needs covet our poor huts in Britain. (51. *A.D.*)

To the surprise of Ostorius the capture of Caratacus did not bring the war in Western Britain to an end. The Silurians became more active than ever after his disappearance from the scene:

> Whether it was that the Romans grew somewhat careless, thinking that they had finished the struggle by removing the king, or whether the enemy burst out into a more bitter passion of revenge from pity for the fate of so gallant a prince. (Tacitus, *Annals*.)

At any rate the war took a turn for the worse after the year 51. The Silurians surrounded and well-nigh cut off a legionary force which had been left to build a fortress in their territory—perhaps the camp still visible at Gaer in Cymddu. The detachment was saved by reinforcements which hurried up from the nearest garrison, (possibly from Isca, but "*castellis*" seems to suggest smaller posts: we should expect "*castris*"), but a prefect, eight *centurions* and very many of the rank and file had been slain. Not long after, this vigorous tribe routed a foraging force, and the cavalry supports which had been sent off to cover it, and were only checked by the arrival of more than one legion on the ground. These fights were followed by a long wearing campaign "like a series of brigand raids in woods or marshes". After two auxiliary *cohorts*, raiding incautiously, had been surprised and exterminated, Ostorius fell ill and died from fatigue, and the wear and tear of constant anxiety, "to the great joy of the enemy, who declared that if not a battle yet at any rate the war had made an end of this by no means despicable general."

Aulus Didius was sent out hastily from Rome to replace Ostorius, and arrived to find matters more unpromising than ever, a legion commanded by Manlius Valens having been defeated in open battle by the Silurians just before he landed. The western war dragged on without any definite result, and he was also threatened with an attack from the Brigantes, among whom civil strife had arisen between the faction favourable to the Roman alliance, and that which wished for war. Cartimandua, the Brigantian queen, who had given up Caratacus, had married a chief named Venutius, but she presently quarrelled with him, and murdered his brother and certain other of his kinsmen.

★★★★★★

A hoard of Brigantian coins dug up at Honley near Huddersfield, in 1893, contained a coin of Cartimandua, the only one yet discovered. The pieces were interesting, the early ones showing the name of an unknown king, Volisius, associated with one Dumnocoverus, while the later retain the name of Volisius but show on the reverse the name *CARTI*—. These inscriptions suggest that Volisius was a king who associated with himself first a colleague (perhaps his son) named Dumnocoverus, and, after the death of the latter, Cartimandua who must surely have been his daughter and heiress.

★★★★★★

He therefore flew to arms, and put himself at the head of the war party, while the queen appealed for aid to Didius. Seeing that the triumph of Venutius would mean a Brigantian invasion of the Midlands, the governor lent her the services of a detachment from the legion at Lincoln, IX. Hispana, then under the command of Caesius Nasica. The fighting began not too favourably for the Romans, but ended with a success, and apparently a peace was patched up between the contending factions, since Cartimandua and Venutius are still found reigning together more than fifteen years later.

Didius ruled for five years—the two last of Claudius, the three first of Nero (52-57). He is said by Tacitus to have been an unenterprising governor, being well advanced in years, and destitute of ambition, since he had already attained to all the honours to which a subject might aspire. He handed over the conduct of all his campaigns to his lieutenants, and thought that he had done enough when he retained what his predecessor had conquered. It seems that the frontier remained fixed, well-nigh as Scapula had drawn it, on the line from Lincoln to the mouth of the Dee, and from thence to Isca—the Silurians and Ordovices retaining their independence, despite of constant raids directed against them from the base-camps on the Severn and Usk.

******

Didius is said by Tacitus to have pushed forward a few forts, but to have done no more, but possibly Deva was made a legionary station by him, as there seem to be signs that it was already occupied not very long after *A.D.* 50, *i.e.*, in the time of Didius rather than that of Suetonius.

******

The northern border would be kept safe through the friendship of the Queen of the Brigantes.

Didius retired in 57: his successor Veranius appeared in the folio wing year, and announced that he was about to assume a more active policy. But he had only just commenced an attack on the Silurians, and ravaged their borders, when he died. In his will was found a curious pledge in which he promised the Emperor Nero that in two years he would guarantee the complete subjection of Britain. After some little delay he was replaced by Suetonius Paulinus, a general of rare merit, and very popular with the army and people, who called him the rival of Corbulo, his great contemporary, who saved the Armenian border and forced the Parthians to peace (59 *A.D.*).

Suetonius changed the front of the Roman advance, and took the land of the Ordovices in North Wales as his objective, partly in order to turn the flank of the Silurians and take them in the rear, but mainly because, as Tacitus tells us, the Isle of Mona (Anglesey), the farthest stronghold of the Ordovices, was the centre of the national religion of Britain, and the refuge of all rebels and deserters. It may have been now that the headquarters of one or both of the legions at Wroxeter were moved to Deva (Chester), on the estuary of the Dee, the natural base for all operations against North Wales, though the change may have been Didius's work. He built a flotilla of flat-bottomed boats on the Dee, with which he intended to carry his infantry across the Menai Strait: the cavalry was to swim across at low water.

Apparently, a year was consumed in these preparations, as it was not until the spring of 60 *A.D.* that the invasion of North Wales began. The governor took with him, no doubt, the whole or parts of the Fourteenth and Twentieth Legions, though a garrison must have been left at Deva to guard the base, while the Second Legion at Isca watched the ever-hostile Silures, and the Ninth at Lincoln was the only solid force left in Eastern Britain. The boats coasted along the rocky shore of North Wales parallel to the advance of the land army, and could have been used to turn the enemy's sea-side flank, if he had made any resistance during the march. But we are not told that the Britons attempted to hold the line of the Conway, or any other of the defensible rivers which flow into the sea between Deva and the straits.

Their efforts were reserved for the defence of Anglesey, where the whole force of the tribe was concentrated to defend the ancient sanctuaries.

Along the shore was seen a dense line of armed warriors, while women were rushing about between the ranks garbed like the Furies, in black gowns, their hair flowing loose, and torches in their hands. The Druids were visible in the rear offering sacrifices to their gods, raising their hands to heaven, and calling down dire imprecations upon the head of the invader.

At first the soldiery, on being thrown ashore, were somewhat impressed by the strange wild scene, and stood as if paralysed under the shower of weapons. But their officers called them on, and they began to exhort each other to have no fear of an army of women and fanatics. In the first charge they broke the Britons, and drove them back on the flames of their own sacrifices. There followed a great massacre of priests, warriors, and women alike; after which Suetonius bid his men cut down the sacred groves, and destroy the altars on which the Druids had been wont to offer human sacrifices, and to seek signs from heaven in the entrails of their victims. At this moment the governor suddenly received terrible news from the rear. All Eastern Britain, where no trouble had been known for more than ten years, had blazed up into sudden revolt.

The immediate cause of this explosion was the recent annexation of the subject-kingdom of the Iceni, in modern Norfolk and Suffolk. Its king Prasutagus had lately died, leaving no male issue, and the Roman Government had resolved to put an end to the existence of his little state, though he had endeavoured to propitiate the young emperor, by naming him, along with his own daughters, as part heir to all his possessions. Apparently, none of the male kin of Prasutagus dared to oppose the annexation, which might have been completed peacefully if the agents employed to carry it out had behaved with common decency and moderation. But the officers sent by the governor to take military possession of the kingdom, and the clerks told off by the procurator (who represented the imperial private estate—*fiscus*—in Britain) to investigate the personal property of Prasutagus, disgraced themselves by their violent and unrighteous doings.

The realm, says Tacitus, was devastated by the centurions, the palace by the procurator's slaves. Many of the richest Icenians were stripped of their ancestral estates—the late king's relatives were treated as if they had been left as slaves to the emperor. The widowed queen Boudicca was arrested and scourged for offering opposition to the officials, and—worst of all—her two young daughters were violated by their ruffianly captors. The whole tribe of the Iceni sprang to arms to avenge these outrages, and were at once joined by the Trinovantes, who had their own special grievances to avenge. The most notable of these was that the owners of an immense area of land round the new colony of Camulodunum had been expropriated without compensation, in order to provide allotments for the veterans there established.

Nor was this all: the settlers habitually subjected their surviving provincial neighbours to violence and insult, and the Britons could get no redress from the government. Instead of strengthening Roman influence in the South-East, as Ostorius had hoped when he founded it, the colony of Camulodunum had weakened it, by provoking the wrath of the surrounding population. Yet the colonists had not taken precautions against their aggrieved neighbours: the place was not provided with a ditch or wall, or a castle of refuge, and the only building in it capable of defence was the large and solid stone temple of Divus Claudius.

Other details are given us by Dio Cassius, which enable us to comprehend more clearly the discontent of the British provincials. It was a very common thing for Roman financiers to persuade or compel tribal magnates to borrow money from them—a thing to which the thriftless and ostentatious Celtic chiefs in Gaul, as well as in Britain, were always prone. The celebrated Seneca, then one of the two chief ministers of Nero, is said to have been the greatest money-lender of all, despite of his philosophy and his ostentatious love of moderation and justice.

At this moment he had just called in loans amounting to 10,000,000 *sesterces* without warning. Hence scores of British landowners found themselves threatened with bankruptcy, or even with slavery. At the same time, the procurator of the imperial private *fiscus*, Decianus Catus, was demanding the instant payment of much money which had been given or lent by Claudius to prominent supporters of the Roman cause.

Thus, the exactions of the local officials conspired with the greed of the financier to turn old friends into enemies. All the chiefs of Eastern Britain, whatever their former politics, listened to the appeal of Boudicca, when she pleaded her own wrongs, and region after region rose, and placed its levies at the disposal of the injured queen, who became not only the trumpet of sedition but the general of the confederate army. For she rode in her chariot at the head of the warriors, and put herself in the forefront of the battle.

On the outbreak of revolt among the Iceni the colonists of Camulodunum at last saw their peril, and, since the governor was absent on his Welsh campaign, applied for aid to the procurator, Decianus Catus. He could only supply them with 200 men, but the veterans and other settlers took arms, and began to think of fortifying the town; this project is said to have been hindered by British residents who were in secret agreement with the rebels. At any rate a sudden onslaught of the Icenian and Trinovantian levies carried the place with a rush, and drove the garrison into the temple of Claudius. This was besieged and stormed on the second day.

The whole of the settlers, Roman and foreign, were put to death with cruel tortures; even the women were stripped naked, mutilated and impaled. Just after this disaster had occurred the *legate* Petillius Cerealis approached, at the head of the Ninth Legion, the only solid force of regulars which had been left in Eastern Britain, when Suetonius went off to the west. The Britons turned upon him and inflicted a complete defeat on his troops. The whole of the legionary infantry was cut to pieces; Cerealis escaped with a few hundred cavalry alone. At once the whole of the neighbouring tribes took arms to aid the victorious Boudicca; the Roman and other foreign immigrants took refuge in the towns of Verulamium and Londinium. The Procurator Catus fled in despair to Gaul.

Such was the news which was brought to Suetonius, on the shores of the Menai Strait, immediately after he had achieved his victory in Mona. He started to fly to the assistance of the isolated Roman towns in the East, and set all the troops that could be spared from North Wales in motion. At the same moment he sent orders to Poenius Postumus, who was in command of the Second Legion at Isca, to bring up that corps to join him.

★★★★★★

The version of Suetonius's campaign here given is suggested by Professor Haverfield, who points out that Tacitus's narrative does not necessarily imply that the *legate* reached London with his whole field army about him, and that the "*jam Suetonio quartadecima legio cum vexillariis,* etc.," of *Annals,* xiv. 34, gives the force present at the battle only, and does not say that it had marched with Suetonius. It certainly seems easier to understand the general's abandonment of London and Verulamium if we believe that he had got ahead of his army. The "*agmen*" which Tacitus speaks of, as accompanied by the fugitive Londoners, must on this hypothesis have been composed of the trifling garrison of London. The "*infrequentia militis,*" which induced Suetonius to retreat, according to this paragraph, does not indeed square in well with the generally accepted idea that he had already 10,000 men with him.

★★★★★★

A rapid rush across the island brought Suetonius to London, whose first definite appearance in British history dates from this year, though we know from its name that it must have been an old Celtic trade centre long before the Romans came to Britain. Tacitus calls it:

A town which though not honoured with the title of a colony was very celebrated for the number of its merchants and the abundance of its resources.

But on reaching London the governor found the situation so much worse than he had expected that he dared neither to hold the town and stand a siege, nor to offer battle to the rebels. It is probable that his own troops had not yet come up in full force. Nor had he yet been joined by the expected Second Legion. Therefore, he bade the citizens of London pack up their goods and retire under his protection. They mostly did so, but many, either from necessity or because they thought that they had friends among the Britons, refused to follow Suetonius. All these were massacred when Boudicca occupied the city after the *legate's* retreat. The sum of the Roman disasters was completed by the fall, about the same time, of the flourishing municipality of Verulamium, which was sacked and burnt with atrocities that rivalled those which had been perpetrated at Camulodunum. The ancient historians state, no doubt with exaggeration, that at Camulodunum, Londinium and Verulamium about 70,000 persons perished, when Romans, continental traders from Gaul and elsewhere, and friendly Britons were calculated all together.

Suetonius, as it seems, had now been joined by all the troops from the North-West, the whole Fourteenth Legion, some chosen *cohorts* of the Twentieth, and auxiliaries enough to make his total force up to 10,000 men. But Poenius Postumus had failed to bring up the Second Legion, and had disobeyed orders by shutting himself up in the camp of Isca, where the Silurians were no doubt threatening him. It was necessary either to fall back on Isca or Deva, the only points in Britain now in Roman hands, or to offer battle at once to the rebels. Probably the fact that his march was clogged by thousands of refugees from London, who would have made farther retreat slow and difficult, induced the governor to take the bolder course.

He turned and faced the pursuing Britons in a narrow position where his wings and rear were covered with woods, so as to make flanking operations impossible. Boudicca and her horde encamped opposite him; they are said to have been a vast host of more than 80,000 men, accompanied by thousands of waggons loaded with their wives, camp followers and provisions.

★★★★★★

The battle spot is impossible to locate. Professor Haverfield suggests that if Suetonius had fallen back from London to pick up his army, or part of it, we must suppose the battle to have taken place somewhere along the line of the road London-Wroxeter (Watling Street), on which the troops must have been moving.

★★★★★★

Flushed by her unbroken series of successes, the furious queen had no thought of tactics, and resolved to overwhelm the Romans by the wild frontal rush of a multitude. She harangued the tribes to a pitch of frenzy, and then flung them forward on the Roman line. Suetonius received the headlong charge with his men halted, but when it was beaten off, took the offensive in his turn and sallied out from his position with the legion in a dense column in the centre, the auxiliaries on each side of it, and the cavalry on the wings. Caesar's old saying that only the first rush of a Celtic army was to be dreaded once more proved true. When the Romans broke out upon the disordered multitude, and pierced its centre, the greater part of the British host gave way and fled. But many thousands were thrust back upon the waggon-*laager* of their own encampment, and were overtaken as they vainly strove to disentangle themselves from it.

The Romans cut to pieces not only the flying warriors but the women and camp followers—the example had been set them by the enemy, who in the sack of three towns had spared neither age nor sex. An incredible number of Britons are said to have fallen—enough to avenge all their late massacres. Boudicca escaped for the moment, but took poison when she saw that the rebellion was doomed to failure.

Suetonius had now to reduce practically the whole island to submission, since the Roman authority had disappeared everywhere during the recent disasters. He was able to do so when his field army had been increased. The Second Legion came up from Isca—its disobedient commander had committed suicide to avoid a court-martial. From the continent there came over 2,000 legionary recruits to replace the lost infantry of the Ninth Legion, eight auxiliary *cohorts*, and a thousand horse. Instead of going into winter quarters, the governor led his troops up and down the rebellious districts, wasting them with fire and sword. Yet the tribes, though suffering terribly from famine, were slow to make their submission. It was said that the new procurator, Julius Classicianus, the successor of Decianus Catus, had given the Britons secret counsel to the effect that the longer they held out the better terms would they get.

This he did, we are told, from hatred of Suetonius, for whose recall he was intriguing at Rome, since he calculated that if the rebellion went on much longer the governor would be superseded, as incapable of terminating the war. After a space Nero sent across to Britain his favourite freedman Polycletus, to make a report on the state of the province: it was apparently favourable to Suetonius, who was retained in command for a year longer, and Succeeded in restoring order within the old boundaries of the province, though he was too busy therein to be able to pay any attention to his original enemies the Silurians and Ordovices. But at the end of 61 he was recalled, on account of a new disaster which Tacitus vaguely describes as "the loss of some few galleys and their crews on the coast." We are left uninformed as to whether the loss was by shipwreck or by capture at the hands of the enemy.

The next governor was Petronius Turpilianus (*A.D.* 61-63), a cautious man, who thought his duty was to restore the administration of the province rather than to court further wars:

And so, since he neither attacked the unsubdued tribes nor was attacked by them, he was able to cloke his want of enterprise with the honourable name of peace.

The boundaries of the province had returned to the position which they had occupied before Boudicca's rebellion, Isca, Deva and Lindum being held as the frontier strongholds, while the Brigantes, Ordovices, and Silurians retained their independence. Doubtless Petronius had enough to do in reorganising the shattered fabric of government within the old limits, and was wise to subordinate all else to that end. His successor, M. Trebellius Maximus, who ruled the province for the space of six years (63-69), a longer term than any previous governor had enjoyed, would appear to have been a man of a similar temperament. Tacitus, in somewhat contemptuous terms, remarks that he endeavoured to keep the province quiet by mere urbanity and good temper, but at the same time accuses him of meanness and parsimony, and states that he kept the soldiery in arrears of their pay.

This makes it appear likely that Trebellius's way of keeping the Britons in good temper was to raise as little money from them as possible, even if military efficiency was thereby endangered. But it must be remembered that his power of resuming a forward policy and completing the conquest of Western Britain was seriously diminished by the fact that Nero, in 68 *A.D.*, withdrew the Fourteenth Legion from Britain for a projected expedition on the Armenian frontier. This left the line facing the Silurians and Ordovices guarded by only two legions, the Second at Isca, and the Twentieth at Deva.

It must be concluded from the fact that this removal was possible that either Petronius or Trebellius had patched up some sort of a formal peace with the mountaineers of Wales. (Tacitus only states that Petronius had made terms with the rebels, and says nothing about his dealings with the rest. *Agricola*, c. 16).

We learn without surprise that the rule of Trebellius was not unpleasing to the Britons, though we need not ascribe his popularity to the fact that the barbarians had "begun to look with less disfavour on the corruption of Roman civilisation," as Tacitus unkindly puts it, (*Agricola.*) Economic administration and courteous treatment are sufficient to account for the phenomenon. It is probable that more solid progress in the assimilation of the province was made in the years 61-69 than in all those which had gone before: in the more stirring times that were to follow the Britons of the south and east gave no trouble whatever, a sufficient sign that they were growing less discontented.

Probably the prosaic but necessary work of roadmaking, and the improvement of towns, was going on apace, when all the resources of the province were no longer devoted to feeding an offensive war. It is quite likely that to this period belongs the development of the great highways of Britain—Watling Street (from London by Viroconium to Deva), Ermine Street (from London by Castor-on-Nen to Lincoln), the Fosse Way (from Exeter, Bath, and Cirencester, by Leicester to Lincoln), and the nameless but important road from London, by Silchester, to Cirencester, Gloucester, and Isca, which was the most important link between South-Eastern and South-Western Britain. All had no doubt been primitive Celtic trackways, which the conquerors straightened out, and converted into good metalled roads at their leisure.

Less important arteries of traffic awaited construction or improvement at a later day; in some outlying or thinly peopled districts the Romans seem never to have cared to build proper "streets," and to have made shift to employ the old tracks during the whole period of their occupation of Britain. This was certainly the case in the extreme west, in the Dumnonian lands of Devon and Cornwall, where Roman milestones have been found, but no properly constructed Roman paved roads of the usual type.

There were many regions of the Midlands which were no better served—where we find scattered traces of Roman habitation, but no metalled *chaussées*. The middle valleys of the Thames and Severn, were, down to the end, very badly served by the provincial road system. The east and west roads, from London to Bath and Gloucester, went by Silchester and Speen, many miles south of the Thames.

There was no corresponding road at all on the north of the river: if a traveller had persisted in going from London to Gloucester through the South Midlands, his only chance would be to take the angular and circuitous route—St. Albans, Towcester, Bicester, Cirencester. (Or rather, to be more exact, not Bicester, but Alchester, which lies a mile or so from the modern town.) Similarly, in the Severn Valley the obvious route—Gloucester, Worcester, Viroconium—does not seem to have existed, the north and south roads in this region running many miles away from the river, the one from Viroconium to Isca through Herefordshire, the other keeping along the slopes of Cotswold, crossing the Avon in its middle course, and joining Watling Street at Letocetum near Lichfield.

The explanation is that the valleys of the middle Thames and

Severn were mainly undrained areas of swamp and jungle, where there lived at most small communities of fishers and hunters. The population lay along the higher and drier ground, and there were as yet no towns to represent the mediaeval Reading and Oxford, or Tewkesbury and Worcester.

The placid and economical Trebellius was still ruling when chaos commenced all over the empire at the death of Nero (68). Britain, however, suffered less from the civil wars of the "year of the three emperors" (69) than most other provinces; its legions followed, at a distance, the motions of those of Gaul, and adhered to the cause of Vitellius, as did the governor. But Trebellius, being unpopular with the soldiery—however much he may have been liked by the provincials—had some unpleasant experiences.

The turbulent legate of the Twentieth Legion, a certain Caelius Roscius, raised a sedition against him, and finally compelled him to fly out of the island and take refuge with Vitellius. For some time the three legates of the legions ruled Britain at their pleasure, but they all adhered to the same cause that the ex-governor had taken up, and after some delay detached 8,000 men, picked legionary and auxiliary *cohorts*, to join the army with which Vitellius invaded Italy. These British troops were too late for the first Battle of Bedriacum, in which Otho fell, but found a notable and much-trusted part of the forces which, a few months later, contended on the side of Vitellius against Vespasian in the second North Italian campaign.

Meanwhile that indolent and short-lived emperor had sent Vettius Bolanus to take the place of Trebellius as governor of Britain, and had also restored to the island the Fourteenth Legion, which Nero had taken away from it, two years before, for his abortive Caucasian expedition. No doubt the garrison had been weakened to the verge of danger by the drafts sent to Italy, and troops to replace them were much needed. The Fourteenth Martia was the corps selected for that purpose, both because it had long served in Britain, and because it had taken the part of Otho in the late civil war, and was therefore not safe to leave in Italy when another contest was impending.

That struggle went against Vitellius, and after his death Vespasian was acknowledged as emperor in every corner of the empire. In Britain the governor, Bolanus, had done little or nothing to aid Vitellius, both because he was an unenterprising person, and because two of his legions had strong sympathies for the other side—the Second Augusta, because of its kindly memory of the time when Vespasian had been its legate in 43-47, and the Fourteenth, because it had always been opposed to the Vitellian faction. So little had Bolanus committed himself to the lost cause that the new emperor actually retained him in command for some months, although he had been appointed by his enemy and predecessor. He is said to have been an easy-going and not unpopular ruler, who shirked the task of imposing the necessary return to discipline upon legions which had got out of hand. The last note recorded of him is that he was compelled to send back to the continent the Fourteenth Legion, which had so recently returned to Britain.

******

During its short second stay in Britain the Fourteenth Martia may have been at Lincoln, along with the Ninth Hispana, as a monument to one of its men has been found there. C.I.L., 187. A concentration at Lincoln may have been due to the impending trouble among the Brigantes, who were just about to take arms.

******

The cause of this transfer was the breaking out upon the Rhine of the great Gallo-German insurrection of Civilis, a rebel of genius, against whom troops had to be concentrated from every corner of the empire. The Fourteenth Martia Victrix never returned to Britain, being replaced, when the war on the Rhine was over, by a newly-raised corps, the Second Adjutrix. But this happened after the supersession of Bolanus by Petillius Cerealis (70 *A.D.*), a hearty supporter of Vespasian, who had atoned by laurels newly won from the German rebels for his old defeat at the hands of Boudicca in 60 *A.D.* For this is the same Cerealis whose legion had been completely cut to pieces by the Iceni after the fall of Camulodunum.

CHAPTER 6

Conquest of Northern Britain. Cerealis and Agricola (71-85 *A.D.*)

With the accession of Vespasian, or rather with the complete establishment of Vespasian's power in the North-West, after the crushing of the rebellion of Civilis, begins a new era of expansion and conquest in the history of Roman Britain. There had, as we have seen, been no considerable annexations made since the governorship of Ostorius Scapula, and no shifting of the legionary stations since the forward move to Deva. The Ordovices and Silurians seemed to have won a permanent independence by their obstinate resistance: the Brigantes of the North had never been seriously attacked.

The new aggressive departure which begins with the governorship of Petillius Cerealis (71-74) may have been first provoked by movements on the part of the Britons, but it is clear that it continued long after any necessity for self-defence was over, and was part of a deliberate policy for bringing the provincial boundary up to the limits which the governor, or his master at Rome, considered natural and convenient. Vespasian was in a much more sound and solid position than his predecessors, and being bred a professional soldier must have had all his ideas dominated by military considerations, in a way which could not be expected of Claudius or Nero. We cannot doubt that he would agree with a lieutenant who demonstrated to him that the continual existence of the independent Silurians and Ordovices, along the whole Western flank of the province, was a tiresome anomaly, and that if the Brigantes gave trouble, there was no reason for leaving them unmolested in their highlands.

The commencement of the new series of wars of aggression, which lasted from 71 to 85, was brought about by domestic strife among the Brigantes. We find to our surprise that the divided kingship among that tribe, which we have already noted in the days of Ostorius Scapula, was still in existence. The queen-regnant Cartimandua and her consort Venutius were both alive in 71, and were engaged, as they had been twenty years before, in perpetual quarrels. These came to a head when the queen, who must now have been well advanced in middle age, publicly repudiated her husband, and married his armour-bearer Vellocatus.

Not unnaturally the insulted chief collected his followers and set to work to expel his wife and her *paramour* from the land. Cartimandua, as she had already done once before in 60 *A.D.*, asked for aid from the governor, pointing out that she had always been the friend of Rome, and that Venutius was the head of the war party. The governor—it is uncertain whether this was one of the last acts of Bolanus, or one of the first of Cerealis—sent some *cohorts* to help her.

★★★★★★

From the place in which the Brigantian civil war and the Roman interference is first mentioned by Tacitus, in *Histories,* iii. 45, we should be inclined to put them in Bolanus's time in the year 69-70. But from the way in which the same incidents are related in the *Agricola* we should suppose that Petillius took up the war.

★★★★★★

But her party was so much the weaker, that the Romans had to be content with bringing her away to a place of safety—the kingdom fell to Venutius, who was the advocate of resistance to Rome, and had no wish to patch up a peace, even when he had got rid of his consort.

Hence open war with the Brigantes began, and did not cease for many a year: the territory of that stubborn tribe was often invaded, and several times subdued, but at the slightest opportunity they were ready to revolt, and the periods of rebellion were so numerous, and so long, that it is difficult to say that the annexation of the land between Humber and Solway was really completed till the reign of Hadrian, sixty years after the Brigantian wars began.

Even after Hadrian's death there was at least one serious revolt, with which we shall have to deal in its due place. The legionary troops available for the conquest of the North were the Ninth Hispana at Lindum, and the Twentieth Valeria Victrix and the newly arrived Second Adjutrix at Deva, each supplemented by a proper complement of auxiliary horse and foot. The bases from which they operated would make it certain that the invasion must have been double, one column taking Lancashire as its objective, the other Yorkshire. It is improbable that the whole garrison of Chester was ever used against the Brigantes: probably one legion habitually remained behind to watch the Ordovices.

The course of the operations is only known to us in the vaguest outline:

> The battles were many and sometimes cost much blood: but the greater part of the Brigantian territory was either annexed or devastated.

Presumably this implies that the plain of York and the flat parts of Lancashire as far as the Ribble were added to the province of Britain, while the valleys of the Pennine Range, the stronghold of the tribe, were frequently invaded but never properly subdued. There is no reason to suppose that Petillius ever reached the Tyne or the Solway, but it is probable that the legion Ninth Hispana was moved up from Lindum to Eburacum (York) before the war had long been in progress, and that the foundation of the capital of the Roman North on the site of a Brigantian village dates from the year 71 or 72.

★★★★★★

Inscriptions show us that II. Adjutrix and IX. Hispana were both at Lindum in the earliest years of Vespasian. We get later traces of IX. Hispana at York, both in inscriptions and tiles: but none of II. Adjutrix, though it was in Britain till about 85 *A.D.*

★★★★★★

We have no trace of a similar advance from Deva to Mancunium, which would have been *per se* equally probable. It is clear, however, that Petillius had begun, but was far from completing, the task of subduing the Brigantes when he was superseded by Sextus Julius Frontinus in 74. Of this governor we have many eulogies as an officer, but he was an author also, and has left behind him books on military stratagems and another on the aqueducts of Rome which chance to have come down to us.

It can hardly have been of set purpose that Frontinus, with the Brigantian war already on his hands, allowed himself to be drawn into a new struggle with the Silurians. We cannot doubt that it must have arisen from incursions into Roman territory on the part of these mountaineers, at a moment when they conceived the governor to be too busy elsewhere to pay much attention to them. But Frontinus, apparently leaving the northern struggle undecided, turned his main strength against the Silurians, and for several years (75-78) devoted himself to their conquest. More fortunate in the Welsh hills than Ostorius or Suetonius, he actually achieved his purpose, and we are told that the tribe was reduced to complete submission before he ended his term of government.

The legion Second Augusta, which must have home the brunt of the struggle with them, was not moved forward to any new garrison in the heart of their territory, but continued to occupy its old post at Isca. But no doubt some auxiliary *cohorts* must have been posted for a time in the inner Silurian territory, at forts such as the Gaer in Cymdu and Gellygaer in Glamorganshire, where there are traces of permanent Roman fortifications. (The coins found in 1908 at the well-preserved fort at Gellygaer were mostly of Flavian date, and the last was a piece of Nerva, 96-98 *A.D.*)

How early it was before the great military road from Gloucester to Isca was continued along the coast to Nidum (Neath) and Maridunum (Carmarthen) it is impossible to say. That South Wales was always considered a district that could not be left without a garrison is made clear by the fact that the Second Augusta remained there down to the fourth century. But whether its later task was to watch the Silurians, or rather to guard against possible pirate raids from Ireland, is not quite certain.

Frontinus was recalled in 78, and returned to spend a long old age in Rome, where he survived in high honour and office till the times of Nerva and Trajan. He was succeeded by Cnaeus Julius Agricola, the father-in-law of the historian Tacitus, whose biography of the great governor is a valuable yet a disappointing work for those interested in the history of Roman Britain. It might have given us all that we could wish to know about the geography and ethnology, the civil and military organisation, of the island-province. But unfortunately, it consists in great part of vaguely epigrammatic laudations of Agricola: it contains no statistics, no accurate dates, very few proper names of the persons, Roman or British, with whom Agricola came in contact, and still fewer geographical names. There is a short sketch of the general topography of the island, but it is almost destitute of names.

Incredible as it may seem, neither the Thames nor Trent, the Severn nor Dee, neither London nor Lindum, Eboracum nor Deva, Isca or Camulodunum, are mentioned in it, and the names of only three or four tribes appear in the whole work. Similarly, there is a short note on the provincial history of Britain; but it consists of little more than a list of the governors, to each of whose names a few epigrammatic sentences of description are added. There is hardly a fact included which is not already known to us from the *Annals* or the *Histories*.

The account of Agricola's governorship, though it takes up many chapters, is almost equally barren of detailed facts; in the tale of his seven years of campaigning the only geographical names that occur are the Clota and Bodotria estuaries (the firths of Clyde and Forth), the isle of Mona, the River Tanaus, the names of the tribes of the Ordovices and Boresti, one single harbour (Portus Trutulensis) and Mons Graupius—the unidentified site of the governor's great battle with the Caledonians.

Apparently, Tacitus intended his father-in-law's biography to be a mere panegyric rather than a serious historical work. The result of this paucity of names is that we are kept wandering in unidentified wastes, not certain whether we are on the Tyne or the Tay, or whether the vaguely indicated enemy is the Brigantes or the Caledonians.

★★★★★★

Most tiresome of all is his failure to give the names of the tribes between Solway and Forth which Agricola fought and defeated, and his omission of any details which would enable us to make out whether, as is very possible, the governor built a regular line of forts from Tyne to Solway.

★★★★★★

At the end of the narrative comes a "purple patch" of wholly disproportionable length, concerning Agricola's battle at the Mons Graupius; it contains two orations of the most unconvincing and commonplace type, by the governor and his shadowy foe Calgacus the Caledonian. The details of the battle itself are hard to follow, but, as has been truly said, "Tacitus was the most unmilitary of all historians," and here is no more faulty than is his wont. He was as uninterested in statistics and organisation as in military affairs; his readers were to be impressed by the noble character of Agricola, rather than instructed in the prosaic details of Agricola's work.

Hence, we have much rhetoric and few facts. There is even some possibility that Tacitus's fervent and uncritical laudation of his distinguished relative are intended to cover a magnificent and ambitious failure. It might be urged that Agricola's expeditions were bold and far-reaching rather than wisely planned, and that his supposed conquests were no more than raids without result, so that Tacitus's account of the campaigns of his family hero may be compared with that of the trans-Rhenane wars of his other idol, Germanicus, in which blood, money, and resources were lavished so as to win some glory, perhaps, but no profit for the empire.

Be this as it may, we must accept with gratitude whatever the great historian has deigned to tell us about the events of the years 78-86, the time of his father-in-law's activity in Britain. It must be premised that Agricola had passed the greater part of his official life in the island. He had seized as a young man on the staff of Suetonius Paulinus, and had witnessed the revolt of Boudicca and its repression. After an absence of some years he returned as legate of the Twentieth Legion, towards the end of the time of Bolanus, and took part at the head of that corps in the Brigantian war of Petillius Cerealis, in which he is said to have won much distinction.

For these services he was promoted to the rule of the Gallic province of Aquitaine—a governorship of the third class, which he held for somewhat less than three years. After this he was recalled to Rome, given the consulship in 77, and then sent out to take charge of Britain, a task very different in responsibility from the management of the civilised and peaceful Aquitaine. But public opinion and the will of Vespasian had pointed him out for the post, as the man who had the

91

best knowledge of the island among all his contemporaries of suitable standing and seniority.

Agricola landed in Britain to take up his charge in the late summer of 78, and had to engage in a difficult expedition before he had been many days on shore. The Ordovices of North Wales, untaught by the disaster of their Silurian neighbours, had raided the Roman frontier just before his arrival, and surprised and exterminated a whole regiment of auxiliary cavalry. It was feared that the recently subdued region might rise again, and that the trouble might spread all over the West and North. Agricola therefore mobilised a competent force, though the campaigning season was nearing its end, and took in hand the subjection of the Ordovices. He beat them in battle among their own mountains, for they had refused to face him in the plain, and then pressed the pursuit with unrelenting vigour as far as the Menai Strait.

For the defeated tribesmen, following the precedent of their fathers in the days of Paulinus, had taken refuge in the sacred island of Mona. Agricola had no such fleet with him as his predecessor had possessed, but dared to attempt the forcing of the straits at low tide. His auxiliary cavalry, with picked swimmers from all the *cohorts*, tried the deep ford, which affords a dangerous and difficult passage, forced their way across, and established themselves on the farther side. The rest of the army followed as best it could, and the Ordovices, cowed by the exploit, submitted without further fighting.

Thus, the tribes of North Wales, like those of South Wales, found themselves subdued, after a resistance which had lasted more than a quarter of a century since Ostorius had first entered their borders. We hear of no further trouble in this region, but since the legion Twentieth Valeria Victrix remained permanently fixed at Deva, we may conclude that Agricola and his successors thought it prudent to keep a solid force at hand, lest rebellion might break out once again in a land so well suited for defensive mountain warfare.

For two years after the conquest of the Ordovices Agricola devoted himself mainly to the reorganisation of the administration of the province. According to his son-in-law he was the most just and wise of rulers.

The Britons were capable of enduring the conscription, the land-tax, and all the other obligations of Roman subjects, if only abuses were avoided: it was abuses that they would not endure, for though they were so far tamed that they would

yield obedience, they would not tolerate being treated as slaves.
...Agricola paid the greatest attention to the public opinion of
the provincials, having learnt by the experience of his predecessors that conquest followed by oppressive administration was of
little profit: wherefore he resolved to extirpate the abuses that
were the causes of rebellion.

A most fruitful source of discontent had been the petty oppres-
sion and peculation of the clerks and freedmen of the governor's staff,
and the officials of the *fiscus*, the imperial private exchequer. Against
such offenders he conducted a long campaign, till he had purified the
provincial civil service. Apparently, the worst grievances of the Britons were to be found in the department of requisitions in kind, for
the service of the army. The commissioners had been making illicit
gains, by tricks of the same sort which we find Cicero detailing, when
he describes the difficulties of his Ciliciax Government, more than a
hundred years before Agricola's day. One was to order the individuals
or communities who had to supply corn to pay in their contributions
at distant and inconvenient places, when they might just as well have
been delivered near home. Agricola is said to have made the taxation
much more tolerable, by redistributing the quota on a new and equi-
table basis, and accepting payments at the place and time most suited
to the contributors.

At the same time, he was doing his best to attract the Britons towards town life and the amenities of civilisation.

He thought that a nation accustomed to live in scattered ham-
lets and with little comfort, and thereby easily persuaded to
war, might be lured to quiet and peace through the pleasures
of life. He exhorted them in public, and aided them in private,
to build temples, market-places and solid houses. He would
praise those who fell in with his ideas readily, and chide those
who hung back, so that rivalry to win his approval acted as a
sort of compulsion. He induced the chiefs to allow their sons
to be trained in the liberal arts, saying that though the Gauls
were better educated the Britons had more natural talent.
Hence it came that provincials who but lately refused to learn
our tongue were found manifesting a desire to shine in Latin
eloquence. The Roman garb even came with fashion, and the
toga was frequently to be seen. By degrees the Britons began
to appreciate those attractive instruments of social corruption,

pillared colonnades, public baths, elegant banquets; all this the simple people called 'civilisation,' but it was really the token of their submission to the conqueror.

It is interesting to find that at this very time educated Britons were already to be found in Rome, apparently in good society. Martial, (*Epigrams* v.), writing in the days of Domitian, (has many compliments for a lady named Claudia who "though descended from the painted Britons had the heart of a Roman," and was noted for her many accomplishments. She was the wife of a certain Pudens, so that intermarriage between the two races had already begun. But while engaged in these peaceful tasks. Agricola was preparing to carry forward the Roman boundaries to what he considered a natural frontier.

The present situation was an impossible one, since of the Brigantian territory half was conquered but the rest was unoccupied and independent. Its inhabitants were perpetually raiding the plains of Yorkshire and of South Lancashire, being still in possession of the mountainous district which separates these two lowlands, as well as of all the moors of the North. The deplorable parsimony of Tacitus with regard to local names prevents us from determining with accuracy what Agricola accomplished in 79 *A.D.*—the year of the death of Vespasian and the accession of the short-lived Titus. We are told that he collected a field force during the summer:

> That he chose himself the sites for camps, and explored in person woods and estuaries: he left no part of the hostile territory undisturbed, but ravaged it all by sudden incursions. When he had struck sufficient terror into the souls of the enemy, he wooed them to submission by his clemency. By which policy many communities which had hitherto dealt with the Roman power as no more than their equal, were induced to give hostages, and to abandon their angry hostility. Their territories were encompassed with garrisons and forts, with such system and care as had never before been displayed in any newly conquered part of Britain.

This vague language is most tantalising. The enemy seem to be the Brigantian clans of the Pennine Range, Northumberland, Cumberland and Westmoreland. The estuaries are presumably those of Tees, Tyne and Solway. The "encompassing" of the communities which surrendered must mean the placing of garrisons and forts up both sides of Britain, along the lines where ran in later days the two great roads from York to Newcastle and from Manchester to Carlisle. If Agricola also drew a line of forts from Solway to Tyne, where the Wall of Hadrian was afterwards to be built, the Brigantes would be literally encircled on all sides. Even the cross-lines across the Pennine Range, from Manchester to York *via* Ilkley, and from York to Carlisle *via* Aldborough, Catterick and Bowes, may have been originally selected as routes, and garnished with forts and blockhouses, at this early date, so as to cut off one community of the Brigantes from another.

But Agricola was not satisfied with the line of Solway and Tyne as a frontier for the province, though it was a good natural boundary, and though it coincided almost exactly with the northern limit of the Brigantian territory. He had heard that there was a still shorter line across the island, ninety miles farther to the north—that from Clyde to Forth—and determined to advance to it—a bold resolve when the Brigantes were still newly subdued, and when he had no nearer bases than Eburacum and Deva.

There can be no doubt whatever that he took in hand during the next four years a task that was too great for the resources that were at his disposition, since, to be really safe, all the newly conquered northern tracts required heavy garrisons, which he could not spare if he was to provide himself with a sufficiently large field army. That he penetrated so far north as he did in 80-84 was only due to the fact that the Brigantes were for the moment cowed: if they had taken arms in his rear, as they did in later years while his successor were ruling Britain, he would have found at once that his northern enterprises were premature and hazardous.

Favoured, however, by the temporary exhaustion of the Brigantes, Agricola accomplished marvellous feats in the third and succeeding years of his governorship. In 80 he started out to subdue the lands north of Tyne and Solway, "opening out new races, for he devastated the land of all the tribes that dwell as far as the estuary called Tanaus" (apparently the Tay, remote as that may seem).

★★★★★★

Or Taus in one MS. We know of no stream called Tanaus: some have suggested the Northumbrian Tyne, but that is too far south. The Tweed would be possible, but we do not know its ancient name: the Forth, which geographically looks most likely of all, had the name Bodotria, so cannot be meant.

★★★★★★

So terrified were the enemy that they did not dare to assail the army, though it suffered dreadfully from bad weather. Hence Agricola had leisure for the building of forts.

Engineers took note of the fact that no other general chose defensive sites with such an unerring eye. No stronghold whose place he had selected was ever taken by storm, or evacuated on terms, or abandoned. The garrisons made frequent sorties: for each had been victualled with a full year's provisions, to guard against the danger of a long siege. So, winter brought no anxiety, and each fort could take care of itself, contemning the enemy, who was reduced to despair. For the Britons had hitherto been wont to consider that they could win back in the winter all that they had lost in the summer: but now they were repelled in summer and winter alike. . . . The next campaigning season (that of 81) was spent in taking solid possession of the lands which had been already traversed.

And if the courage of the army and the glory of the Roman name had but permitted it, a final frontier might have been fixed in Britain. For Clyde and Forth (Clota and Bodotria) running up far into the land from the two separate tidal seas, are separated by no more than an isthmus. This line was made safe with garrisons, and all the nearer sweep of land was grasped, the enemy being driven off, as it were, into another island. (*Agricola*.)

Here again, as in 80, we are lamentably hampered in our comprehension of Agricola's work by the want of detailed geographical names. The identification of the Taus (or Tanaus) with any other river than the Tay seems impossible, considering that we are told that in the year 81 lands previously traversed were firmly occupied, and a line drawn at Forth and Clyde. Therefore, the campaign of 80 had gone at least as far as these estuaries; and if the troops reached Stirling in a raid, why should they not have reached Perth? That Agricola's routes in arriving at the isthmus were mainly along the eastern side of the Lowlands may be inferred from the fact that his exploration and conquest of Galloway were deferred to the year 83, and are narrated in a separate chapter of his biography. But since Carlisle had been occupied at the time of the surrender of the Brigantes, and must from the necessities of its situation have been a very important base when expeditions farther north were in question, we may suspect that Agricola's invasion was carried out in two columns.

The right hand one must have advanced along the valley of the

North Tyne, up which the later Roman road to the Forth was drawn, and would cross Cheviot so as to drop down into the valley of the Teviot near Jedburgh. From thence its progress would be under Eildon Hill, where the great camp of Newstead (Trimontium) must surely have been one of Agricola's chosen sites, and then across the Lammermuirs, descending on to the Firth of Forth at Inveresk and Cramond, both Roman stations of importance in a later age. Probably this line of invasion was taken by the Ninth Hispana, the York Legion, and its auxiliaries. Meanwhile detachments of the two Chester Legions, Twentieth Valeria Victrix and Second Adjutrix, and their auxiliaries, starting from Carlisle, might fix their first camp in hostile territory at Birrens (Blatum Bulgium),—a considerable station in later days, at least, though we know not what it may have been under Agricola,—and then ascend the valley of the Annan, and after crossing the watershed descend into Clydesdale. (Unfortunately, there has apparently been no discovery of clearly Flavian date at Birrens, so the hypothesis stated here is unverified.)

This double line of invasion seems much more probable than a single advance from the Tyne to the Forth. Nor would it present any dangers, since we are told that the tribes of the Lowlands failed to combine, and never offered battle to the invaders. Among the numerous Roman camps in their territory it is difficult to separate those founded by Agricola from those of later days, but Birrens in Dumfriesshire, Newstead, under Eildon, and Barr Hill, on the line between Forth and Clyde, must surely have been of his selection, and possibly also Cramond, Inveresk, Chesterhill near Biggar, and the large camp near Carstairs.

It is curious to find no trace, either from Agricola's time or later, of either castles or lines of communication along the coast of Northumberland, Berwickshire or East Lothian. All expeditions to the north from the valley of the Tyne seem to have avoided the shore, and to have followed the inland road from Corbridge by High Rochester (Bremenium) to the central course of the Tweed by Jedburgh and Newstead. It is strange that Tacitus makes no mention of the names of the tribes whom Agricola met between Solway and Forth, but they must have been the three races whom Ptolemy places in this direction: the Otadini on the east from Tyne to Forth, the Selgovae from Solway to Clyde, and the Dumnonii in the north, on both sides of the isthmus formed by the two firths.

The Novantae, in Galloway and along the Irish Sea, would not be affected by these invasions of 80-81 *A.D.* There are no signs that any of these were powerful or vigorous tribes, and they may even, for all we know, have been vassals of the Brigantes. It is at any rate clear that the Lowlands were thinly peopled, though Ptolemy gives us the names of some dozen "cities" of one sort or another among them. None of these had a future before them: of the Lowland towns of mediaeval Scotland—Edinburgh, Glasgow, Ayr, Dumfries, Roxburgh, Berwick— not one seems to be on a site indicated by the old geographer.

Agricola's next summer of campaigning (82) was dedicated to the conquest of Galloway.

> In his fifth year he started by going on shipboard, and tamed by many successful combats tribes hitherto unknown. He then garrisoned the part of Britain which looks out on Ireland, more with a view to future operations than because there was any-thing to be feared. For he considered that Ireland, which lies in the midst between Britain and Spain, and is adjacent also to the Bay of Biscay, might be made a flourishing and useful part of the Roman Empire. Though smaller than Britain, it is larger than any isle of the Mediterranean Sea. Its soil and climate, the character and manners of its people, do not differ much from those of Britain.
>
> It is easier of approach, and its harbours are known through commerce and merchants. Agricola had sheltered one of the Irish kings, who had been expelled in civil strife, and kept him at hand in friendly guise, to use if opportunity offered. I have often heard my relative say that Ireland could be conquered and held down by one legion, and a moderate contingent of auxiliaries. And its conquest would be useful with regard to the Britons, if Roman arms were everywhere, and independence were no longer visible in any direction. (*Agricola.*)

It is clear that no firm hold was established on Galloway; all that Tacitus seems to imply is that troops were placed at points on its coast, from which an expedition to Ireland could be easily conducted. It was well for the governor's reputation that such an attempt was never made, for his estimate of the force required to subdue and garrison the sister island was obviously far too low. It reminds us of Strabo's *obiter dictum* that Britain itself would require but one legion and some auxiliaries to hold it down. Four legions, and the corresponding con-tingents of non-legionary troops, were actually employed in Britain for thirty years before the frontier even reached Tyne and Solway!

Ireland would have absorbed at least half that amount of troops, besides a large addition to the British fleet. If Agricola had invaded it with a smaller force, he would have been beaten off; if he had taken over all his field-army (which would really have been necessary) there is not the smallest doubt that the Brigantes and all their northern neighbours would have revolted. The governor would then have had to return, in a not very dignified fashion, and to repeat all his work of 80-82 over again. And his task would have been harder than before, because he would have lost his reputation for infallibility and invincibility. But he found other work to do, and the Irish prince who was to play the part of Adminius and Bericus was never utilised.

In his sixth year (83), instead of attacking Ireland, Agricola made himself busy north of the isthmus between Clyde and Forth, where he had so recently established his line of garrisons. His advance to that line had alarmed the tribes of the North, they had leagued themselves together, and were not only ready to defend their independence, but to take the offensive and threaten his lines of communication with his southern bases. Apparently conscious that the whole country behind him, as far as Yorkshire, might revolt, if the northern tribes burst into the Lowlands, the governor resolved to take the offensive himself, and give the enemy enough to do near home. His fleet was sent to coast around the headlands of Fife, and to explore the Firth of Tay: the land army marched parallel to its advance, in three columns, one of which kept in close touch with the naval forces.

In this fashion the lands between Forth and Tay were overrun: the enemy was discovered after a time: "all the tribes that inhabit Caledonia"—a name now heard for the first time in Roman history—had united to form a single host. Their force was imposing, and was exaggerated by rumour to an innumerable multitude, so that many of the Roman officers advised their general to retire behind the Forth before he was compelled to do so. Agricola thought that he was strong enough to face the danger, and his confidence was justified by the event. The whole Caledonian host concentrated upon the column which consisted of the Ninth region, the weakest of the three divisions in which the Roman army was moving. (Weakest apparently because it had vexillations detached in this year for Domitian's German war, as a continental inscription shows.)

They attacked its camp at night, succeeded in bursting in, and were in a fair way to overcome its obstinate resistance when Agricola arrived at the head of the other corps, assailed them from the rear and inflicted on them a decisive defeat. The barbarians retired into their woods and marshes, disappointed, but still unbroken in spirit. Agricola then went into winter quarters, but whether in Lothian or in Fife it is impossible to determine, since Tacitus gives us no means of guessing.

The last of the great offensive campaigns of Agricola fell into the following year (84).

★★★★★★

Tacitus makes no break between the sixth and seventh campaigns of Agricola, so that we cannot be sure where the winter-quarters come in. But since the battle speech in the seventh campaign alludes to the attack on the Ninth Legion as having taken place in the preceding year, the halt probably took place at the time indicated above.

★★★★★★

The soldiery are said to have started with the intention of "penetrating Caledonia, and finding the end of Britain, even if it were necessary to fight all the way". But it is hinted that their general's plans were more modest—though what his exact purpose was Tacitus will not tell us. He informs us that the fleet was sent up the eastern coast, to keep the natives uncertain as to his exact line of invasion, while the field army, now strengthened by some British levies, advanced till it reached the Graupian Mount, on which the Caledonians lay.

★★★★★★

Presumably Southern Britons, as they were "*longa pace exploratos*" which could not include Brigantes or Ordovices or other recently subdued people. This is the only mention in Tacitus of British auxiliaries serving with the regular army (*Agricola*, §29).

★★★★★★

The enemy had sent his non-combatants and cattle up into the remoter valleys, and the tribes had bound themselves at a solemn congress, accompanied by sacrifices, that they would not flinch from each other. Thirty thousand warriors are said to have been collected, not all foot (as might have been expected) but partly charioteers and horsemen.

The Graupian Mount cannot be identified. From the fact that it had been deliberately occupied by the enemy before the Romans came up, it must clearly have been some well-known position of strategical importance. Agricola, advancing from the valley of the Lower Tay, must have taken one of three lines, either that which follows the river and leads into Athole, past Dunkeld, "the gate of the Highlands," or the route more to the east which goes towards Aberdeenshire *via* Cupar Angus and Forfar, or else the coast road which, starting along the Firth of Tay, goes by Dundee and Arbroath towards the same destination, keeping south of the Sidlaw Hills.

The Mons Graupius has been looked for in all these directions, since the older view that it was a general name for the range which divides the basin of the Tay from that of the Dee has been abandoned. Yet the ancient hypothesis, and a misreading of Grampius for Graupius, has imposed the wholly fictitious name of the "Grampian Hills" on modern geography books, which invariably mark the range that separates Aberdeenshire from Perthshire and Forfarshire with that designation. Something is to be said for each of the three routes named above: Dunkeld and its neighbourhood would be a very natural place for the mustering of a Highland host, even at this early date, and if Agricola marched with the intention of fighting the enemy wherever he might be found, Delvine or some similar position in front of Dunkeld would be a likely enough battle spot.

✶✶✶✶✶✶

For a long discussion of localities, ending in the selection of Delvine near Dunkeld, see Sir James Ramsay's *Foundations of England*, i. 71-75; General Roy, the first scientific investigator, pitched on Stonehaven, north of Montrose, arguing from the situation of real or supposed Roman camps. Mr. Skene contended for the neighbourhood of Blairgowrie, on the central route. But since modern explorations have shown that the great camp at Inchtuthill was probably Agricola's, the Delvine site seems best. See *Proc, Scottish Antiquaries*, 1901-2.

✶✶✶✶✶✶

On the other hand, the North British tribes seem to have been stronger and more numerous along the comparatively fertile and accessible lowlands of Forfarshire and Aberdeenshire than in the woods and moors of Athole, and a position somewhere about Cupar Angus best covers those regions against an enemy advancing from Perth. Yet again Agricola had a fleet, and the temptation to keep in touch with it might well lead him along the coast-route by Dundee. In that case the natural position for the Caledonians to occupy would be somewhere north or south of Montrose. Yet since there is no mention of the vicinity of the sea to the battlefield in Tacitus, which even he would hardly omit in such a case, it seems safer to conclude that one of the two other routes was adopted by Agricola, and that the excursion of his fleet along the coast had been intended merely to distract the enemy. The student may make his choice between the neighbourhood of Dunkeld and that of Cupar Angus as the situation of the Graupian Mount. Certainty is impossible.

The topography of the battlefield is as vague as its situation. We should gather from Tacitus that the Caledonians were arrayed at the point where the foot-hills of some considerable range touch the plain—their chariots and horsemen on the flat, their infantry in successive lines on the rising slope. The Romans were drawn up below them in front of their camp, with 8,000 auxiliary infantry forming the main line, 3,000 horse equally divided between the two wings, and the legionary foot (which consisted of the whole or the greater part of at least two legions) in reserve outside the camp. The whole force must have amounted to at least 16,000 men: it is improbable that the Caledonians can have put more in line, though they are credited with 30,000 men by Tacitus. But no Highland Army throughout recorded history ever attained the historian's figure. A lively harangue is put into the mouth of Calgacus, the most noted of their chiefs, but it is obviously a rhetorical composition, as little to be trusted as any other set speech.

The operations are difficult to follow, but we gather that the Caledonians took the offensive, and that first the horse and chariots assailed the auxiliaries. As long as the fight was at arm's length, the long claymores and darts of the barbarians contended at no great disadvantage with the short sword and the lance. But when Agricola bade his infantry close, the enemy was driven back, their lack of armour and the inferiority of their long blades in hand-to-hand combat putting them at a great disadvantage. They then tried to get round the wings of the advancing auxiliaries, by throwing their reserves or rear lines upon the Roman flanks and rear. But the masses which attempted to execute this movement were charged and broken by Agricola's cavalry.

The whole Caledonian Army then sought refuge in some woods, which lay at the back of their position, and made pursuit difficult. Among the trees they turned upon the first of the victorious auxiliaries, and checked them: but on the approach of formed *cohorts* they gave way again, and melted off in small bodies through fastnesses where they could not be followed. Agricola lost one *praefect* of a *cohort*, a certain Aldus Atticus, and about 360 men; he estimated the loss of the enemy at 10,000 men, an impossible figure, though no doubt many Caledonians had fallen in the *mêlée*, before they could escape into the woods.

But the battle had not made the Romans masters of Caledonia: next morning they could see the smoke of many villages on the horizon: this meant that the enemy had burnt their abodes, and were going up into the mountains, in order to continue the war. Only one tribe, the Boresti, probably the people of Forfarshire, submitted and gave hostages. The season was now far advanced, and seeing that it was no triumphal march to Cape Wrath that awaited him, but the continuance of a campaign in the wilderness. Agricola took his army back to winter quarters somewhere nearer his base—presumably on the Firth of Forth. He directed his fleet, however, to undertake a daring voyage round the northern end of Britain, and to return by the Irish Sea and the Channel.

★★★★★★

The account of this voyage is not given by Tacitus in its natural place, Agricola, §38, where it is only said that the governor ordered the fleet to circumnavigate Britain. But the details are given in §10. That this was the voyage in question is proved from *Dio Cassius*, xlvi. §20.

★★★★★★

This was accomplished without disaster: the fleet touched at the Orkneys, where a landing was made and the submission of some natives received. It is said to have seen Thule a "land of snow and winter" in the far distance—apparently this must have been Fair Isle or even Sumburgh Head at the south point of Shetland. Then coasting down the western side of Britain, past a hundred rugged isles, the galleys rounded Land's End, ran up the Channel, and reached Portus Trutulensis (probably a misreading for Portus Rutupensis) in time to winter.

★★★★★★

The fleet reached Portus Trutulensis "*proximo Britanniae latere lecto omni,*" the "nearer" shore being the Channel coast, and Rutupiae a well-known station for the fleet, it seems likely that Trutulensis should be Rutupensis (*Agricola*, 38).

★★★★★★

This was, strangely enough, not the actual first passage of the Pentland Firth by Roman soldiers. Tacitus records that in the preceding year, 83, a *cohort* of Usipii, untrustworthy German levies, who were quartered somewhere on the west coast of Britain (probably in Galloway) mutinied, murdered their officers, seized three ships, and coasted amid a thousand dangers (They are said to have been driven to cannibalism from sheer famine during their long voyage.) round the northern cape of Britain, from whence, striking across the North Sea, they reached Germany, only to be fallen upon by the Suebi and Frisii, who slew some and made slaves of the rest. It was through certain captives, who were sold in the markets of the Rhine, that the Romans heard what was the end of the mutinous *cohort*. Dio Cassius says that the story of their adventures had reached Agricola by the autumn of 84, and was the cause of his sending his fleet to make from east to west that passage of the Pentland Firth which the Usipii had already made from west to east. (*Epitome of Di.*)

Before the campaigning season of 85 came round, and, as it appears, during the early months of that year. Agricola was recalled by Domitian, and probably superseded by one Sallustius Lucullus, who was certainly governor of Britain a year or so later. Tacitus ascribes the sudden summons to Rome received by his father-in-law as caused by the emperor's jealousy for one who seemed to be acquiring a military reputation of a splendid and unique character. He says that Domitian imagined that everyone was comparing the real victories of his *legate* with the hollow and fictitious triumphs which he himself had claimed over the Germans in *A.D.* 83.

> He feared above all things that the name of a simple citizen should be exalted higher than that of the sovereign:.... to be considered the only great general is a prerogative of the emperor.

But though Domitian may have been both jealous and timid, he had good political reasons for recalling Agricola. The great general had now been campaigning for seven years in Britain, and despite all his victories the end of the war still seemed far off. It must certainly have been most expensive both in men and in money, but this was not the worst. The emperor had matters on hand upon the continent, which seemed to him more important than the conquest of Northern Britain. His German war of 83 had been brought to a successful close, but it had ended in a forced annexation of great districts beyond the Rhine, for which garrison troops were badly needed.

And it appears that in 85 new fighting began in Germany, while in 84 there seem to have been serious troubles on the Danube—at any rate in that year Domitian was saluted as *imperator* for the sixth and seventh time on account of victories in Pannonia or Moesia. Troops were so badly needed that a detachment (*vexillatio*) of the Ninth Legion was actually borrowed from Britain in 83, though Agricola was in the midst of his sixth campaign. Apparently in 85, just after his recall, the whole legion Second Adjutrix was hastily brought over and moved to the Danube, where it took part in the Dacian wars. There is good reason, therefore, to think that Domitian put an end to Agricola's aggressive campaigns in the North mainly because he could not afford to allow them to continue, when troops were required to guard much more vital points of the empire. (For a good note on Domitian's probable motives see Gaell's *L'Empeuur Domitien.*)

Nor, despite of all the innuendos of Tacitus, does it seem that the emperor failed to show his appreciation of the great services which Agricola had done to the empire. Alone of all the generals of his time he was granted triumphal honours, and (no small favour under "the bald Nero") he retained his life and his high position till the day of his death in 93, surviving unmolested through eight years of a tyranny that was ever growing worse. Even his son-in-law does not pretend to credit the story that he died by secret poison administered by Domitian's orders, though (after his usual wont) he inserts the rumour in his biography.

CHAPTER 7

From Domitian to Commodus (86–180 *A.D.*)

The moment that Agricola was recalled, the greater part of his northern conquests were lost to the empire. Their fabric was too slightly built to withstand the shock of his departure; perhaps it might have crumbled under his own hands, if he had been allowed to persist a little longer in his progress towards Cape Wrath and the Pentland Firth. Nothing is more clear than that his Caledonian campaigns were only possible because the Brigantes kept quiet, and it seems that, soon after his disappearance from Britain, that unquiet race burst out into fierce and obstinate rebellion. The army of the province was not numerous enough to garrison every strategical point up to the Tay, and at the same time to provide a competent force for field operations.

When Agricola was fighting at the Graupian Mount the line of communication behind him must have been desperately thin, for (as has been already said) there was no solid base nearer than Eburacum. The camps and castles on Tyne and Solway, on Forth and Clyde, were not self-sufficing centres of military strength, but newly-established strongholds in an enemy's country, which needed to be revictualled constantly, and to have every item of munitions of war, perhaps even of food, brought up from the distant South.

Whether the Brigantes flared up in insurrection the moment that Agricola had departed, or whether they waited till, very shortly after, one of the four British legions—the Second Adjutrix—was withdrawn to the Danube, we have no means of knowing. The later British wars of Domitian are not chronicled even in the unsatisfactory style in which those of his earlier years are preserved. Presumably the garrisons left by Agricola beyond Tyne and Solway were attacked by the Caledonians. The Brigantian rising may have preceded the retirement of the Romans from the North, and so have caused it: or on the other hand the rising may have been the result of that retirement.

Whichever was the case, we know that the Lowlands were evacuated, and that there was war with the Brigantes during the later years of Domitian's reign. Juvenal speaks of the daily life of the professional soldier as being "to destroy the huts of the Moors or the castles of the Brigantes." (*Satires*.) In another passage he guesses that the best and greatest news that Domitian would have liked to receive was that the Briton Arviragus (a Brigantian king, no doubt) might have fallen dead from his war-chariot. (*Satires*.)

The evidence of archaeology clearly proves that the hold of Rome on anything north of the Tees and Morecambe Bay in this period was precarious. There are no inscriptions that can be dated before the year 120 north of York and Lancaster, and inscriptions are the best proof of settled and permanent occupation.

The evidence of the coins dug up at many fortified places—Brough on the Derwent, Slack by Huddersfield, Templeborough near Rotheram, Melandra Castle near Glossop, Castleshaw above Oldham—shows that garrisons had to be kept up, even at the south end of the Pennine Chain, from the time of Domitian down to that of Hadrian. If the Peak district and the West Riding had to be held down by force, it is clear that things must have been far worse on Solway or Tyne. Nothing north of York, where the Ninth legion was firmly established, can have been perfectly secure. We must think of Sallustius Lucullus and Metilius Nepos, the two governors of Domitian's later years whose names have survived, as campaigning continually, and not always with success, on the moors and hills between the Ouse and Mersey, as well as on more northern ground.

It is noteworthy, however, that we have no evidence from the spade or from literary sources to show that troubles were prevalent in the other quarter where they might have been expected, the west side of Central Britain. Indeed the occupation of some of the Roman forts in

Wales seems to have ceased about the time of Trajan, as if they were no longer required for the keeping down of the population, and *legionaries* drawn from the Welsh garrison of Isca Silurum were being freely used in Brigantian territory in Hadrian's day—a clear proof that they had no pressing work nearer home. (The last coin from the great fort of Gellygaer is of Nerva. See J. Ward on that station, in the recently published monograph dealing with it, 1909).

Indeed, this was the period in which all Southern Britain was being rapidly and steadily Romanised, after the fashion set by Agricola. Wars had ceased out of the land south of Humber and Mersey, and the road-system and the commerce that followed it were penetrating all the province, save the remote south-western peninsula beyond Exeter, and the inaccessible hills of Mid Wales. It was now as Juvenal sarcastically remarked that:

> The fluent Gaul was giving lessons to the British pleaders, and that Thule was seriously thinking of hiring a professor of elocution.

The towns were growing in size, wealth and splendour; Nerva made Glevum a colony (96-98), and probably Lindum attained the same dignity within the same generation. Glevum, which had long ceased to be a garrison town, must have gained its distinction purely as the commercial centre of the Severn Valley, whose fertile southern slopes are more thickly strewn with the remains of Roman villas than almost any other district of Britain. Lindum, also happily placed on a high road in the centre of a well-cleared district, evidently survived as an already existing town of importance when the legion which had been its garrison was moved on to Eburacum early in the Flavian period, perhaps about 80 *A.D.* Most of all must London have been growing in importance, though it never attained either colonial or municipal rank.

But more objects of artistic merit and intrinsic value are dug up from the ruins of Roman London than from any other town in the province. We may guess that its public squares were better decorated than those of many places that had higher official rank, when we look on the splendid head of the bronze statue of Hadrian in the British Museum, almost the best piece of Roman work that has been found in this island. It was dredged up from the Thames, a beautiful fragment, probably dropped by some fifth-century spoiler, who had broken up the colossus purely for the sake of the fine yellow bronze of which it was composed.

The lesser towns of the south, centres of tribal commerce, or places happily placed at the junction of great high-roads, like Calleva or Corinium, or sought for other reasons like Aquae Sulis, (the earliest Bath inscription is as old as Vespasian), the spa frequented by so many invalids of all ages, were all steadily growing in prosperity, and no doubt acting as centres for the diffusion of Roman civilisation and the Latin tongue.

Nothing can be more definite and well marked than the evidence that the higher civilisation of the conquerors destroyed within two or three generations the lower national culture of the conquered. Celtic art had a peculiar character of its own, which it is impossible to mistake, and countless British finds bear witness to the fact that it was alive and flourishing when Claudius crossed the Channel. (For all these see Haverfield's "Romanisation of Roman Britain," in *Proceedings of the British Academy* for 1907.) But it could not stand against the world-culture of the Romans.

The Briton preferred the classical type when it was presented to him, even in inferior and second-hand examples, to his own ancestral work, just as the native artisan of India today is prone to cast away the time-honoured patterns of the East and to copy the most commonplace European models. On the whole it is true to say that from the second century onwards there was hardly any Celto-Roman art in Britain, but only Provincial-Roman art, an art that cannot easily be distinguished from that which prevailed in other remote and rough western parts of the empire, such as Lusitania or Armorica.

Even the ordinary better-class crockery of daily life was imported from Gaul, or copied at first and second hand from the Aretine ware of Italy itself The careful archaeologist detects a few weak survivals of old Celtic tradition in the so-called "Castor ware" of the East Midlands, or the pottery of the New Forest, both of which show scroll work and returning spirals with affinities to the pre-Roman style, and delight in conventionalised animal and vegetable forms that are not copied from the usual provincial types of the West. But such exceptions were survivals of an isolated sort in an ocean of commonplace work, directly borrowed from the conquering race.

Nor is it even the case that the towns, with their partially immigrant population, shared in the monotonous culture of the empire, but that Celtic life survived in the villages. Just as the better houses in a south country hamlet copied the hypocausts and tessellated pavements of the Roman, in poor style and with cheap material, so did their inhabitants grow into using mean imitations of Roman utensils, pottery, and metal-work. Rural Britain soon grew to be provincial and not barbarous in its outer aspect, though it was but a poor province, and though the village people were as far behind the southern Gauls of the open country, as the towns people fell short of the inhabitants of Arles or Narbonne in wealth and splendour.

We must only except from this generalisation certain districts of Britain where the population was very thin, where the great roads never penetrated, and where no towns arose to diffuse civilisation around them, such as the Dumnonian peninsula west of Exeter, Mid-Wales, and the wooded districts of the western Midlands, where the whole land was covered by the vast forests of which Arden and Wyre were the medieval survivals.

The Romanisation of exterior culture was accompanied by the Romanisation of religion. Like so many other provincials of the West, the Britons proceeded to make rough identifications between their own divinities and the Romano-Greek pantheon of their conquerors. Mabon was identified with Apollo, Sulis with Minerva, Belatucadrus with Mars, and so forth. In the process of time the Celtic appellation became a mere epithet of the Divinity, or was forgotten altogether. The larger half of the altars and shrines discovered in Britain are simply set up to honour the ordinary gods of the Roman world.

But in some cases, the native divinities lingered on as objects of local worship, and we find all through the second century dedications to forgotten powers with strange names such as Nodons (or Nudens), Antenociticus, Ancasta, Cocidius, and Coventina (this last a spring-goddess on the Northumbrian wall).

So little remains to us of the prehistoric Celtic mythology that we can generally make no guess as to the character of these local survivors from it. It is interesting to find that the well-known Roman practice of making divinities out of personifications of regions, virtues, moral qualities, etc., was fully acclimatised in this province. Not only Britain herself, (she is "*Britannia Sancta*" in a York inscription, C. I. L., 232), but Brigantia, the personification of the North, had altars and statues.

★★★★★★

She is "*Dea Brigantia*" in some cases. She is found adored at Birrens (Dumfriesshire), Addle (near Leeds), on the Irthing near Naworth, and elsewhere in the North. Her statue is a Minerva-like figure with helm and shield.

******

Victory, Fortune, Peace, Bonus Eventus, even Discipline (a deity not always worshipped in practice by the British army) are adored by various votaries. Caesar-worship, the most typical development of the religion of the Roman empire, is found widely spread. The number of dedications to the divinity of the emperor (*Numen Augusti*) or emperors, or to his or their "genius" which are extant, is as great as that of the dedications to any one of the old gods. Equally characteristic signs of the cosmopolitan nature of the pantheon of the Roman world are the number of deities adored in Britain who are neither members of the orthodox Olympian family nor survivors from Celtic heathendom. Merchants and soldiers from every land, Gaul, Spain, Germany, or Syria, brought with them their devotion to strange divinities, Ricagambeda and Harimella, the Dea Syria, Mithras, Contrebis, and all manner of other aliens, and raised altars to them on the western soil to which they had been led by the chances of trade or of military service.

******

Mithras got a wonderful popularity in the third century, and was worshipped not by Oriental immigrants only but by many a western citizen or soldier. His chapels have been found under the wall of Severus.

******

Of the political organisation of Britain, outside the few towns which had been granted the rights of a colony or a *municipium*, we could till lately do no more than make speculations. Inscriptions mentioning the *civitas* of the Catuvellauni and the Dumnonians had been found, (both found on the Northumbrian wall C. I. L., 775 and 863), but they were too short to allow any deductions to be made from them. Fortunately, a monument was discovered at Caerwent in 1903 which made it clear that Britain was, like Gaul, organised in large cantons bearing the names of the old tribes. This particular one which has come down to us is an inscription put up in honour of an ex-governor by decree of the Senate "of the community of the state of the Silures". (The governor's name, at the head of the inscription, is unfortunately knocked away.)

If this South Welsh tribe, in one of the remoter corners of the land, had a regular canton and senate, and were organised into a "*civitas*," we cannot doubt that all the other regions of the south were governed by similar institutions. The inscription seems to belong to the end of the second or beginning of the third century, but there is no reason

110

to think that the system of which it gives us such useful information had not been introduced long before. Very probably it went back to the Flavian emperors, and it certainly cannot have been later than the Antonines. It is to be imagined that the "*civitates*" of Britain were fairly large, that they represented units into which many of the smaller tribes of the first century had coalesced.

It may be noted that in Ptolemy's statistical picture of Britain there are only seventeen tribes south of the line from Tyne to Solway, which represented in his day the boundary of the province. We do not find in him the names of the small tribes mentioned by Caesar, the Bibroci, Ancalites, Segontiaci, or Cassi, nor of Tacitus's Deceangi or Jugantes. It seems certain that the race had been gathering together into larger units since the day of Caesar: though whether this mainly came about owing to the wars of the house of Cunobelinus and its rivals, before the coming of Claudius, or whether it was the work of the Roman administrator a generation or two later, we cannot tell.

But it is pretty certain that cantonal names of the second century, like those of the Belgae or the Cantii, and probably of the Atrebates also, represent several of the older and smaller units confederated together. Of the seventeen civitates some must have been immeasurably larger and more wealthy than others: some, the Cantii, Belgae, Iceni, had very large and well-peopled territory: others like the Durotriges of Dorsetshire, and the Atrebates of Berkshire, had narrow limits: others again like the Cornavii in the Midlands or the Dumnonii in the extreme southwest, represented very thinly peopled and poor districts. Yet, as the inscription quoted above shows us, there was certainly a *civitas* of the Dumnonii—and presumably, therefore, all the other tribes had each become a regular canton.

The North, however, had yet to be organised, and reduced to obedience, when Hadrian came to the throne in 118. His reign, as it seems, started with an outbreak of the Brigantes on a larger scale than usual, and with results more than normally disastrous. We have allusions only to it in the classical authors, but Fronto's statement that "a great number of soldiers were slain by the Britons in the reign of Hadrian" (Fronto, *De Bello Parthico*, see Mommsen's *Roman History, v.*) must surely be put in juxtaposition with the fact that the garrison-legion of York, the IX. Hispana, suddenly disappear from the imperial muster rolls at this moment. (It was still existing in Trajan's day, as an inscription at York dated in the year 108-109 shows. C. I. L., 241.) It was the rarest thing in the world in the earlier empire for a legion to be reduced: indeed this only happened as the result either of utter extermination (such as that of the XVII., XVIII., XIX., who fell to the last man in Varus's German disaster) or of disbandment for specially bad cases of treason and mutiny (the fate of the old First Legion and certain others that joined Civilis in *A.D.* 70).

We can hardly doubt that the former was the case with the IX. Hispana: that it must have been exterminated in some unrecorded Brigantian battle. This, probably, was the reason why the emperor crossed himself to Britain in 120, probably bringing with him the Sixth legion, which we know to have been transferred from the Rhine to Britain at this moment. It replaced the vanished IX. Hispana at York, and is found garrisoned there down to the last years of the Roman dominion in Britain, when the famous *Notitia Dignitatum* was drawn up about 400 *A.D.* An inscription found in Italy gives us the information that detachments (*vexillationes*) of three other Rhine legions (VII. Gernina, VIII. Augusta, XXII. Primigenia), also came over to Britain for the "*expeditio Britannica*" of Hadrian, a fact borne out by the fact that a shield-boss belonging to the second of these corps has been found in the Tyne near Newcastle, and an inscription belonging to the last-named exists at Abbotsford.

It is one of the saddest mischances of British history that we have no detailed account of Hadrian's British expedition. The man himself was a character of strange and fascinating interest—by nature a dilettante and a man of pleasure, he was by the chance of an intrigue placed at the helm of the empire. He rose to the occasion, and made an admirable emperor, though the routine of his work must often have been most distasteful to his wayward spirit. The literary and artistic matters in which his real interest lay had to be put behind him, while he was absorbed in questions of frontier policy, taxation, or political organisation. But his insatiable and intelligent curiosity as to the world at large, and his resolve that if things had to be done they must be done well, earned him through twenty years of incessant travel and heart-breaking toil, and at the end a grateful empire rightly honoured "*Divus Hadrianus*," of the *animula vagula blandula*, that loved jests and pleasure yet turned unwillingly but manfully to hard work.

On crossing the British Channel in the third year of his reign, Hadrian, as his biographer Spartian informs us, "found many things to put right in Britain"—the reorganisation of a depleted army and the repression of the revolt of the Brigantes were but a part of his work. Yet no historian has thought fit to leave us a record of what the emperor's jesting friend Floras called his "walking about Britain." Only coins commemorate his review of the British legions, his "advent," and his "restoration" of the province. The great work which he left behind him, as the memorial of his reign, was the first wall between Tyne and Solway, which marked a determined and successful effort to put an end to the disorders of the north. It was built after his departure, as the dating of the inscriptions found on many points of its course indicate. He left Britain, apparently, in 121 *A.D.*, and the wall-inscriptions mainly date from 123-4, when the governor Aulus Plaetorius Nepos was busy all along the chosen line, with detachments of military masons drawn not only from the VI. Victrix, the York Legion, and the auxiliaries of the North, but from the other British legions, II. Augusta from Isca, and XX. Valeria Victrix from Deva. We cannot, however, doubt that the wall was the emperor's own inspiration, and that he had surveyed the ground on which it was to run, while he was present in person in the British Islands.

Clearly, he must have visited York, to inspect the newly arrived legion, and to form his own views as to the best way of dealing with the troublesome Brigantes. And, once in Brigantian territory, he must have been drawn up to take a view of the short line between Tyne and Solway, on which he must have found, occupied or unoccupied, Agricola's forts, and to form his own conclusions as to their suitability as a base for operating against the rebels. The idea of shutting in these hill men by drawing a line of garrisons along their northern frontier probably dated back to Agricola, as we have seen in the last chapter, yet these garrisons had proved inadequate to restrain Brigantian revolts, for the enemy could pass between and around them, and could summon through their gaps succours from the remoter North.

Though the country between Tyne and Forth was, as far as we can judge, thinly inhabited, it must nevertheless have owned a certain amount of untamed raiders, and beyond Forth the Caledonians were both numerous and enterprising. The design of Hadrian's Wall seems to have been to oppose a very solid barrier to the peoples of the North—all its fortification is turned in that direction—and at the same time to provide a chain of garrisons which would be useful against the Brigantes; though the main task of repressing the latter would fall upon the troops sown thick in foils and castles among the strategical centres of the Pennine Chain.

The works which fall into the period 121-124 and must be associated with the name of Hadrian are (setting aside the isolated castles south of the line from Tyne to Solway) (1) a great ditch between mounds, which archaeologists have usually called the *vallum* though the *limes* would be a better name; and (2) a wall carefully built of sods running close on the northern side of the ditch, at a distance of not more than a few hundred yards from it; (3) between wall and *limes* runs a fine military road.

The *limes* is essentially a non-military work. It may mark the definite civil boundary of the province of Britain, and this was probably its object, but it cannot serve any end of defence It consists of a deeply cut ditch, the earth of which has been thrown up into high banks on each side of the artificial hollow, probably with additional soil from remoter ground added. The bank on the northern side is the loftier of the two, and single: that on the southern side is double, there being a smaller mound on the very edge of the ditch, and a larger one some twenty feet further out. The central hollow itself seems to have been flat-bottomed, and with sides sloping outward at a rather obtuse angle, so that it averages fifteen feet broad at the bottom and thirty at the top. Its depth is only some seven or eight feet. It is separated by a berme, some twenty-five feet wide, from the northern mound.

On the south side there is no berme, the smaller of the two banks running quite close to the edge of the ditch; this accumulation of soil may have been the result of a supplementary cleaning out of the ditch at some time after its original excavation. The engineer who was responsible for the first digging probably caused the earth to be carried twenty or thirty feet away from the edge of the ditch on both sides, lest it should slip back again. The cleaner of the ditch more carelessly threw his upcast all on to the southern side, and left it quite close to the brink. The mounds, it must be repeated, are wholly unsuitable as a line of defence either against the north or the south. They are rough deposits of excavated earth, not shaped away so as to give a sharp face either on one side or the other.

Nor is there any trace of a road, either on the berme behind the northern mound or at the bottom of the ditch—the only places where a road could conceivably have run. There are no regular bridges or crossing-places discernible along the eighty miles of the *limes*. But where it lies close behind forts on the line of the wall, which we are now about to discuss, it has generally been worn down or filled up. This seems to prove that the garrisons of such forts in later ages found it inconvenient, and either gradually trod it into non-existence, or deliberately threw rubble into it, in order to level it up for convenient egress.

(2) To proceed to the wall. Much evidence has been produced to show that the solid stone structure now visible on the Northumbrian Moors is not Hadrian's original work, but a reconstruction by Severus. (Since this paragraph was written in 1909 the wall excavations of 1910-11 have produced some evidence which appears to make the case less clear. I must now reserve judgment till the controversy has been thrashed out.) It has been held that since Hadrian generally chose the best course possible, the later stone wall runs exactly on top of his structure: there is only one considerable section where his work still remains intact: this is a stretch of between two and three miles, to the west of the fort of Birdoswald (Amboglanna), where the wall of Severus takes a curve slightly to the north of Hadrian's line, in order to obtain a rather better and more commanding slope.

At this point we can survey the wall of 121-3, while elsewhere its course lies buried below the stones of 208-11. We find that it was, like the later Clyde to Forth wall of Antoninus Pius, built of turf solidly laid in regular courses, and not of stone. This is exactly what we should expect from looking at the one classical author who speaks of the two walls in relation to each other. Julius Capitolinus (*de Antonio Pio*) says that Antoninus Pius, "*Britannos per Lollium Urbicum legatum vicit, alio muro cespiticio submotis barbaris ducto.*" This translated in the most natural fashion should mean that the first wall (Hadrian's) as well as the second (that of Pius) was a *murus cespiticius*, made of sods, like that which we can trace today from Forth to Clyde.

It was the fact that the turf wall of Hadrian was buried, save for one section, under the stone wall of Severus, that led many antiquaries, neglecting the evident stretch of turf wall near Birdoswald, to attribute a stone wall to Hadrian, and to ignore the clear testimony of several classical authors, which tells us that Severus also built a stately wall from Solway to Tyne. Recent explorations have shown that slight traces of the turf-wall and its ditch may be found elsewhere than at Birdoswald, especially at Chesters, and the adjacent bridge over the North Tyne. (See Haverfield's *Excavations at Chesters, in September, 1900,* and *Excavations on the Roman Wall.*) But owing to the excellent choice of a line made by the engineers of 121-23, those of 208-11 hardly ever diverged from it, and Hadrian's turves were easily to be demolished by the spade: hence the small amount of relics left from it are a testimony to its good design.

Hadrian's Wall, then, a *murus cespiticius* strengthened with forts at frequent intervals, must be considered to be represented, as far as direction goes, by the stone wall still visible, save on the single section, already repeatedly named, near Birdoswald. It runs roughly parallel to the *limes*, sometimes within a few yards of it, sometimes at a distance of as much as 500 yards from it. For the *limes* seeks the shortest and easiest course, since it has no military purpose, while the wall habitually diverges from the line of the *limes*, in order to seek higher and more defensible ground, wherever the latter is taken along localities unfavourable for defence against an attack from the North.

At the highest point of its course, between Aesica and Procolitia (Great Chesters and Carrawburgh), the wall climbs to the edge of a steep ridge, with frequent cliffs along its northern face, while the ditch and mounds forming the *limes* pursue their even way at the south foot of the slope, at distances varying from 250 to 500 yards from the summit of the ridge. In short, the wall dominates the whole of the ground over which an attack from the North would come, while the *limes* would be completely commanded by an enemy established on the higher slopes of the ridge along which the wall runs.

The full length of Hadrian's wall is stated by his biographer Spartianus at eighty Roman miles, which fairly corresponds with the seventy-three English miles between Segedunum (Wallsend) on the Tyne and Bowness (Gabrosentum?) on the Solway. The wall continues for some miles at each of its ends after the *limes* has come to an end. The latter stopped when it reached tidal water at the head of the Solway Firth; the wall was extended some way along the estuary, in order to prevent out-flanking by enemies who might cross the tidal flats at low water, or come across the head of the firth in small boats. (See later, under the reign of Severus, for statements by Roman historians as the way in which the uncivilised Briton or Caledonian would cross tidal marshes where the legionary could not follow him.) Hadrian's forts along the wall may probably have been the same fifteen which are visible today along the wall of Severus.

In some cases, they were certainly smaller than those which now exist; and they may often, or always, have been earthen strongholds instead of stone ones. The considerable number of inscribed stones, bearing the names of the emperor and his *legate* Aulus Plaetorius Nepos which are to be found along the wall, may have stood originally in the stone structures, gates, stores, official residencies, etc., belonging to the forts. None of them, unfortunately, record the character of the building which they commemorated. The majority, however, state that the building, whatever it was, had been the work of a legion; several have the name of the legion from Isca, II. Augusta, or that of the Chester Legion XX. Valeria Victrix. More than one has been taken from its original place, in order to be used in building or repairing the stone wall of Severus, ninety years after it had been set up in Hadrian's time. The Romans had as little scruple in using up old material in this fashion as had the mediaeval builders, who afterwards wrecked Severus's Wall in order to build churches or farmhouses. (See Professor Haverfield's paper on the Epigraphy of Hadrian's Wall in *Proceedings of the Society of Antiquaries*, for 1892.)

There are enough inscriptions belonging to the Antonine period along the line of Hadrian's Wall to enable us to say that, although the building of it was largely done by the legions, yet the garrisoning of it was handed over entirely to the auxiliary *cohorts* and *alae*. Indeed, many of these units, first placed on the wall by Hadrian, seem to have retained their position there for a century, some for two centuries and more. The First Dacian *cohort*, whose name Aelia shows that it was raised, or at least honoured, by Hadrian, seems to have been at Birdoswald (Amboglanna) from its first coming to Britain down to the moment when the *Notitia Dignitatum* was drawn up about the year 400 *A.D.*

Several others of the auxiliary garrisons can be traced back from the *Notitia* well into the time of the Antonines, and if we find them localised by 150 or 160 in the places where they still lay in 400, we may fairly suppose that their original placing goes back to the first builder of the wall himself. Other units which leave record of themselves on the Wall in the second century have been superseded by newcomers in the third. But on the whole, there was singularly little change in the composition of the army of Northern Britain from first to last.

******

A bronze tablet found at Riveling near Sheffield (C. I. L., 1195) contains a list of *cohorts* and *alae* serving in the eighth year of Hadrian's Tribunician Power within Britain. There are twenty-one *cohorts* and six *alae*. Of their names those of three *alae* are lost. There remain three *alae* and all the twenty-one *cohorts*. Of these troops serving in 124 there still survive in the *Notitia Dignitatum*, compiled about the year 400, at least two *alae* and nine *cohorts*. After the wear and tear of nearly three centuries this is astonishing. Moreover here are several more units, whose names do not happen to occur in this tablet (since no soldiers

117

belonging to them chance to have been granted privileges in it), yet which were certainly in Britain under Hadrian and still survive in the *Notitia, e,g.,* I. Aelia Dacorum, named above in the text.

★★★★★★

In dealing with the British Army of the second, third and fourth centuries, we must guard ourselves against the natural idea, drawn from our knowledge of earlier Roman days, that the soldiery, whether legionary or auxiliary, were wholly alien to the population of the province. From the time of the Antonines onwards it is certain that both legions and *cohorts* were growing more and more closely connected by ties of blood with the provincials among whom they were quartered. The change had begun in the time of Vespasian. Down to his reign the recruits of the legions in the West had been largely Italians, all citizens born, the remainder being supplied by a *delectus* held mainly in the old senatorial provinces, which had long been incorporated in the empire, and had lost all national feeling, such as Baetica and Gallia Narbonensis.

The men so drawn were of free birth, and received the citizenship on being enrolled: they mixed freely and without difficulty with the purely Italian element among their comrades. The legion was usually Roman in feeling, and alien to the district in which it was quartered. Such were the corps which fought in Britain under Aulus Plautius or Suetonius Paulinus. But Vespasian put an end to the levying of *legionaries* in Italy, and seems to have laid down the rule that only the Praetorian Guard should for the future be raised from the inhabitants of the peninsula. Legionary tombstones show that while plenty of Italians were serving in every western legion when Vespasian came to the throne, and for some years later, they had almost disappeared from the ranks by the end of the reign of his son Domitian.

So far as the inscriptions allow us to trace the nationality of legionary recruits after the change made by Vespasian, it would seem that in the days of his dynasty, and in the following time of Nerva and Trajan, the policy was canned out of keeping the composition of the legions very heterogeneous. The *delectus* was carried out in different provinces every year, so that each corps was formed of *strata* (so to speak) of different provincials. A western legion would have all its recruits one year from South Gaul, and the next from South Spain. But in the time of Hadrian (a great innovator in all things) a new tendency comes to the front. We get a decided commencement of local recruiting, of the

118

telling-off of the conscripts of each province to the legions quartered in it or near it.

Nothing could better mark the complete absorption of old tribal nationalities in the common Roman name, than the fact that it had now become possible to think of levying homogeneous legions from the population of the provinces in which they were quartered. In Britain this plan was not carried out so fully as in Gaul or Spain, because the civilised Latin-speaking communities suitable for the providing of legionary recruits were few. But nevertheless, the legions became largely Britonised in another way: an enormous proportion of recruits in the second and following centuries were provided from the legions themselves, by children born in the camp who took up their father's profession.

And as the legionary almost invariably married a provincial wife, from the distinct in which he was quartered, his sons were semi-British. There was a danger, therefore, that as the proportion of locally connected recruits continued to grow, the legions would grow "particularist," and think of themselves as provincials rather than Romans. This danger did not happen in the days of the Antonines, but showed itself clearly in the following century, when each provincial army represented not merely a military but a racial unit, with a close *esprit de corps*, and a rancorous jealousy of the legionary armies of other provinces. This simple fact was at the bottom of all the civil wars of the third century.

If the legions grew Britonised from Hadrian's time onward, the case was far more so with the auxiliaries. Vespasian was the innovator in this branch of army organisation, as well as in the branch of recruiting for the legions. But his changes had not been in the same direction. Under the early empire, down to 69, an auxiliary *cohort* was normally both raised from the tribe whose name it bore, and quartered fairly near its recruiting centre. Batavians served with the army of the Lower Rhine, Gauls with the army of the Upper Rhine, Moors in Africa, and so forth.

But the great revolt of Civilis, which gave so much trouble to Vespasian, showed that it was dangerous to keep auxiliary *cohorts* garrisoned among their own countrymen. From that time the large majority of them were sent to do duty far afield—Moors even to northern Britain, Britons to Dacia, Syrians to the Danube. This arrangement rendered the preservation of the national character of each regiment very difficult: instead of requiring recruits to be brought from thousands of miles away, the local military authorities would be tempted to accept eligible men who could be obtained nearer the place where the *cohort* was quartered. By the time of the Antonines the composition of the auxiliary regiments very largely ceased to bear any relation to their titles.

Some corps kept up their national recruiting better than others: in Britain it seems that the Tungrian and Batavian auxiliaries were still mainly Tungrian or Batavian in the third century. But *cohorts* or *alae* brought from much further afield, like Dacians, Thracians, or Moors, could not be kept national, and got more and more filled up with local recruits. We have clear instances of Brigantians serving in their own country in a *cohort* that was nominally Thracian, and so forth. (*E.g.,* one Nictovelius son of Vindex "*nationis Brigans*" in the second Thracian *cohort* C. I. L. 1090.) When in the third century the empire was broken up for long years into fractions dominated by different rulers, *e.g.*, in the long "Gaulish empire" that lasted from 258 to 274, or the "British empire" of Carausius and Allectus, which lasted from 287 to 296, a *cohort* of Thracians or Moors garrisoned in Britain cannot have had for many years a single recruit of its nominal nationality, since Mauretania or Thrace were not in the hands of the usurping emperor acknowledged in Britain. The *cohorts* continued to exist, but were completed with western, and mainly no doubt British, conscripts.

Hence from the time of Hadrian onward the auxiliaries, even more than the *legionaries*, began to be closely connected with the province in which they were quartered, and to possess a provincial particularist feeling, identical with that of the people among whom they dwelt.

Hadrian reigned for seven or eight years after the *limes* and the turf-wall from Tyne to Solway had been completed in 123-24. The frontier stood still, at the line where he had drawn it, only for a few years longer, for in 140-41 it was earned forward to the line of Forth and Clyde by Lollius Urbicus, the governor of Britain under Antoninus Pius. What led to this advance it is difficult to conceive: possibly the Brigantes were considered to have been finally tamed; they had settled down into a more or less delusive quiet, since the garrisons along the wall had encompassed them and cut them off from any connection with the North.

On the other hand, the tribes between Solway and Forth, the Otadini, Novantae, and Selgovae may have been giving trouble, yet have seemed weak enough to be easily subdued, since there is every sign that their country was but thinly inhabited. The way to tame them would be to encompass them with another wall, just as the Brigantes had lately been surrounded by the first wall. Troops for the holding of the first line might seem procurable without danger from the garrisons of the forts in Brigantia, and on the Tyne-Solway wall, where the number of *cohorts* could safely be cut down if the unruly tribe was truly broken in spirit.

What happened can only be gathered from inscriptions—the only mention of the movement in the historians is the single sentence in Julius Capitolinus which has been already quoted. But the inscriptions show us that Lollius Urbicus took detachments from all the three British legions, the second, sixth, and twentieth, and a number of auxiliary *cohorts* drawn mainly from the Wall-garrisons, and with them advanced across the Lowlands, and seized the narrow neck from Clyde to Forth, which Agricola had already discovered sixty years before, "the place where Britain is narrowest from ocean to ocean," as the geographer of Ravenna very correctly observes.

He then built a solid wall of turf, and dug a deep ditch in front of it, from Carriden on the Forth, near Abercorn, to Old Kilpatrick on the Clyde, a distance of a little less than 37 miles. Ten strong forts were dotted along this line, at intervals from each other much less than those between the fifteen forts on Hadrian's wall. A great road was constructed to join the new wall to its military base on the south. It started from Corstopitum (Corbridge) on the Tyne, and ran to Abercorn on the Forth, having dotted along it large permanent forts at Habitancium (Risinghame) and Bremenium (High Rochester) in Northumberland, at Newstead on the Tweed near Melrose (Trimontium?), and at Inveresk and Cramond, on each side of Edinburgh.

Possibly a corresponding highway for the western side of the Lowlands may have been begun, but it was never completed. For a very large permanent camp was built at Blatum Bulgium (Birrens) in Dumfriesshire, and a visible road connects this fortress with Luguvallium (Carlisle) and the Solway end of Hadrian's Wall. But north of Birrens there is no clear continuation of this track, as might have been expected, towards the western end of the wall of Lollius Urbicus. No Roman road can be discovered along the course of the Clyde, the direction which a way from Birrens to Old Kilpatrick must have taken. And Roman remains of all kinds are not common in Lanarkshire, while they are found in considerable quantities all along the road through Northumberland, Tweeddale. and Lothian, on which Habitancium, Bremenium and Trimontium lie.

The conquest of the western Lowlands, the modern Lanark, Ayr, and Galloway, can have amounted to nothing more than the submission of the local tribe, the Novantae, who did not receive garrisons among them like those on the eastern side, the Otadini and Selgovae. If any great camp, like those of High Rochester or Newstead, had been reared in this direction it could not have escaped notice. The complete occupation and settlement of the district on the Irish sea must have been postponed till that on the eastern shore should have been thoroughly finished. And this time was never to come, for the forty years of the occupation of the Lowlands were not a period of quiet advance, but one of trouble in the rear.

The large majority of the monuments found beyond the Cheviots may be dated to the years of Antoninus Pius following the conquests of Lollius Urbicus (140-161); there is hardly anything from the time of Marcus Aurelius (161-181); and absolutely nothing from that of Commodus. (Of course, undated inscriptions are hard to attribute with certainty. But such seems to be the case. The large majority of the inscribed stones belong to the first building operations of Lollius Urbicus, in 140-41.) Coins give the same evidence: the finds along the wall of Lollius Urbicus, and at the camps behind it, like Cramond, Newstead, and Birrens, consist of coins of the time of Trajan, Hadrian, and Pius in great quantities, of a certain amount of those of Marcus Aurelius, and barely one or two of Commodus and his wife Crispina. (See Haverfield's list of Scottish coin-finds in Appendix I. to the Antonine Wall Report of the Glasgow Archaeological Society, 1893.) Clearly the evacuation of the region must be placed at the very commencement of the reign of the unworthy son of the philosophic Marcus.

The reason why Roman conquest never bit deep in the Lowlands would seem to have been that about the end of the reign of Pius, in the governorship of Julius Verus (*circ.* 155-158) the last great revolt of the Brigantes took place. It is only recorded in a parenthesis in Pausanias's description of the Peloponnesus, a very strange place in which to find a notice of a purely British affair—and the note which there occurs is very puzzling in its language. Pausanias says that Antoninus had to punish the Brigantes by annexing a great part of their territory, because they had dared to make armed incursions into "the Genunian part" which was subject to the Romans. If we did not know that the Brigantes had been already taken completely into the Empire by the building of Hadrian's Wall many years before, we should have supposed that what Antoninus did was to appropriate part of the lands of a tribe which had hitherto not been fully subdued.

But considering the situation of affairs in 155 *A.D.*, this is an impossible rendering. The term "the Genunian part" is equally puzzling: there is no mention elsewhere either in historians, geographers or inscriptions of Genunians. And we are at a loss why they are called a "part," and of what they were a part—was it of the Brigantes themselves? Or is the curious phrase a translation of some Caledonian local name—since the Picts at a later time divided themselves into "parts" each with the word Dal (which has that meaning) prefixed to it. (See for this hypothesis Rhys's *Celtic Britain*.) And why is stress laid on "the Genunian part" being subject to Rome—as if the Brigantes themselves were not also within the empire?

The whole statement of Pausanias is a riddle, and all that we can deduce from it is that the Brigantes attacked other Roman subjects, whether north or south of Hadrian's Wall, and were severely punished for it, by part of their territory being removed from the authority of the tribal *civitas* and put under some other form of administration. That the subjection of the Brigantes did not take place without a severe struggle seems proved by the fact that military building all round their territory can be traced in the governorship of Julius Verus, whose inscriptions show that he restored forts as far south as Brough in Derbyshire, and as far north as Newcastle-on-Tyne, Birrens in Dumfriesshire and Netherby at the north-east end of the Solway Firth. (See Professor Haverfield's Note on the Brough Inscription, 1903).

It would seem that the revolt under Pius was the last struggle of the Brigantes, and that (whether because of the partition of their territory, or because their spirits were tamed at last) they gave no further trouble. Some, if not all, of the garrisons in their southern limits were evacuated in the third quarter of the second century, no doubt because they were no longer required. Such small traces of civilised Roman life as are found in their land seem to commence about the same time. Probably York got a new lease of life when the country outside its own immediate circle of plain became safe and peaceful.

Isurium (Aldborough), fifteen miles further up the Ouse, must have developed into the flourishing little town that can be restored from its remains, about the same time. Corstopitum (Corbridge) the northernmost town, as opposed to a mere military station, in Britain, may have made its start earlier, as being the base-depot for the road that led to Antoninus's wall, and well protected by the line of garrisons close in front of it. But it must have profited much by the submission of the Brigantes, since it would become the market-town of the northern members of the tribe, as Eburacum and Isurium were for those who dwelt farther south. Luguvallium (Carlisle) may have fared the same, but its remains have never been properly explored: a certain number of tombstones of civilians found in its cemetery prove that it was not a wholly military settlement.

But the pacification of Britain south of Hadrian's Wall was not followed by that of the regions north of it, by Clyde and Forth. And probably the last Brigantian War was precisely the circumstance that prevented the work of Lollius Urbicus from being completed. The troops on guard along Antoninus'Wall may have been in part recalled, and certainly no advance can have been made in the settling up of the Lowlands, while the land south of them was aflame. Nor did better times come with the accession of Marcus Aurelius (161 *A.D.*). In the reign of the philosopher-emperor the Roman world began to show, for the first time, an alarming lack of stamina and recuperative energy.

Whether the famines and pestilences which raged through the greater part of Marcus's time were the cause, or only a symptom, of decay, it is not necessary to decide. But it is clear that the time of advance was over. Britain was one of the provinces where trouble began early: the new reign had hardly started when we are told that a British war was impending, and that Aurelius had to send Sextus Calpurnus Agricola, one of his best officers, to deal with it. This trouble must have been caused by revolts of the tribes in the Lowlands, complicated by irruptions of the Caledonians from the north, for it clearly did not affect the region south of Hadrian's Wall.

The name of the second Agricola is found in several British inscriptions, but they do not suggest trouble on this side of the wall—consisting mainly of altars erected by some of the garrison troops at Carvoran, with a dedication in honour of the emperor at Ribchester. Similarly the traces of the next governor, Ulpius Marcell us, who may have been ruling Britain about 165 or 170, do not imply disorder—an aqueduct was put up at the fort of Chesters (Cilurnum), hard by the North Tyne, bearing his name, and an altar at Benwell, another Wall-station. This sort of record of building and peaceful religious dedication does not suggest a time of strenuous warfare.

But in the parts north of Hadrian's Wall the case is different, and there is strong suspicion that matters were not going on in a satisfactory fashion. The numerous inscriptions from that region which bear dates from the reign of Antoninus Pius have no successor from the time of Marcus, and his coins also are not found in such profusion as those of his father-in-law. It is quite probable that a distinct retrograde movement had already set in, and even that the wall from Forth to Clyde may not have maintained consistently through the whole of Marcus's lifetime. It is certainly strange that not a single inscription from that line mentions his name, though so many bear that of Pius.

★★★★★★

But we must of course remember that most of these were connected with the building of Antoninus's Wall, or of forts, so that Marcus, who had not to do such building, would naturally be less commemorated.

★★★★★★

The deduction would seem to be that while Hadrian's Wall was safe in the period 161-180, we cannot be sure that the northern wall was intact. But there is no reason to think that the whole of the Lowlands were lost at this time; even if the wall was sometimes pierced, the road must still have been open to it, and the great intermediate forts, Habitancium, Bremenium, Trimontium were still held in force. The crisis was not to come till the next reign.

CHAPTER 8
Roman Period: Commodus to Carausius (A.D. 180-296)

While our evidence concerning the state of the frontier of the British province under Marcus Aurelius is fragmentary, and leads to the deduction that Hadrian's Wall and all that lay behind it was sate, but that there was perpetual strife and little progress north of that wall, we have decidedly clearer signs of disaster in the time of Commodus. Except at three or four isolated points, all traces of Roman occupation beyond the line of Tyne and Solway cease about the year 181. These exceptional spots are Habitancium (Risinghame) on the road from Corbridge, Bremenium (High Rochester) farther to the North on that road, and close under Cheviot, and on the western front Castra Exploratorum (Netherby) and Bewcastle, in front of Carlisle.

★★★★★★

At High Rochester, despite its advanced position, thirty miles in front of the Wall, important military buildings were being constructed, as we shall presently see, as late as the time of Alexander Severus, more than fifty years after the accession of Commodus.

★★★★★★

These were all firmly held down to a late date in the third century. But all north of them was clearly abandoned soon after the year 180. The excavations at the more important Lowland stations, such as Newstead and the castles on the Antonine Wall, show that these fortresses were either stormed by an enemy or evacuated in dire haste by their garrisons. When inscribed altars are found choking the main well of a station, we may recognise either the mischievous hand of the triumphant barbarian, or the despair of a departing occupant, who never dreams of returning.

These are traces of the "British War" which filled the earlier years of Commodus, and for which he was most undeservedly voted the title of Britannicus by the subservient senate. It seems to have filled the years 181-87 *A.D.*, and to have started with a disastrous Caledonian raid. The short account of it in Xiphilinus's Epitome of Dio Cassius is the only coherent narrative that is left to us.

> Certain of the insular nations having crossed the wall that divided them from the stations of the Romans, did dreadful damage, and cut to pieces a certain general together with the division which he commanded.

Commodus sent against them a very aged officer, Ulpius Marcellus, who had already been governor of Britain twenty years before, in the time of Marcus Aurelius. This grim and severe personage, concerning whose austerity and sleepless vigilance curious tales are told, is said to have inflicted many defeats on the barbarians. But the war undoubtedly went on after his time, and ended with the abandonment of the wall of Antoninus and all the stations of the Lowlands, and a retreat to the line of Hadrian's Wall. We have no information as to whether the Caledonian invader was assisted by a rising of the Otadini and the other tribes between the walls, a thing in itself most probable. But the Brigantes, though tamed only forty years before, do not seem to have been tempted into insurrection.

The epilogue of the British war of Commodus was a series of desperate mutinies on the part of the legions, who may possibly have been goaded into sedition by the austerity of Marcellus. There follows the astonishing statement that they sent a deputation of 1,500 men to Rome to demand the death of the Praetorian Praefect Perennis, the rather inexplicable cause given for their action by Lampridius is that:

"During the British war he removed senators from military command, and substituted men of equestrian rank for them, whereupon he was called the enemy of the army and dragged out to be torn to pieces by the soldiers" (186 *A.D.*).

Helvius Pertinax, afterwards emperor, succeeded Ulpius Marcellus, and met with similar mutinies. In one of them he was so maltreated that he was left for dead upon the ground. We are told that he punished the soldiery in the most bitter fashion for their outrages, and reduced them to order. But Pertinax then asked and obtained his own recall from the emperor, saying that the troops would not settle down, on account of the intense hatred that they bore him for restoring discipline.

Yet on his first arrival the legions are said to have wished to make him emperor "since they wanted to set up an emperor at all costs, and thought him specially fitted for the post". Despite his unimpeachable conduct, Commodus's informers are said to have tried to persuade their master to accuse Pertinax of treason. But he refused to listen, and when he recalled him gave him the honourable post of Director of the Corn Supply of Rome.

It was presumably Pertinax who brought the war to an end, since we are told that it was still going on when Perennis fell a victim to his unpopularity with the army. From 187 onwards the frontier is once more at Hadrian's Wall: the peace may probably have been accompanied by some vague admission of Roman supremacy by the British tribes just outside the wall. But it seems that the Caledonians must have made a southern advance, at the expense of these Britons, occupying some part of the land just south of the Forth, up to the Pentland Hills. One of the subterranean dwellings or "weems" characteristic of the Picts has been found near Crichtoun in Midlothian, with its roof partly composed of Roman-hewn stones from the station of Inveresk.

This implies a permanent Pictish occupation, not mere ravaging. Between Pict and Roman the unfortunate Britons between Forth and Tyne must have been in a miserable condition. Probably they were forced to join the invader whenever he came forward, and then bore the brunt of Roman retaliation.

A few years later (192 *A.D.*) we find the British province in the charge of D. Clodius Albinus, who may have been the immediate successor of Pertinax in command. He was of an ancient and wealthy family, had served with credit in his youth, and is said to have been good-humoured and liberal, qualities which gave him a popularity with the soldiery which neither Marcellus nor Pertinax could command. He was withal, rather ambitious, given to vainglory, but lacking in decision. On a false rumour of the death of Commodus reaching Britain, he is said to have harangued the legions in terms which were taken to hint at his willingness to make a grasp at the diadem.

This was reported to the emperor, who sent out Junius Severus to supersede him. But Commodus died in real earnest, assassinated by his own courtiers, before Albinus was removed, and the latter found himself still in command of the British Army during the chaotic year 198, which gave every opportunity for a man of energy. The senate, as it will be remembered, named Pertinax as Augustus, but the Praetorians slew him, put the empire up to auction, and sold it to the wealthy but incapable Didius Julianus. Thereupon the three great frontier armies of the Roman world each proclaimed its commander emperor, the Danube army acclaiming L. Septimus Severus, the Syrian Army Pescennius Niger, and the British Army the not-unwilling Albinus.

This triple nomination was destined to bring about an abnormal situation of affairs both for Britain and for the Empire. Severus, who succeeded in reaching Rome and slaying Didius Julianus before the other would-be emperors could even make a start, saw that he would have to fight both Niger and Albinus. But preferring to face them in detail, and fearing the fierce British army more than the Orientals, he sent to Albinus, offering to recognise him as his junior colleague, and to leave him complete control of Britain, in return for his alliance against Niger. The British pretender showed greater simplicity and a more halting ambition than had been expected.

Apparently, he thought that the Antonine practice of imperial adoption might be renewed, that he might be the Hadrian of the new Trajan, serve him loyally, and ultimately succeed to his throne. Accordingly, he accepted with thanks the title of Caesar offered to him by Severus, and remained in Britain, where he ruled with some success, instead of crossing to Gaul and summoning the German legions to join him. This condition of affairs lasted for over three years, during which Albinus reigned in Britain alone, though his name was added to that of Severus in official documents and inscriptions throughout the west. (There is a notable one in the museum at Mainz, but none, oddly enough, in Britain.)

But this compromise, which foreshadowed the British Empire of Carausius, only lasted till Severus had made an end of Pescennius Niger and the Syrians, and had then devoted another year to the reorganisation of the East. He had children of his own, whom he intended to make his associates in the imperial dignity and by 196 the unfortunate Albinus had become unnecessary to him. The excuse made for attacking him is said to have been that it was discovered that many important senators had been sending him secret letters, bidding him seize Rome while Severus was still absent and busy in the East. But Albinus, whatever answer he may have made them, had taken no steps to break his contract with Severus: indeed, we are told that he had shown himself indolent and easy-going, and displayed intense satisfaction in the title and state of Caesar.

Meanwhile Severus brought up the Illyrian Army to the Western Alps, and then declared war on his colleague. Seeing that he must choose between defending Britain, or seizing Gaul and winning over its legions, Albinus took the bolder step. He declared himself Augustus, mobilised every corps that could be spared from the island, hastily crossed the Channel, and called upon the Gauls to join him. Some of the cities and many troops did so, but more hung back, prudently determining to join the victor, whoever he might be. But Albinus was able to push on to Lugdunum before he met with resistance. In front of that great city he was confronted by Severus and the army drawn from the Danube.

Then followed the greatest battle between Romans that had been seen since Philippi, for the forces on both sides were larger than those which had fought under Otho and Vitellius at Bedriacum in 69. The fight was long and doubtful "for the Britons," says Herodian "are no whit inferior in courage or sanguinary spirit to the Illyrians". The wing of Severus's army in which he himself fought was completely routed by the charge of Albinus's legions, and the emperor had his horse killed under him, and had to fling away his purple cloak to escape notice.

But at this moment, when the Britons seemed sure of victory, a fresh corps under one Laetus, which had been marching to join Severus, came suddenly upon the scene, checked the rout, and beat back the exhausted and disordered troops of Albinus. Their arrival decided the day: the British army fell back in complete disarray, and was pursued and slaughtered up to the very gates of Lyons. The victors pushed their way into the city along with the fugitives, and not contented with massacring their armed opponents, burnt and plundered the houses of the citizens. Albinus was taken alive in the city, and promptly decapitated by his captors, who took his head to Severus. Thus, ended the first "British Empire," which had lasted over three years (193-97).

The whole of the garrison of Britain must have been completely disorganised by the departure of Albinus with its picked corps, and the destruction of many thousands of veterans at the Battle of Lugdunum. Severus paid some attention to the island after his victory: to curb the power of future governors he divided the province into two halves, "Upper" and "Lower" Britain, so that for the future there were two co-ordinate and rival authorities in the island. The probable boundaries of the two new units may be guessed from the fact that Dio Cassius mentions that the Sixth Legion at York was in Lower Britain, while both the Second Augusta at Caerleon and the Twentieth Valeria Victrix at Chester were in Upper Britain.

This suggests a boundary drawn from the Mersey to the Humber: but other hypotheses are possible. This note of Dio, confirmed by numerous inscriptions, shows that Severus did not disband the remnants of the legions which had pressed him so hard at Lugdunum, but reconstructed the three corps, probably filling up their depleted ranks with conscripts drawn from other regions than those which had produced the men who fought so furiously against him in 197.

As to the auxiliary *cohorts*, we find a great number of those which had served under Hadrian in Britain still existing in the third century: but it is likely that some perished for ever on the field of Lyons. Be this as it may, it is probable that for some years after the civil war had ended the garrison of Britain was both under its normal strength and in a disorganised condition. Nor can we doubt that the old disease of mutiny, which had raged so severely under Commodus, must have been seething under the surface, when the troops were forced to obey the conqueror who had slaughtered thousands of their comrades and slain their chosen emperor.

It is by the weakness and discontent of the British Army that we can best explain the disasters which befell the province in the middle years of the reign of Severus. The troubles commenced by incursions of the Southern Picts into the region of Hadrian's Wall. These people are now (for the first time) called Meatae: the Epitome of Dio gives us the information that by this date all the smaller tribes of North Britain—the Boresti, Vacomagi, Taexali, etc., of Tacitus and Ptolemy—had merged themselves into the two confederacies of the Caledonians and the Meatae, "of whom the latter dwell close on the wall that divides the island in two" (no doubt the turf-wall of Antoninus is meant) while the former possessed the remoter regions of the North.

In the time when Virius Lupus was governor of Northern Britain (197-205?) the Meatae attacked the province: the legate was resisting them, and had apparently won some small successes, (Xiphilinus. lxxv. 5. So there must have been some small local captures), when it was reported to him that the Caledonians were about to intervene, despite of the treaties which were in existence with them—presumably agreements made either by Pertinax or Clodius Albinus. Thereupon Lupus, with unseemly haste, bought peace from the Meatae by giving them huge subsidies. Of course, no permanent quiet was secured by this cowardly policy. In 205-8 we find Alfenius Senecio, the successor, of Lupus, busy in repairing the Northern fortifications, and finally reporting to Rome:

That the barbarians were in a state of disturbance, overrunning the country, driving off booty, and laying everything waste, so that there was need either for large reinforcements, or even for an expedition headed by the emperor in person. (Herodian.)

★★★★★★

Note: Inscriptions on the quarries overhanging the River Gelt show that they were being worked in the Consulship of Aper and Maximus (207). An inscription at Bainbridge (C. I. L., vii. 269) shows buildings by the Sixth Nervian *cohort* under Senecio's orders.

★★★★★★

Severus was at this moment free from foreign troubles, having brought to a successful end his great Parthian war. His position was quite safe at home, his mental vigour was undiminished, though he had begun to be afflicted with violent fits of gout, and, as we are told, he was anxious to find a good excuse for removing from Rome his two young sons, Antoninus (Caracalla) and Geta, who were beginning to alarm him by their dissolute life and unseemly addiction to the shows of the amphitheatre. Accordingly, he announced his intention of taking up in person the charge of the Caledonian war, and of utilising it for the purpose of giving the young princes their first experience of military life.

He carried out his promise with great energy, crossing Gaul with unexampled speed, and arrived in Britain long before he was expected, and that although his gout lay heavy upon him, so that he had to be carried for many stages on a litter. The moment that he reached Britain he began to make elaborate preparations for a long campaign, calling up troops from all quarters—the Praetorians no doubt accompanied him—and he probably made large drafts from the Rhine Army. Hearing of his sudden arrival, and terrified at the strength of the force that was being collected, the Caledonians and their fellows sent ambassadors to Severus, begging for peace, excusing their past transgressions, and proffering all sorts of guarantees. The emperor deliberately wasted time before giving them an answer, in order that his preparations might be finished, but finally sent them away. He had never really intended to treat, being fully determined to complete the conquest of Britain, by canning the boundaries of the empire up to the Northern Ocean.

We are told that among the preliminary measures of Severus was the construction of many bridges and causeways over marshy places, more especially over certain tidal swamps, where the rising and falling tide made passage difficult and dangerous for the legions.

> Though the barbarians were wont to wade through them and to traverse them immersed as high as the waist; for going naked as to the greater part of their bodies, they despise the mud. Indeed, they have no proper knowledge of clothing, and wear collars and belts of iron round their waists and necks, thinking these the best of ornaments and a sign of wealth, as the other barbarians consider gold to be. (Herodian.)

It is difficult to locate this bridge and causeway-building, which (since it is described as preliminary to the actual campaign) must have been somewhere quite close to the frontier. The region about the head of the Solway Firth suggests itself as a possible place; but the Romans had already a solid road turning the head of the tidal sands of Solway, and going as far as Blatum Bulgium (Birrens) in Dumfriesshire, which is recorded as the Northern terminus of the British road-system in the Antonine Itinerary. The only other district where large tidal marshes could give difficulty is the estuary of the Forth below Stirling; but this seems a very advanced position for the Roman Army to be occupying before the actual commencement of the war.

Yet there is no other large stretch of tidal swamp on the eastern side of Britain anywhere north of the Wall, in which causeway building could be of any military use, and it is quite conceivable that the Meatae had drawn back behind the Forth, as a sign of their peaceful intentions, at the moment when they sent their ambassadors to propitiate the emperor.

Be this as it may, Severus commenced his advance in the spring of 209, and made two long campaigns, without desisting from his original plan of complete conquest: from the first to the last he never seems to have left the field, save to take up his winter quarters at York. The troops were probably, like those of Agricola, compelled to remain from October to March in camps established far within the enemy's territory. For if they had withdrawn behind the Forth, or to the shelter of Hadrian's Wall, the whole of their work would have had to be commenced *de novo* as each spring came round. We have no consecutive narrative of the war, but only a series of depressing pictures of its monotonous and deadly futility.

The army underwent indescribable labour in cutting down woods, levelling acclivities, making marshes passable, bridging rivers, but fought not a single battle, nor even saw an enemy in regular array. Occasionally the barbarians threw herds of sheep or oxen within reach of the soldiers, in order that they might be enticed to pursue them, and so worn out by fatigue. The army also suffered dreadfully from the rains, and whenever they were scattered in detachments ambushes were laid for them. Many men are said to have been despatched by their own comrades, when they were too worn out to walk any longer, lest they should fall alive into the hands of the barbarians. It is said that in one way or another 50,000 men perished.

So far, the epitome of Dio. Herodian in less dismal language gives much the same story.

The moment the army had passed the rivers and the earthen walls which form the boundaries of the empire, there were numerous small affrays and skirmishes, and retreats on the part of the barbarians. But to them flight was easy, and they hid themselves in woods and mosses, having the necessary local knowledge. But all these things were adverse to the Romans, and served to protract the war.

★★★★★★

The statement of Herodian that the boundary of the empire was protected at this time by ῥεύματα καὶ χώματα is very important. If a stone wall had already existed from Tyne to Solway, he must have used the word τεῖχος, for χῶμα means an earthen structure and nothing else. But since he mentions χώματα and not one χῶμα, both the walls of Hadrian and Antoninus Pius must be meant, and both must have been earthen. What were the rivers? Perhaps the lower course of Forth and Clyde. He can hardly mean Tyne and Irthing.

★★★★★★

133

But Severus was not a man who could easily be turned back from his purpose. Despite of all difficulties of weather and of territory, he forced his way to the Northern Ocean "until he drew near to the extreme end of the Isle of Britain," according to his biographer. But it is improbable that in reality he got any farther than the eastern end of the Moray Firth, where the promontory of the Taexali (Kinnaird Head), with the land falling away from it to west and south, may well have seemed to his army the very end of the earth. It is a sign of his active and curious mind that he caused investigations to be made at this northernmost point of the explored world into the parallax of the sun, and the length of the days and nights both in summer and winter. (*Epitome of Dio.*)

Doubtless he was set on verifying by actual investigation the calculations already made by geographers, such as Ptolemy, as to these facts, for one of the localities whose exact situation and whose extreme hours of light and darkness had been calculated by the Alexandrian scientist, was the "Winged Camp" in the territory of the Vacomagi, a locality which, being somewhere in the north-east of Scotland, must have been very near the last point of Severus's advance. Possibly some unhappy corps of the imperial army had its winter quarters for 209-10 fixed in bleak Aberdeenshire, and came to know only too well the length of its winter nights.

As far as the evidence and the probabilities go, it would seem that the main seat of Severus's campaigning was the eastern side of the Highlands, that starting from the Wall of Antoninus he worked up the comparatively flat and easy country along the North Sea, the land of the Meatae,—which was afterwards to be known as Fortrenn—leaving the Caledonians proper in the recesses of Athole and Badenoch and the remoter North comparatively unmolested, though no doubt raids may have pushed up past Dunkeld "the gate of the Highlands" into the valley of the Upper Tay, or up Strathearn, or along the whole southern side of the Moray Firth. The series of Roman camps traceable north of Antoninus's Wall starts with that of Ardoch, ten miles north of Stirling: there are others at Comrie, Strageath, Abernethy, Gask and Inchtuthill, all in the basin of the Tay. (But Inchtuthill is probably one of Agricola's camps.) But the reported Roman traces farther north, in Forfarshire and Aberdeenshire, need verifying.

Awful as were the sufferings of the Roman Army, Severus's steady and undeviating advance, and his evident intention to persevere till he should have finished his undertaking, ended by cowing the spirits of the barbarians. They sued for peace at the end of the second campaign, that of 210, not only doing homage and surrendering arms, but consenting to cede a great tract of territory, presumably the lands from Forth to Tay, where the Roman garrisons were now securely established, as well as anything that they may have been occupying south of the Wall of Antoninus. It was time, for the emperor's sake, that the war should end; he was now sixty-five, his health had completely broken down, his fits of gout were growing more persistent and dangerous, and he had accomplished more marches in his litter than on his horse.

Not the least of his trials, as we are told, came from the conduct of his eldest son. Geta had been left in the South to govern Britain, but Antoninus had accompanied his father through both campaigns. Though showing a very meagre interest in the war, he had been doing his best to court the favour of the army, deprecating the labours which Severus was imposing on the soldiery, tampering with the loyalty of ambitious officers, and making open and indecent preparations for his father's death, as his health grew worse and worse. He is even said to have schemed to murder his unhappy parent, though we can hardly believe the story that he drew his sword upon him as they were riding to a conference with the Caledonian chiefs, and only sheathed it when the staff, who were riding behind, uttered a unanimous shout of horror. The tale must surely be either a sheer invention, or a misrepresentation of some incident capable of misinterpretation which actually happened.

Severus retuned to York in the autumn of 210, leaving garrisons behind him in the newly annexed districts, and rested there for the winter His arrival in the city is said to have been accompanied with many strange and unfavourable omens, but the worst was his own broken form and haggard face. Yet his mind was still strong: he is actually said to have quelled a mutiny from his litter, and to have remarked to the repentant soldiery, pointing to his swollen limbs, "that they should remember that it is the head and not the feet which commands". But his health steadily grew worse, the effects of the late campaign conspiring with the undutiful conduct of Caracalla to bring him low.

At midwinter the last blow was given, by a report that the Meatae had attacked the garrisons, and that the Caledonians were joining them. Severus swore that they should be punished, and began to make preparations for a new campaign in March, warning the soldiers, as it is said, that no quarter should be given on this occasion. But the excitement was too much for him, he had to take to his bed and to delegate the task of marching against the Picts to his son, who showed no relish for it. A few days later he died (Feb. 4, 211): his end is said, probably without good grounds, to have been hastened by physicians suborned by his unworthy heir.

No sooner was Severus dead than Antoninus proceeded to patch up a peace with the Caledonians and Meatae. He withdrew every garrison that had been left in the North, and they in return gave some hostages and some easy promises of homage. Then he departed for Rome, there to slay his brother, and reigned with brutal tyranny for six years, till he was overturned and slain by the rebel Opelius Macrinus (217).

It might have seemed that all the work of Severus was wasted, since under Caracalla the line of Roman defence was drawn back to where it had stood at the death of Commodus;—the wall from Tyne to Solway once more forming the frontier, with its outposts at Bremenium, Castra Exploratorum, etc. But this was not so, Severus left as legacy to his successors a vastly improved boundary, having replaced Hadrian's earthen wall by a solid rampart of stone of far greater military value. It may seem strange that the emperor who had designed to add all Caledonia to his realm should have devoted attention to a structure which would have lain right in the midst of his dominions, and would not have guarded any frontier, if his plans had been carried to a successful conclusion. Yet there seems no reason to doubt that the stone wall of Northumberland, as we see it today, was the work of Severus. Spartianus, a writer who had good authorities before him, and wrote only three generations after this time writes:

> The chief glory of his reign was the wall which he drew right across the isle of Britain, from sea to sea.

The same statement is made by Aurelius Victor, who copies Spartianus's very words; Orosius adds some details:

> He thought fit to divide the conquered part of the island from the untamed tribes without by a wall: and so, he drew a great ditch and a most solid wall, furnished with frequent towers, for a distance of 132 (a misreading for 82) miles between sea and sea.

Eusebius makes the same miscalculation. A similar statement is found in Eutropius, with the opposite blunder of a calculation of the wall at 32 instead of 82 miles, as also in Cassiodorus. It is impossible to ignore all this evidence, though much of it is late. And when we find, by the evidence of excavation, that the present stone wall between Tyne and Solway is built upon the top of an older wall of turf, which in one place only diverges from its line for a couple of miles, (these two miles are just west of Birdoswald), but is otherwise identical with it, it would be useless to dispute that the first is Hadrian's building, the second that of Severus.

In several places, it may be added, forts, which form an integral part of the stone wall, are found built across the filled-up ditch of the earthen wall. (See Haverfield's Report on the excavations at Chesters in 1900.) And the filled-up ditch has its bottom filled with a muddy deposit, which implies the accumulation of many years, while above this mud is the gravel and debris thrown in to level the surface, when the new fort was constructed. The wonderful remnants of the stone wall, which we follow as it charges steep ravines or soars above the very edge of precipitous crags, with its fifteen great forts and its innumerable mile-castles, must be assigned, therefore, to the reign of Severus, though the inscriptions of his date left along it are no more numerous than those surviving from Hadrian's earlier earthen structure.

If it be asked why Severus built it, considering his northern ambitions, the reply seems to be that the commencement of the work dates back to before the time of his personal visit to Britain. He arrived in 208, and probably late in the year: but inscriptions show that the wall-quarries were being energetically worked in the consulship of Aper and Maximus (207), (C. 1. L., vii. 912), long before his landing in Britain, as well as in that of Faustinus and Rufus (210) the year of his second Caledonian campaign. (C. 1. L., vii. 871), Conceivably the conversion of the wall into a stone structure was one of the defensive measures taken in hand by the governor Alfenius Senecio, before the war grew so dangerous that he implored the presence of his master in Britain.

Yet we cannot suppose that it was finished before Severus's arrival. Did the emperor employ the large army which he collected in 208 upon the completion of the wall, as we know that he employed it during the winter of 208-9 on the building of roads and causeways through tidal marshes? If this work was well advanced towards completion before the actual campaigning began, it is quite conceivable that, when the Caledonians had made their submission in 210, Severus may have thought it worthwhile to utilise the services of the greater part of his army, which must have returned from the north in that autumn, in finishing the structure, even though it would be a superfluous precaution in case the conquest of Caledonia turned out to have been successful and permanent. We know that emperors, when they had a very large army collected, and actual campaigning was not on hand, often employed its energies upon building work, on the principle that idle hands always find mischief.

It may be remembered that Probus, two generations later, tried precisely this expedient on the Danube, till he worked his army so hard that a mob of soldiers suddenly burst out into mutiny and killed him. Conceivably the sedition that Severus is said to have suppressed in the autumn of 210 may have been caused by precisely the same sort of discontent at forced labour. But all this is hypothetical: whatever his reasons, we must believe that Severus built the stone wall which still remains as the chief wonder of Northern England.

There seems every reason to believe that the measures taken by Severus for the defence of Britain were more effective than those which were employed by other third century emperors for the protection of the Rhine and Danube frontiers. It would not be sufficient to argue from the silence of historians concerning serious troubles in Britain that none such occurred: for the annals of the time between Severus and Constantine are short, and scrappy in the extreme. Only those who have read the miserable stuff served up by the *Scriptores Historiae Augustae*, and the later epitomists, understand how little is known of the third century. We get trifling personal anecdotes instead of continuous history, and often events of serious permanent importance have to be inferred because they are not narrated. But this much is clear, that throughout the decades in which the defence of the outworks on Rhine and Danube was being broken down, the British frontier left by Severus was maintained.

The *Limes* beyond the Rhine was broken up and evacuated: Dacia was lost for ever: but the garrisons on the wall from Tyne to Solway stood at the end of the century exactly where they stood at its beginning. We find inscriptions on the Wall, showing building or repairs, which date not only from the reigns of Elagabalus and Severus Alexander, when chaos had not yet come, but from the darker times after the house of Severus had disappeared. Most striking of all is it to discover, at the remote outposts far north of the wall, records of elaborate constructions of edifices which were rather luxuries than necessities.

At Netherby there was a riding school (*Basilica exercitatoria equestris*) erected in 222. At High Rochester (Bremenium), the most northern point of all, a *ballistarium*, or storehouse for military machines, dates from the same period (219-22). If the advanced posts were thus adorned, the Wall, far behind them, must have been absolutely safe. On it are found the names of the unfortunate Gordian III. and his murderer Philip, (who gives his name as an honorary title to the Cuneus Frisiorum at Papcastle), and, what is more surprising, those of ephemeral rulers like Gallus and Volusian, (their names are found in a dedication at Penrith), and the Gaulish usurpers Postumus and Tetricus.

★★★★★★

Under whom there seems to have been repairing done just south of the wall, a military store, etc. at Lanchester (Co. Durham) restored (*conlapsa restituit*) and a bath and Basilica built (*balneum cum basilica a solo instruxit*) at the same place. C. I. L., vii. 445-6. Three or four military units become *vexillatio* or *numerus Gordianus* in his time, at High Rochester, Ribchester and Lanchester.

★★★★★★

During the existence of the so-called Gallic Empire under Postumus and his successors (258-74 *A.D.*) Britain, whether with enthusiasm or not we cannot say, acquiesced in all the proclamations of new monarchs on the Rhine, and showed no wish either to cling to the legal emperor at Rome, or to set up provincial pretenders on its own account. On the whole it is probable that the adherence of the island to the secessionist empire was willingly given, for in the later attempts of the West to break loose from Rome, after Tetricus had made his tame submission to Aurelian, the Britons are found taking a leading part in the particularist movement. This was the revolt of Bonosus and Proculus, of whom the former was the son of a British father and a Gallic mother. He may be noted as the first pretender of British blood who made a grasp at the imperial diadem.

These two conspirators are said to have expected to obtain assistance from all the Gauls and Britons and even from the Spaniards. They proclaimed themselves emperors at Cologne, and maintained themselves for some time, indeed there seemed to be some chance that they would be as successful as Postumus had been twenty years before. But when the legitimate emperor Probus came up against them he was joined by all the Trans-Rhenane Germans, whom the usurpers had vainly supposed that they had won over to their alliance. Bonosus and Proculus were defeated and slain, but not even then, if we are to believe Zosimus and Zonaras, did Probus finally recover Britain.

Another pretender, whose name is not given, was set up in the island: he fell by treachery not by force of arms. For one, Victorinus the Moor, who had formerly been the rebels' friend and patron, pretended to flee from Probus as if in danger of his life. But when he had been welcomed in Britain, he took the opportunity of secretly murdering his host at night, and returned to report success at Rome. Thereupon the rebellion came to an end, and the province returned to its allegiance (277 *A.D.*?) It is recorded that Probus sent over to Britain, no doubt organised in military units—*cunei* or *numeri*—all the Vandal and Burgundian warriors whom he captured in his German campaigns. They are said to have been intended to act as a counterpoise to the local troops, with whom they could have no community of feeling.

There is no reason to believe that during all the years of murder and civil war which lie between the death of Severus and the accession of Diocletian Britain was to any great extent molested by her old enemies the Caledonians, while domestic turbulence no longer took the form of tribal rebellion against the Roman imperial system as a whole, but rather that of adhesion to usurpers who were not recognised in the capital. The century was probably quite a prosperous period for Roman Britain. The laudatory description of the province which we get at the end of the period from the Panegyrist Eumenius is sufficient proof that it was in a flourishing condition.

It would have been fruitless to write of its lively seaports, its wealth in corn and cattle, its numerous mines, its large revenues, if all had been laid waste either by the barbarian or by civil strife. All the disasters of the empire during the third century had come from invaders who arrived by land, and since Britain was protected against its only land neighbours, the Caledonians, by Severus's Wall, it escaped the misfortunes of Gaul, Dacia and the Balkan Peninsula.

But at the very end of the century traces of danger from the side of the sea at last appear, and against such a danger the island had not yet been secured. There had always been a *Classis Britannica*, as inscriptions show, but it was a small affair, and insufficient to guard the whole of the North Sea and the Channel. For reasons which we cannot fathom, (but not solely as Zosimus would have it, because they were fired by ambition to copy the great sea raid of the escaped Frankish *cohort* from Pityus, i. 66), the Franks—the newly-formed league of German tribes on the Lower Rhine—and the more distant Saxons began to take to the sea and to act as pirates in the last years of the third century. Why they had not done so before is a problem as difficult to solve as the similar question as to why the Scandinavian Vikings did not start on their great raids before the age of Charlemagne.

Perhaps the recent disasters of the empire had encouraged them to feats of unprecedented boldness: perhaps the Ocean flotilla of the Romans had been allowed to sink into practical non-existence during the existence of the ephemeral Western state founded by Postumus. At any rate, we find that, about the time of the accession of Diocletian, the coast-lines of Northern Gaul and Eastern Britain were beginning to be infested by Frankish and Saxon pirates. The evil does not seem yet to have bitten deep, and the enemy were mere raiders in open boats, not owners of a properly constructed war navy.

But the nuisance became serious enough to require special attention, and Maximianus Herculeus, the colleague of Diocletian in the Western half of the empire, was forced to strengthen, or perhaps to create, naval forces for the discomfiture of the pirates. This command was practically the same which was afterwards known as the "Count-ship of the Saxon Shore," for in the fourth century the tracts on both sides of the Channel exposed to the pirates received the name of *Littus Saxonicum per Gallias* and *per Britannias*. The count had in the end not only the charge of the fleet but that of certain fortified ports and sea-coast castles, but whether this arrangement existed from the first we have no opportunity of knowing.

To command the fleet destined to cope with the pirates Maximian appointed one Carausius, an experienced officer of North-Gaulish blood, who is called both a Menapian and a Batavian.

★★★★★★

He is called *Menapiae civis* by Aurelius Victor, whence many of our own earlier writers ascribed his origin to the British Me-napia (St. David's), arguing that if he had been a Gallic Mena-pian the author would have styled him *civis Menapius*. But the fact that Eumenius, a contemporary, calls him *Bataviae alumnus* would seem to make it clear that he was really a Belgian. And the evidence for Menapia as a town is not clear. If he had come from thence Carausius would more probably have been called *Civis Demeta.*

★★★★★★

The new admiral commenced his career with marked success, destroyed many of the marauding Teutons, and recovered much plunder from them. But he was presently accused before Maximian of being less anxious to prevent the raids than to catch the raiders, when they were laden with spoil. And the proceeds of his captures were said to benefit himself and his crews, rather than the imperial exchequer, or the robbed provincials. It was even hinted, with or without justification, that he had a tacit understanding with some of the Franks. Learning that the emperor intended to seize him and perhaps to execute him, Carausius took the bold step of appealing to his followers to join him in rebellion. He proclaimed himself emperor and landed in Britain, where he was joined at once by a legion and many auxiliary *cohorts*.

★★★★★★

So, says Eumenius. But there is no reason for supposing that the legion was taken by surprise or the *cohorts* "surrounded" in any physical sense. The Panegyrist is merely lavishing abuse on the usurper.

★★★★★★

Apparently, an appeal for insurrection was seldom made in vain to the turbulent soldiery of the province. Ere long the whole island came over to his standard, with much enthusiasm; for while some of the coins which he struck to commemorate his accession show emblems and inscriptions witnessing to the "concord of the army," others represent Britannia herself welcoming Carausius with the inscription *Expectate Veni*, as if she had long been yearning for a saviour. (Sometimes Britannia bears a sceptre, at others a long caduceus, and at others, again, a military standard.) The type is unique in Roman numismatic history, and despite of the habitual flattery to which the mints were prone in choosing designs, must surely have had some real provincial feeling behind it.

Carausius reigned in Britain for over seven years (286-93 *A.D.*), apparently with great success and with undisputed sway. He increased his fleet by building many more galleys, raised new levies to strengthen his army, and hired a great force of barbarian mercenaries from the Franks. (Eumenius tells us that he conscribed Gaulish merchants, perhaps mainly seafaring traders.) But his ambition was not merely to be Emperor of Britain but to reconstitute the old "Empire of the Gauls." He had a hold beyond the Channel, owing to his possession of Gessoriacum (Boulogne), which was one of the arsenals of his fleet, and he tried from thence to extend his power all over Gaul.

He seems to have been for some time in possession of a considerable tract of its northern coast, for it is pretty clearly proved that he had a mint at Rotomagus (Rouen) during part of the early section of his reign, and he was tampering with the loyalty of the legions of the Rhine Army, who had not forgotten the old times between 258 and

274 when they were independent of Rome.

★★★★★★

The mint at Rouen seems to be conclusively proved by Mr. Percy Webb's articles on the coins of Carausius in the *Numismatic Chronicle* for 1907-8. The tampering with the Rhenish troops seems inferable from the fact that Carausius struck a considerable amount of money marked with the crests or emblems of these legions—First Minervia, Thirtieth Ulpia, and two or three more. As they were not actually under his command, the move must have been intended to appeal to them to join the other Western legions. It is notable to find that Victorinus, Carausius's predecessor, in a similar usurpation, did exactly the same thing twenty years before, striking coins in honour of legions which were outside his sphere of influence.

★★★★★★

But his wider schemes proved unsuccessful: he failed to extend his power in Gaul, the troops on the Rhine did not join him, and he lost all his possessions beyond the Channel save the single town of Gessoriacum, which he maintained for several years. Yet his naval power was too great for Maximian. The emperor built a new fleet to attack him, but it was repeatedly beaten through the unskilfulness of the untrained sailors, who proved unable to endure the fogs and crosscurrents of the Channel. (Eumenius.) After several repulses Maximian and his colleague Diocletian, who had many other troubles on hand, stooped to the necessity of making peace with Carausius, and acknowledged him as their colleague, while he undertook to desist from his designs on Gaul. The peace was marked by the issue from the mint of London of numerous coins struck in honour of Diocletian and Maximian, and of others representing the busts of the three emperors side by side, with the legend *Caravsivs et fratres svi*, and the reverse *pax avggg*, "the peace of the three Augusti" (289 *A.D.*).

After this Carausius reigned for several years in great prosperity. His large fleet kept the province safe from the Saxons, and his coins commemorated a "*Victoria Germanica*" which must refer to some triumph over them. With the Franks he had made peace, and kept many of them as auxiliaries. The Caledonians must certainly have been kept in due check, since milestones with the name of Carausius were erected just behind Severus's Wall—a certain proof that law and order were safe in that quarter.

A sign of care for trade and commerce was the restoration of the silver coinage, which had ceased to exist throughout the empire for many years, having been replaced first by half-alloyed pieces and then by mere silvered bronze. While the rest of the empire was using this depreciated stuff, Carausius issued a large coinage of pure silver *denarii*. It was only some years later that Diocletian copied him by issuing a similar reformed coinage for the rest of the Roman world. If the care of the usurper for other economic needs was as enlightened in other respects as in this, he may well have been justified in placing the legends *uberitas avg. felicitas temporum* and *restitutor saecvli* on his money. We know from similar evidence that he celebrated secular games, though how he managed to find a centenary anywhere about the year 290 *A.D.* it is hard to see, since the Emperor Philip had conducted the last games of the sort with great pomp less than fifty years before, in 248 *A.D.* (Perhaps he reckoned from Domitian's secular games of 88 *A.D.*, counting Philip's celebration as incorrectly calculated, just as Domitian had ignored the celebration by Claudius.)

Probably almost equal importance was attached to the ceremonies at which Britain put up the "*Quinquennial*" and "*Vicennalian*"Vows for the safety of its Caesar. But Carausius was not destined to see twenty years of power; his reign was to last for less than eight.

In 292 Diocletian and Maximian, having put down the rest of their enemies, thought it time to turn their attention once more against the British usurper. War was declared on him, and the charge of it was given over to Constantius Chlorus, the Caesar whom Maximian had just adopted as his junior colleague. Under his auspices the struggle took an indecisive turn, for though he succeeded in recovering Gessoriacum, the one foothold which Carausius had retained upon the Continent, he was utterly unable to obtain command of the seas. While the Channel was held by a fleet superior both in force and in efficiency, nothing could be accomplished against the insular realm.

When the renewed war had been some two years in progress, and showed no signs of coming to an end, Carausius was basely murdered by one Allectus, of whom we know nothing save that he was the underling (*satelles*) of his victim. But since the assassin was not crushed at once by an enraged soldiery, it is probable that he was holding some great office under Carausius which had made it possible for him to secure the favour of at least some part of the army. He may even have been his designated successor, since we know from numismatic evidence that Carausius had nominated a "*Princeps Juventutis*," a title only given to persons who had been formally nominated as heirs and colleagues by the reigning emperor. (No emperor seems to have taken the title for himself, after he had become Augustus. It was reserved for "Caesars," heirs designate and colleagues.)

It is much to be regretted that we know so little in detail concerning Marcus Aurelius Carausius, the first sea-king of British history.

★★★★★★

Carausius had a fourth name, which began with Mavs—and was evidently Gallic in character. But the inscription from which we get it does not give it in full. No doubt it was his original proper name, and Aurelius only an assumed one.

★★★★★★

His numerous and often well-executed coins show him to have been a broadly built, bull-necked, square-headed man, well advanced in middle age—he must have been considerably over forty, by his portrait, at the moment of his usurpation. Of his designs and ambitions we have all too little evidence, but it seems clear that those who have represented him as a mere "particularist," a British patriot, are in error. Not only did he make a serious effort to conquer Gaul, but he may have even aimed at the sovereignty of the whole empire. One of his most frequent coin-types is that of *renovatio romanorvm*, surrounding the Roman wolf and twins, a clear sign that he wished to be regarded as a Roman reformer, not as a British separatist.

Other coins are struck in honour of *roma aeterna*. Though he honoured some twenty gods and goddesses—(including Jupiter, Apollo, Mars, Sol, Hercules Paciter, Diana, Neptune, Oceanus, Venus, Vulcan, besides Victory, Fortune and many other half-abstractions)—there was only one of them who was local and provincial—Hercules Deusoniensis, a divinity worshipped on the Lower Rhine. (Possibly Carausius had learnt to worship this local god in his own youth, for he came from the region where this form of Hercules was venerated.) And this worship may have been part of his propaganda for an appeal to the sympathy of the Rhine legions.

The first person who had commemorated that divinity was Postumus, the founder of the empire of the Gauls Carausius thrice assumed the title of Consul, and probably took up all the other usual attributes of imperial authority: it is likely that he kept some sort of a senate to vote and ratify his behests. It is most unfortunate that inscriptions from his reign are practically non-existent: a single long commemorative dedication might give us a clearer conception of his constitutional status and political ambitions than all his numerous coins, from whose types we have to reconstitute them for lack of literary evidence.

Allectus appears to have been a man inferior in every respect to the master whom he had murdered: certainly, he lacked his courage and his military skill. Probably his throne was from the first a tottering one, since his predecessor must have left behind him many friends and admirers. We have a hint that he was obliged to rely almost entirely on his barbarian mercenaries, for when he had to fight for his life and crown, he took the field with them almost alone, presumably because he could not trust the legions. According to the story of his enemies the British provincials found that their persons, their families and their property were exposed to the rapacity of a licentious foreign soldiery, and yearned to be quit of the "tyrant" at the earliest possible opportunity.

This much is certain, that the fall of Allectus was sudden and ignominious. He reigned for some three years, during which his enemy Constantius was occupied in building large fleets at all the harbours of Northern Gaul. Apparently, he made no attempt to take the offensive, and to destroy these armaments before they grew overwhelmingly strong. In the third year (296) Constantius sailed for Britain, with his fleet divided into two great sections, one of which issued from Gessoriacum, the other from the mouth of the Seine.

Allectus's own vessels, which were still numerous, were lying off the Isle of Wight waiting for the latter division; but a chance fog hid from them the course of their enemies, who were carried farther down channel than they had intended, but came to shore quite unopposed—presumably somewhere west of the island. The *praetorian praefect* Asclepiodotus, who commanded this squadron, burnt his boats, after the manner of Agathocles, and pressed inland. Meanwhile Allectus, abandoning his fleet and his fortified ports, hastened to throw himself between the invaders and London, with a force composed only of his marines and his Frankish mercenary troops.

★★★★★★

The marine troops must evidently be the *"veteres illius conjurationis auctores"* who, according to Eumenius, were the only troops, over and above the Franks, whom Allectus took out to the battle. Probably the usurper was at Portchester looking out for the arrival of the expedition from the Seine, for we are told that on hearing of Asclepiodotus's landing *"classem portumque deseruit"*. If the fleet was *"apud insulam Vectam in speculis,"* its base must have been Portchester or possibly Clausentum (Southampton).

★★★★★★

He was beaten, after a fight in which, according to the prejudiced testimony of his enemies, he displayed military incompetence verging on insanity. (Eumenius.) He himself perished unnoticed in the rout, for he had thrown away all his imperial insignia save one garment. (So, he had kept one imperial garment, presumably the purple tunic below his *cuirass*.) The downs for many miles were thickly sprinkled with the bodies of the Franks, easily recognised by their barbarous dress and long red hair, but very few Roman citizens fell, for Allectus had shrunk from putting his legions in line, no doubt because he mistrusted them. (Eumenius.) The engagement must have taken place somewhere on the road from Salisbury and Winchester to London, and possibly near Woolmer Forest, where an enormous hoard of copper coins of Carausius and Allectus was found some forty years ago, evidently a hastily buried regimental treasury.

Constantius himself meanwhile, who had sailed from Boulogne, had apparently come ashore unopposed in Kent, while one division of his squadron, going farther north than it had intended, in that same fog which had favoured the landing of Asclepiodotus, ran into the mouth of the Thames.

★★★★★★

This may be gathered from the fact that Allectus is said to have been avoiding Constantius when he attacked Asclepiodotus. "*Te fugiens in tuorum manus incidit.*" Probably the usurper was merely striking at the nearer enemy. Starting from Gessoriacum, Constantius must have come ashore somewhere in Kent or Eastern Sussex. We are told that the squadron on the Seine only put to sea when it heard that the Caesar had already sailed from Boulogne. We should guess that the northern expedition must have reached Britain first; yet it had no fighting to do, or Eumenius would have said something in praise of his master's valour, instead of merely commemorating his good fortune.

★★★★★★

This detachment, reaching London, found the town in a state of confusion, for the surviving relics of Allectus's mercenary array of Franks had fled thither, and were plundering the citizens, preparatory to embarking in their own boats and fleeing to the Rhine-mouth. Vast numbers of the robbers were slaughtered in the streets, to the great pleasure of the Londoners, who were glad to be rid of the usurper and his unruly auxiliaries. It was not unnatural, therefore, that Constantius was welcomed with enthusiasm when he appeared in person. The whole province returned to its allegiance with alacrity, and the Caesar found no further operations necessary, since even the barbarians beyond the wall sent him submissive messages and kept quiet.

He had no reason to go further, unless he had wished to explore the boundaries of Ocean himself, which Nature has forbidden.

CHAPTER 9

The Roman Period: Diocletian to Honorius (296-410)

The defeat and death of Allectus brought Britain once more into the general system of the Roman Empire, and enabled Diocletian to subject it to the same reorganisation which he was already carrying out in the remaining provinces. He had divided the Roman world into four portions, two of which (the East, and Italy with Pannonia and Africa) were governed directly by himself and his senior colleague Maximianus Herculeus, while the other two (Gaul with Spain, and the Balkan Peninsula) were administered by the two junior emperors, the Caesars Constantius Chlorus and Galerius Maximianus. (Galerius, however, did not get Thrace, which went with the East, while Constantius had the outlying province of Mauretania Tingitensis in Africa.)

Britain, of course, fell into the share of Constantius, and looked for the future to Trier, the capital of the western section of the empire, instead of to Rome, as the administrative centre from which it was to be governed. Constantine completed and modified Diocletian's arrangements, and in the fourth century we find Britain a "*diocese*" of the "*Praefecture* of the Gauls." Each of these *dioceses* consisted of several old provinces: the British one being composed of the two units "Upper" and "Lower" Britain which had been created by Severus, just as, *e.g.*, the Spanish *diocese* was formed by the union of Lusitania, Baetica and Tarraconensis. Inside the *diocese* wholly new subdivisions were created, much smaller than the old provinces.

Those of Britain were four in number, Britannia Prima and Secunda, Maxima Caesariensis and Flavia Caesariensis. A fifth was added in 369 when Valentinian made certain northern tracts of the *diocese*, lately recovered from the barbarians, into the province of Valentia. We are unfortunately wholly without information as to the situation of these units. The sole facts presented about them are that Corinium (Cirencester), as is shown by an inscription found there, (see chapter 10), was in Britannia Prima, and that Valentia was in the North.

148

★★★★★★

The boundaries shown in all old and (alas!) some new atlases are taken from the ingenious forgery of Professor Bertram, an eighteenth century Dane, who foisted on the learned world a catalogue, fathered on the chronicler Richard of Cirencester, of roads, towns and provinces in Britain manufactured by himself.

★★★★★★

The essential core of the system of Diocletian and Constantine was the division of military from civil power in each section of the empire, with the object of preventing provincial insurrection headed by viceroys who were also commanders-in-chief—the disease of the third century. Accordingly, the vicar or governors-general of the *diocese* of Britain, was a civilian, who was at the head of all the administrative and financial machinery, but had not direct control over the military officers who commanded the troops of Britain. Under the vicar were four other civilian governors for the four provinces, a *consularis* in Maxima Caesariensis, three *praesides* in Flavia Caesariensis and the two Britanniae.

The troops on the other hand were entrusted to three commanders, the *Comes Britanniarum*, the *Dux Britanniarum*, and the *Comes Littoris Saxonici*, all of whom reported directly to the *Praetorian Praefect* of the Gauls, and not to the vicar. The title of *comes*, it must be remarked, was in the fourth century superior to that of *dux*, quite contrary to the usage of the Middle Ages. The *Dux Britanniarum* commanded in the North, having under him the garrison of the wall: the Count of the Saxon Shore was in charge of a fleet, and of the coast-garrisons from the Wash to the Solent: he was the successor of Carausius for all intents and purposes.

The *Comes Britanniarum*, who was the senior officer of the three, was probably in command of the other two: his own troops formed a small reserve army, which could be brought up to aid any threatened point in time of need. We do not know where they were normally cantoned: perhaps a large proportion of them may originally have been in the West Midlands and South Wales, where down to the third century two legions had been stationed at Chester and Caerleon. But our only list of the stations of the British Army is that in the *Notitia Dignitatum*, an official directory drawn up about 400 A.D. Vast changes must have taken place between the fall of Allectus and that date. Yet it is curious to find that even in 400 many of the old arrangements of the third century still subsisted. The Sixth Legion was still at York, and of the regiments in the North about half were those which had been there ever since the time of Antoninus Pius.

✶✶✶✶✶✶

So slightly changed is the garrison of the wall in the *Notitia*, when compared with its garrison in the time of Severus, that Mommsen started a theory that the list in the Notitia was not a genuine directory to the cantonments of the British Army in 400, but a screed copied from some much earlier document, to hide an unsightly gap in the military organisation of the empire, caused by the destruction of the British garrisons in the recent disastrous wars with Pict, Scot and Saxon. This theory will not hold water for a moment. Though there is certainly a much greater similarity between the army of 200 *A.D.* and the army of 400 *A.D.* in Britain than in any other province, we yet find in it regiments whose nomenclature belongs distinctly to the reign of Honorius.

Not to speak of the *Equites Honoriani Seniores*, whose title dates these clearly enough, we have a regiment of Taifalae, a tribe never mentioned till the late fourth century, and several *numeri* with names like Defensores, Directores, Solenses, Victores Juniores Britanniciani, Catafractarii Juniores, which have the stamp of the post-Constantinian epoch. Still there is a wonderful survival of old regiments, and a lack of new ones with the grotesque names common on the Continent, like Ursi, Exculcatores, or Seniores Braccati.

✶✶✶✶✶✶

It was probably to a great extent in consequence of the division of military from civil authority, introduced by Diocletian, that for more than fifty years after the fall of Allectus Britain was vexed by no further insurrections. Perhaps the unhappy memory of the last years of the "British Empire" under Allectus had cured the soldiery and the provincials alike of seditious tendencies. But something also must be allowed for the fact that during the early years of the fourth century the island was more frequently the residence of an emperor than had ever been the case before. Both Constantius and his son Constantine the Great were resident in Britain for long periods, as was natural with Caesars who only ruled the West, and had no concern with troubles on the Danube or the Euphrates.

It was during a stay in Britain in 306 *A.D.* that the former emperor contracted his last fatal illness, and it was at Eburacum that he expired a short time after. He had been joined just before he crossed the

Channel by Constantine, who had up to that moment been retained as a hostage by Constantius's colleague Galerius Valerius Maximianus. A chance allusion in Eumenius tells us that the elder emperor's last journey was not caused by absolute military necessity:

> He was not seeking British trophies, as the vulgar believe: he was not set on annexing the woods and marshes of the Caledonians and the other Picts, nor the neighbouring Ireland, nor distant Thule, nor the Fortunate Isles—if indeed they exist.

But another, if a later authority, tells us nevertheless that Constantius made a campaign against the Picts, and gave them a severe chastisement, returning to York to die immediately after—perhaps from fatigue or disease contracted during his expedition (July 25, 306.) (The anonymous chronicler whose excerpts about Constantius, Constantine and others are found at the end of the history of Ammianus Marcellinus.) The chance that the emperor died at Eburacum caused that city to be the place where his son Constantine was proclaimed his successor, much to the vexation of Galerius, who had not intended that he should inherit his father's share of the empire. But the young prince assumed first the title of Caesar, and afterwards that of Augustus, which Galerius had intended to confer on his dependant the Illyrian Severus.

The story that Constantine was born in Britain has no foundation: at the moment of his birth (274) the usurper Tetricus was reigning in Britain and Gaul, while Constantine's father, a nephew of the legitimate emperor Claudius Gothicus, was following the fortunes of Claudius's duly elected successor Aurelian. Equally destitute of foundation is the legend that Constantine's mother Helena was a British princess, the heiress of a mythical King Coel. These are late Celtic tales, and we must believe the fourth-century historians who tell us that the first Christian emperor was born "*ex obscuriori matrimonio*," if not that Helena was the daughter of a Bithynian innkeeper, whom Constantius had picked up while campaigning in the East.

Immediately after his proclamation Constantine crossed over to Gaul, to guard his father's old dominions from the grasping hand of Galerius. How many times he returned to Britain, before he began the great series of campaigns which ultimately made him master of the whole Roman world, we do not know. At least one such visit is mentioned in the statement of the chronicle of Eusebius Pamphilus that:

> After he was firmly seated in power, and had seen to the peoples in his father's share of the empire with benevolent care, he

151

passed over to the British tribes, which lie within, on the very borders of Ocean, and put them in order.

And again, we are told that:

At the commencement of his reign the Britons who dwell along the Western Ocean were subdued by him.

This must probably refer to campaigning north of the wall, on the borders of the Irish Sea. But it is hard to believe that any proper annexation of the Western Lowlands can have been made by him.

★★★★★★

It is well, however, to remember that after the abandonment of Britain by the Roman Government in the reign of Honorius, we seem to find the British tribes of the Lowlands merged with those on the wall, and acting together in union. See also *Britain & the Anglo-Saxon Invasion, 410 A.D.-802 A.D.*, concerning the general, Coroticus, who bore sway in those parts in the middle of the fifth century. It is possible that the campaigns of Constantine led to a more real exertion of suzerainty north of the wall than had been existing before.

★★★★★★

Probably the Selgovae and Novantae, or the tribes who had succeeded to the former holdings of these peoples, did him homage and gave hostages. If there had been any serious fighting or notable victories in Britain, in the period of Constantine, it would almost certainly have been recorded on the coinage—that public gazette of the Roman Empire. But while the chastisement of Franks, Alamanni and Sarmatians, ((Francia Devicta, Alamannia Devicta and Sarmatia Devicta are all found about 320 *A.D.*) and the valour of the Gaulish and Illyrian armies are recorded on the money of Constantine and his elder son Crispus, there is no mention of British victories.

Perhaps it is not without significance that the favourite type of the London mint during the middle period of the reign of Constantine is *Beata Tranquillitas*—though it must be owned that the same inscription appears also on the coinage of Trier, which was quite close to the site of the Frankish wars.

Archaeological and literary evidence, however, join in suggesting that the period between the tall of Allectus and the middle of the fourth century was probably the most prosperous epoch which the British provinces ever knew. The general laudation of the fertility and wealth of the island in which the Panegyrists indulge is corroborated by such practical evidence as the fact that Constantius collected masons and artisans for the rebuilding of the Gallic Autun in Britain, "*quibus illae provinciae redundabant*." We find milestones of Constantius and his son, testifying to the care for, and repairing of, the old roads, on the most exposed edges of the land, *e.g.*, on the highways just south of Hadrian's Wall and the coast of South Wales.

The London mint was pouring out enormous quantities of money from the time of the arrival of Constantius in 296 down to the later half of Constantine's reign. Why it was closed somewhere at the end of the lifetime of the latter emperor it is impossible to say; but this was the case, and no more coins were issued there save during the usurpation of Magnus Maximus nearly fifty years later.

★★★★★★

The date can be fixed at somewhere about 335 *A.D.*, because of the absence of coins of the sons of Constantine with the title of Augustus, which was conferred on Constans and Constantius II. in 337.

★★★★★★

The agricultural prosperity of the island is vouched for by the fact that it was sending corn to the provinces of the Lower Rhine even in the time of Julian (360 *A.D.*) when evil days had once more begun to dawn upon the empire. But the greatest and most widespread mass of evidence concerning the tranquillity of the province comes from the use of the explorer's spade. Of the countless Roman villas of Britain that have been excavated, nearly all seem to have been occupied, and many to have been built, during the Constantinian epoch.

The mines of Mendip, which had apparently been neglected for more than a century, were being worked with energy in the first half of the fourth century. The few traces of Roman occupation in Cornwall and Western Devon belong mainly to the same time; they only begin in the late third century. The more important of them, two milestones and an ingot of tin stamped with the imperial marks, come from the days of the descendants of Constantius Chlorus. (See Professor Haverfield's papers in *Proceedings of the Society of Antiquaries*, 1900, and *Numismatic Chronicle* of the same year.)

The majority of the coins dug up in the extreme south-west also belong to this epoch. We should know much more of the administration of Britain if the practice of marking every new building with a dedicatory or commemorative inscription, so universal in the second century, had continued into the fourth. But the historical inscriptions of this age can be counted on the fingers of one hand, if milestones are set aside. The two most important, the Cirencester dedication alluded to in a later page (see chapter 10), and the Yorkshire inscription near Whitby, are later than Constantine—one seems to date from Julian, the other from Honorius. It is not correct to ascribe this silence of the fourth-century officials and soldiery of Britain to the introduction of Christianity, and the consequent cessation of the erecting of altars to the gods, or to the *genii* of the *cohorts* and legions.

There is, as we shall see, reason to believe that Britain was still predominantly pagan down to the end of its connection with the Roman Empire. A more potent cause was the increase of the barbarian element in the army; the "*cunei*" and "*numeri*" of Germans from beyond the frontier, who formed an ever-growing proportion of the garrison of Britain, did not commemorate themselves or their gods as the old auxiliary *cohorts* had done.

But it is curious to find a noteworthy lack of ordinary sepulchral inscriptions of private persons in the fourth century; there are a very few Christian tombs—the small number need not surprise us—but it is much more surprising to find a lack of those of the ordinary heathen type, which ought to have been set up by the hundred during a period which seems to have been one of considerable prosperity. Conceivably the fourth century tombs, like the fourth-century public buildings, lay on the surface-*stratum* of Roman Britain, and were handiest for the Saxon spoiler, or the medieval seeker after hewn stone, to destroy or to carry away. The memorials of earlier days may have escaped in greater numbers because they were already buried below later Roman work. (Yet it is curious that the London mint put Christian emblems on its coins before those of Trier, Lyons, or Arles. See *Corstopitum* Report, 1910.)

When Constantine died in 337 Britain fell into that share of the empire which he left to his eldest son, Constantine II. But that ill-fated prince died early, slain in battle with his younger brother Constans, whose dominions he was endeavouring to annex (340). All his lands fell to the victor, who reigned over the whole West from 340 to 350. It is in his time that we have the first note of renewed danger from the barbarians reported from Britain. The Picts seem to have made a sudden and dangerous assault on the districts along the wall, perhaps assisted by the Scots, an enemy of whom we have not heard before, but of whom we shall have much to tell.

It seems likely that they actually burst through the Wall, though of definite evidence for this disaster we have only the fact that Corsto-pitum, the largest town behind it, shows signs of having been burnt at a date after the death of Constantine (337) and before the time of Julian or Valentinian (360). The books of the history of Ammianus Marcellinus which deal with the reign of Constans have unhappily perished. We only know from allusions, in a later part of his work, that Constans went in person to Britain, and imposed terms of peace upon the invaders.

★★★★★★

Speaking of the events of 360 Ammianus (xviii. 2), says that Julian was disturbed by the fact that the Picts and Scots *rupta quiete condicta* (terms had therefore been imposed upon them) were again wasting the lands near the *Limes*, and that the Caesar doubted whether he ought not to go at once against them, "as we have already related that Constans went". But he did not do so.

★★★★★★

The line of the wall was restored and regarrisoned. From another source we know that the danger had been so fierce and sudden that the emperor crossed the Channel at midwinter to bring prompt help. (Julius Firmicus; So the empire was in some sense extended; probably by terms of submission being imposed on a new enemy, the Scot.) A large bronze medal of Constans, commemorating his embarkation at "Bononia Oceanensis," seems to refer to this abnormal voyage. Its date was apparently 343 *A.D.*

Constans, though a prince of some vigour and merit, perished suddenly and miserably, in strife with the rebel Magnentius. This person was the second usurper of British blood who wore the purple, Bonosus (as we have already remarked) being the first. He had served with distinction in the guards under Constantine the Great, and had been made a count and entrusted with the command of two legions by Constans. Having slain his master in Gaul, he was recognised as emperor by both Britain and Spain, and ruled them for three years (350-53). He made his brother Decentius his Caesar and colleague, and these two Britons were obeyed at Rome as well as in all the West, till Constantius, the last surviving son of Constantine, came up against them with the armies of Illyricum and the East, and beat them in three desperate battles, one at Mursa in Illyricum the other two in Southern Gaul.

After his last defeat the usurper committed suicide, to avoid falling

155

into the hands of a foe who had his brother's blood to avenge, and was known for his calm and deliberate cruelty, Magnentius had met with many supporters in Britain, as was natural considering that he drew his origin from her, and had been notably helped by Gratianus, once local commander-in-chief (*comes Britanniarum*). After his fall Constantius sent into the island one Paul the notary, a secret spy and inquisitor whom he often employed on matters of police, bidding him seek out all traitors and send them to Rome.

Paul did his work in such a reckless and cruel fashion, arresting and imprisoning multitudes of innocent persons, that Martinus the *vicarius* (governor-general) of Britain openly withstood him. Whereupon Paul presumed to declare the vicar himself a traitor, and came to arrest him. This so enraged the governor that he drew his sword, and tried to cut down the notary; but having missed his blow and failed to slay Paul, he suddenly turned his weapon against himself before he could be seized, and escaped capture by suicide. We are told that his fate moved universal pity, as he was the justest and most kind-hearted of men. Paul brought back to Constantius a multitude of chained captives, who suffered the scourge and the rack. Some were finally put to death, others sent into exile.

We hear nothing more of Britain for seven years, but in 360, when Constantius was still emperor and his cousin Julian was ruling as his lieutenant in Gaul, troubles of the same kind that had been seen in the days of Constans broke out in Britain. The Picts and Scots broke the peace imposed upon them seventeen years before, began to ravage the lands about Hadrian's Wall and caused a panic throughout the island. The Pict is but the Caledonian under a new name; the Scot deserves a word of further notice. The Romans applied the name to all the inhabitants of Ireland, but the Scot proper was the *Scuit*, the "man cut off" or "broken man," (*not*, I think, the "tattooed man" the explanation of Isidore of Seville), who was to the other Goidels what the Viking was to the Danes four hundred years later. The name was not national, nor often used in Ireland itself.

It was applied in a particular sense, however, to a tribe in the extreme north-west of Ireland, in the modern county of Antrim, who seem to have been exiles driven out of lands farther west and south by other peoples. Their country was called Dalriada, a name that was afterwards transferred to that district of the Highlands, across the water in North Britain, which was destined to be colonised by these Scots. It is curious to find that just south of the Irish Dalriada there was another small territory held by a fragment of the Picts, who, at some unknown date, had found their way to Ireland.

Moreover, somewhere in the fourth century, as we must suppose, another section of the Picts established themselves on the north shore of the Solway Firth, in the modern shires of Kirkcudbright and Wigtown, intruding among the British Novantae and Selgovae, who held that territory at an earlier time. (Ptolemy, writing in the second century, knows of no tribe save Novantae and Selgovae in the Western Lowlands.)

These Picts were known as *Niduarii* from their dwelling on the west bank of the Nith (Nidus), but apparently earlier Novius, as in Ptolemy.) They were certainly lodged there before the end of the fourth century, as the Christian missionary Ninian was working among them at that date. It seems more probable that they were an offshoot of the Irish Picts of Ulster, than that they had pushed south from the Highlands behind the Forth, and settled beyond the Britons of the Clyde Valley, whom the Northern Picts never succeeded in conquering.

Such a settlement in Britain would be quite in keeping with what is known of other Irish movements at this time. For there seems to be no doubt that another Hibernian tribe, the Desse or Daesi, thrust out of their old home in County Meath by their neighbours, passed over into Britain and settled in the land of the Demetae in South Wales, where in the fifth century they were occupying the districts of Gower and Kidwelly.

★★★★★★

See Bury's *Life of St. Patrick* and the long passage concerning the Desse in Zimmer's *Nennius Vindicatus*. But I cannot agree with the conclusions made by the latter that the Irish immigrants came as early as the third century, and remained in possession of Demetia permanently, till they were absorbed by their Brythonic neighbours. The definite statement in the *Historia Brittonum* that they were expelled by Cunedda's family is too strong, and Zimmer omits the tale of Urien Reged and his conquest of these Goidels of South Wales.

★★★★★★

As we know that this region was securely held by the Romans in the time of Constantine, whose mile-stones and road-building can be traced along its coast, we must suppose either that the immigrants were received as peaceable settlers by the imperial government—a thing common enough in that epoch—or that they came later than

340, and that their movement was part of that general assault on the Roman borders in Britain of which we get the first trace in the reign of Constans. It is even conceivable that their arrival formed precisely the crisis which drew Constans to Britain in midwinter, and that their submission to him after some fighting was the "extension of the empire" on which Julius Firmicus congratulated that emperor.

But whatever was the character of the first coming of the Irish to Britain, and whatever was the cause of their arrival, it is certain that by the year 350 *A.D.* they had commenced that series of destructive raids which was to last for about a century. As was the case with the Vikings 400 years after, the first attacks seem to have been sporadic and tentative, but after a time the number of the invaders increased, and their fleets were led not by mere adventurers but by tribal chiefs, and even by the high-kings of Ireland themselves, of whom two Niall (*circ.* 405) and Dathi (*circ.* 425) are recorded in the earliest annals of their island as having perished beyond seas—one in the British Channel, the other in Gaul.

The front of the Irish invasion was from the Solway Firth to the Bristol Channel, (the iron-bound northern coast of the thinly peopled Devon and Cornwall cannot have tempted them), the poorest and most rugged face of Britain, yet one where plunder sufficient to tempt the pirate was to be got, in favoured districts such as the lowlands about Carlisle, the lower valleys of the Dee and Mersey round Deva and Mancunium, the south coast of Glamorgan, and most of all the rich and well-peopled plain of Gloucester.

We may reasonably attribute to the Scots the destruction of the many Roman villas of the Constantinian epoch on both sides of the Severn mouth, which evidently came to an end by burning. It was apparently in this region that one of their bands captured, along with other prisoners, the boy Patricius, who was destined to become the Apostle of Ireland—but this was in the year 405, long after the date which we have now reached.

★★★★★★

See Bury's *Life of St. Patrick* for an elaborate argument to prove that the Saint must have been carried off from the region of the Severn Mouth rather than that of the Clyde. His birthplace was Bannaventa, which must probably be one of the two Banwens of Glamorganshire.

★★★★★★

It is highly probable also that it was the Scots who made an end of Deva, and even of Viroconium, whose destruction may have come early, for its ruins have yielded no coins later than the year 380. (But the site is so imperfectly explored, that this deduction would be dangerous. If sacked in 380, Viroconium might surely have been restored.) But the coast of Cumberland, south of Hadrian's Wall, was certainly another focus of Scottish raids. It must have been against them that a guard was kept by the numerous auxiliary regiments whom the Notitia records as placed from Gabrosentum at the mouth of the Eden to Morecambe Bay, with reserves among the Westmoreland Hills.

The Scots and Picts are often found acting together: it must have been in this region that they would most easily meet, the one coming down from the Highlands, by way of the Clyde and the Annan, the others coasting along Galloway, and ready to outflank the line of the Roman Wall by landing south of it and taking it in the rear.

In the series of invasions, growing every year more serious, which began in 360 *A.D.*, we first hear of the Picts and Scots alone. They ravaged the lands along the Wall, and so attracted the notice of the Caesar Julian who, being distracted by dangers on the Rhine, refused to cross to Britain, but sent over his *magister equitum*, Lupicinus, with four regiments of German and Illyrian auxiliaries.

But the death of Constantius II. and his own accession to the throne seem to have distracted Julian's attention from Britain, and two of the newly landed corps were withdrawn to the East. It does not seem, however, that the raids on the North can have been very serious as yet, for Julian was not only able to ignore the military needs of Britain, but to draw great stores of corn from it for the devastated Rhine provinces, and even to cut down certain of its military expenses, which were nominally spent on the soldiery, but really went into the private purse of the governors. (See Julian's *Letter to the Athenians*, 360 *A.D.* Such exports were not unusual. Previous drafts of corn from Britain are mentioned in 358 by Zosimus, iii. 5).

During the short three years during which Julian ruled as sole emperor after the death of his cousin Constantius, we have no further notice of Britain: all the attention of the historians was drawn to his vain struggle to arrest the progress of Christianity, or with his Persian wax's. It is not till the "Apostate" had perished, and his short-lived successor Jovian had followed him to the grave, that in the reign of Valentinian we again are permitted to get a glimpse of insular affairs. In 364 we are told by Ammianus that Britain was being harassed by the joint assaults of four enemies. Not only were the Picts and Scots on the war-path, but the province was also being attacked by the Saxons—an enemy of whom we have heard nothing since the day of Carausius—and also by the Attacotti "a warlike race of men", (Ammianus, xxvii.)

Who those last invaders can have been is somewhat of a puzzle? They are only mentioned at this particular date, and save Ammianus no ancient author names them except St. Jerome, who vouchsafes the startling information that they were a British tribe who practised cannibalism! who, when they carried off swineherd and swine together, preferred a steak from the human rather than the porcine captive. (Jerome, *Adversus Jovinianum*, ii.) The saint states that he himself had seen certain of these monsters in Gaul. This is quite possible, for the Roman Army, when the Notitia was drawn up, contained no less than four regiments of Attacotti. But that any British tribe at this date should have been given to cannibalism is incredible, all the more so one out of which the Romans were raising many auxiliaries.

The fact that the Attacotti are called Britons is sufficient proof that they were neither Irish nor Saxons. They are also carefully distinguished from the Picts by Ammianus: we are therefore driven to believe that the name must represent some of the Brythonic tribes between the Walls of Hadrian and Antoninus, disguised under a new designation, which perhaps represents a temporary confederacy. Seeing that we find them serving in considerable numbers in the Roman army a generation later, this seems a probable explanation; the land between the Walls would be a very natural region from which to enlist auxiliaries.

When mentioning the Picts on this occasion, Ammianus takes the opportunity of stating that they were at this time divided into two leagues or sections, the Dicaledonians and the Verturiones. The former seems to Represent the Northern tribes, who dwelt along the so-called Ducaledonian Ocean: the latter appeal's to be a new name for the Southern Picts or Meatae, of whom we heard in the time of Severus. Their designation is connected with the later Fortrenn, the title given by the Britons to the region to the north and east of the Tay.

The assault of Picts, Saxons, Scots and Attacotti upon Roman Britain is ascribed to a "conspiracy" among the four barbarian races, so that it would appear that they were deliberately acting in unison and playing into each other's hands. Their attacks grew more frequent and formidable as the years of Valentinian's reign went on, till in 367 *A.D.* we learn that the whole defence of Britain was shattered, owing to two simultaneous disasters, Nectarides, Count of the Saxon Shore, being defeated and slain by the pirates of Germany, while Fullofaudes the "*Dux Britanniarum*" or commander of the Northern garrisons, at York and on the wall, fell into an ambush and perished—no doubt at the hands of the Picts.

The defence of the wall was broken down, many of the surviving troops disbanded themselves, and the barbarians came flooding into the Midlands. The emperor Valentinian, after sending in quick succession three generals to Britain, who accomplished nothing, gave the command of the province in 368 to Count Theodosius, an experienced officer of Spanish extraction, and the father of a better-known son of the same name, who was destined to wear the purple some twelve years later.

Theodosius was allowed to take with him the Batavians and Heruli, the best auxiliary troops in the Gallic Army, and the Jovii and Victores from the imperial guard. So far south had the barbarians spread, that he was forced to make London the base of his first operations—presumably therefore York and Chester had been evacuated by their legions and had been sacked by the enemy. We are told that the invaders offered no opportunity of a pitched battle to Theodosius, that they were scattered over the country in numerous bands, each intent on its own particular raid. His only difficulty was to locate them, since their movements were rapid and uncertain. But by means of the information furnished by captives and deserters he succeeded in hunting down and destroying many parties, and cleared the southern parts of the province of them. He then increased his force by offering free pardon to all deserters who should return to their standards, and calling in many disorganised detachments, who had retired into remote corners of the province, and had there been living at free quarters.

It was apparently in the next year (369) that Theodosius, with an army that had been strengthened both in numbers and in efficiency, cleared the North, right up to the Wall, and reoccupied many cities and forts which, though they had suffered damage of all kinds, were capable of restoration. At the same time, he had to crush the beginnings of a provincial rebellion; one Valentine the Pannonian, a political exile, was detected tampering with the soldiery—no doubt with the disorganised bands which had only lately returned to their allegiance—in order to induce them to declare him emperor. He was detected in time, captured, and executed, along with two or three of his confidants; but Theodosius refused to make any further inquiry into the plot, lest by arresting many conspirator's he should cause general distrust, and give occasion for provincial tumults to break out.

This being done, he repaired and re-garrisoned the wall and the camps behind it, and restored the old course of civil and military administration, wherever it had been swept away. He made one change, we are told, by abolishing a frontier institution called the Arcani. These were a body of men, evidently Britons, who had been stationed far out beyond the *Limes*, for the purpose of discovering by constant explorations, and reporting to headquarters, any signs of movement on the part of the Picts or other neighbours. They were accused and convicted of having repeatedly given notice to the enemy of the movement of Roman troops, in return for bribes. Such treason would be almost inevitable if the Arcani were mere Britons of the frontier— Brigantes or Otadini—who were near kinsmen of these hostile tribes between Solway and Clyde who were now known as Attacotti.

The work of Theodosius was evidently very thorough. We are told that he not only cleared the land of invaders, but pursued them out to sea.

He followed the Scot with wandering sword, and clove the waters of the Northern ocean with his daring oars.

He trod the sands of both tidal seas. (the Irish and the North).

The Orkney isles dripped with the blood of the routed Saxon.

There must be much exaggeration in these lines of Claudian—we can hardly believe that Theodosius reached the Orkneys, or that the Saxons would have chosen these islands as their refuge: and our suspicion turns into certainty when we read that slaughtered Picts lay thick in the fabulous Thule. But nevertheless, the poet must have had some facts on which to base his hyperbolical account of the naval exploits of Theodosius. There need be no doubt that he reorganised the fleet no less than the army—there are two naval regiments marked on the Notitia as lying on the North-west coast, (the Barcarii Tigridenses and Cohors Aelia Classica, at Arbeja and Tunnocellum), and the whole establishment of the "Saxon shore" was restored, which must have included, as of old, a squadron of ships no less than the land troops registered as belonging to it. All this must represent the re-arrangements of Theodosius, for all that had existed before him had been swept away for the moment.

Having completed this work of reorganisation, Theodosius returned to his master Valentinian, who received him as if he had been some dictator of the old days of Rome, a Furius Camillus or a Papirius Cursor, and gave him the important post of *Magister Equitum Per Gal-*

lias. The emperor also decreed that the newly recovered Northern province of Britain should be named Valentia, in allusion to his own name. Conceivably it was also at this same time that Londinium was given the honorary title of Augusta; but this may have been the work of Constans, twenty years before. (This is the first mention of the new name. It was still Londinium in 330. The coins of Magnus Maximus (383-88) and the Notitia (400?) both call it Augusta.)

It is in error that some historians have supposed that Theodosius added a new province to the Roman Empire, and that "Valentia" means the land between the walls of Hadrian and Antoninus. The words of Ammianus are clear:

> Theodosius restored the province that he had recovered, which had been lost to the barbarians, to its ancient state, so that it had once more a legitimate ruler, and was afterwards named Valentia by order of the emperor, who had as it were triumphed over it.

There is no extension of the border implied in these words.

It would seem that Britain had a rest for some ten or fifteen years after the victories of Theodosius, and that the great general himself was dead—slain in Africa by orders of the cowardly Valens, who suspected him of aiming at the crown—before troubles once more began. The only note that we have in these fourteen years (369-83) is that Valentinian transferred over to Britain a certain king, Fraomar, chief of the Buccinobantes, a section of the Alamanni; the territory of this race had been so devastated that they were moved wholesale to serve as a "*numerus*" of military settles on this side of the Channel, no doubt in some region that had been depopulated by the late incursions of Picts and Scots (371 *A.D.*).

The awful defeat of Adrianople (378) in which the Goths slew Valens, the Emperor of the East, and so for a time got possession of all the inland of the Balkan Peninsula, had no effect in the West. Here matters seem to have been fairly quiet, under Gratian, the son and successor of Valentinian (375-83). But the woes of Britain recommenced with civil strife; Gratian, though a youth of many merits, was unpopular with his soldiery, who accused him of loving barbarians over-much, and neglecting his military duties for the chase.

An insurrection against him was headed by Magnus Maximus, a Spanish officer of mature years, who had seen much service in Britain under Theodosius, and was still in office there fifteen years after. (As he had a son almost grown up to manhood, and had been already an officer in 368, he must have been at least forty when he rebelled.) We are told by Orosius that the legions invested him with the purple almost against his will, and that:

> He was an energetic and just man, and would have been well worthy of the title of Emperor if he had not come to it by breaking his oath of allegiance.

Zosimus, however, who, like Orosius, wrote little more than thirty years after the insurrection of Maximus, declares that he was the secret instigator of the revolt, having conceived a great hatred for Gratian, because he had not received the promotion which he thought his due. Apparently, therefore, he was not Count of the Britains, commander-in-chief in the island, but must have held some subordinate military post, such as that of duke, or Count of the Saxon Shore.

Magnus Maximus seems to have reigned for some short time in Britain alone, where he opened the long-disused mint of London, (where a few coins were also struck in Theodosius's name), and repelled an incursion of the Picts and Scots, who probably saw an opportunity for raiding presented to them by the outbreak of civil war. (For this campaign we have only the evidence of Prosper Tiro, who misdates it, placing Maximus's rebellion in 381 and the Pictish War in 382.) But in the same year that saw his proclamation he concentrated the picked corps of the British Army, and crossed into Gaul. He had already been tampering with the officers of the Rhine legions, which came over to his cause *en masse*, Gratian started to fly to Italy, but was murdered at Lyons by one of his own officers, who wished to commend himself to the usurper by this treacherous deed.

Spain submitted to Magnus Maximus immediately after, without fighting, and he thus became master of the whole West. Valentinian, the younger brother of Gratian, still reigned at Rome, but was too young and weak to revenge his brother's murder. His ministers patched up a peace with Maximus, which lasted two years. In the third the usurper resolved to cross the Alps with his British and Gallic legions (387). He was almost unopposed, and Valentinian and his family fled to Constantinople, to throw themselves on the mercy of Theodosius the Younger, the son of the murdered general, who had been reigning in the East since 379.

It seems clear that the depletion of the British garrisons by Maximus, at a moment when the Picts were already on the move, marks a stage in the final ruin of the province. It is, at any rate, taken as a starting point by Gildas and the *Historia Brittonum*, who date from it the beginning of the end. Many of the displaced troops never came back. Maximus, who had inherited from his predecessor a German war on the Rhine, and also feared the latent hostility of the Emperor of the East, kept his army concentrated in the South, anxiously expecting hostile moves on the part of Theodosius, the protector of the young Valentinian II.

The war which he had dreaded came at last in 388: after much hard fighting in the passes of the Eastern Alps the Gallic and British legions were defeated by the Eastern Army, and Maximus, falling into the hands of the victor, was beheaded at the third milestone from Aquileia (388). His son and colleague Flavius Victor was murdered soon after by Count Arbogast, who had been left in command in Gaul, and thought that his submission to Theodosius would be received more kindly if accompanied by the head of the unfortunate Caesar.

The British home-garrisons, left without a leader, and probably engaged in an uphill battle with the Picts and Scots, returned to their allegiance, and found themselves the subjects of the young Valentinian II., to whom Theodosius now handed over the dominions of the whole Western Empire. But this young prince was murdered only four years later by Arbogast, the same ruffian who had put to death Flavius Victor, and had thereby won undeserved pardon and promotion. Another civil war followed, in which the ever-victorious Theodosius put down Arbogast, and his puppet the pretender Eugenius. But this virtuous and hard-working emperor died in the next year, leaving the Roman world to be divided between his two young sons, Arcadius and Honorius (395).

The latter, an unhappy boy of eleven, was the tool or victim of a series of unscrupulous ministers throughout his life, and when he reached full age showed neither courage nor capacity. The few acts in which he was personally concerned prove that he lacked all his father's good qualities, and was cowardly, treacherous and ungrateful. But during the first years of his minority the Roman frontiers were still maintained with more or less success by the great general, Stilicho, whom Theodosius had left as a legacy to his son, and who acted as regent in the whole West. As authority for the activity of this energetic (if selfish and grasping) personage in Britain we have only the verses of his panegyrist Claudian. But after allowing for a due percentage of flattery and exaggeration, we can extract a certain amount of definite information from his lines. Evidently the lands on this side of the

Channel were, at the end of the reign of Theodosius, in a condition of perpetual war. The province of Britain is introduced, speaking in the first person:

I was perishing at the hands of the neighbouring tribes, when Stilicho took up my defence: the Scot was stirring up the whole of Ireland, and the sea foamed with his hostile oars: it is Stilicho's work that I no longer fear the darts of the Scot, nor tremble at the Pict, nor look out along my line of shore for the Saxon, who might arrive with every shift in the wind. (*In primum Consulatum Stilichonis*, ii.)

In another poem, written a few months earlier, Rome says:

What is my strength, now that Honorius reigns, recent events show: the sea is more quiet now that the Saxon is tamed, Britain is secure now that the Pict has been crushed. (*In Eutropium,* i.)

There must have been enough truth in this to permit Stilicho, who was no fool, to accept it as genuine praise. Evidently a serious effort had been made both to beat off the maritime incursions of Scot and Saxon, and to stop the inland raids of the Pict. Whether Stilicho himself visited Britain we cannot say: he was certainly busy in Gaul for long periods, and may well have crossed the Channel. But Claudian only speaks of his care and providence: he does not definitely declare that he beat off the raiders in person. These poems date from the year 399, and the dating of the pacification of Britain by the fact that Honorius is emperor, shows that it cannot have taken place earlier than 395.

******

I cannot follow Professor Bury's view that Stilicho's activity in Britain may possibly date from the reign of Valentinian II. (*Life of St. Patrick*). His whole argument hinges on the statement that Claudian in the *In Eutropium* "emphasises a defeat of the Picts and does not refer to the other foes of Britain." But this is not so Claudian says:—

"*domito quod Saxone Tethys*
Mitior, et fracto secura Britannia Picto."

He does therefore mention Saxon as well as Pict: and we cannot draw the conclusion that the lines in the *de Consulatum Stilichonis* do not refer to the same events as those in the *In*

Eutropium. There is no proof that Stilicho ever worked under Valentinian II.; probably Theodosius always kept him under himself.

★★★★★★

Presumably, therefore, the province had been enduring perpetual raids ever since Magnus Maximus took away great part of its garrison in 383, during the twelve years during which it gave its allegiance to Maximus himself (383-88), to Valentinian II. (388-92), to Eugenius (392-94) and to Theodosius the Great (394-95). It is obvious that neither Maximus nor Eugenius, whose whole interest lay in their contest with the Eastern Empire, can have had much attention to spare for Britain. And the reign of the boy Valentinian II., which was notoriously a time of chaos and decay, is equally unlikely to have seen any amelioration in the state of the island. But Stilicho evidently reorganised its defences very thoroughly during the first four years of Honorius.

The result of his rearrangements must be the state of things shown in the *Notitia Dignitatum,* a document which, though it dates from the very last period of the Roman Empire in Britain, is yet the only complete summary of its military and civil organisation that we possess. It evidently belongs to the date 400-402 *A.D.*, and probably to the earlier rather than the later of those three years. The first thing notable in it is that the army of Britain had suffered less change than those of most of the other frontier provinces during the fourth century. The great change instituted in the defence of the empire by Diocletian had been the division of the troops into a sedentary frontier army, on which fell the ordinary work of protecting the *limites*, or the river banks on the border, and a movable field-army formed out of an enormous imperial guard, and so called "*palatine*" legions or regiments.

But this second force, which acted as a reserve for the "*limitary*" army, did not go out with the person of the emperor only, as the old *Praetorians* had done, but was sent in smaller or larger detachments whenever there was abnormal pressure on any section of the border. On the Continent there were many provinces where the Palatine Army was as numerous as the frontier guard: this was specially the case in Gaul and on the Danube. But in Britain the central reserve, which was commanded by the *Comes Britanniarum*, the senior military officer on this side of the Channel, only included three regiments of foot and six of horse. The bulk of the local army was under the *Dux Britanniarum*, whose rank was below that of the count, and was devoted entirely to the protection of the Northern regions.

167

The headquarters of the *Dux* was undoubtedly York, where the Sixth Legion still remained on guard. Yorkshire and Lancashire, to use modern terms, had three cavalry and ten infantry regiments of auxiliaries, scattered about in cantonments which were evidently designed to protect the whole countryside against sudden incursions of enemies from the sea. But the greatest accumulation of forces was on the line of Hadrian's Wall, which, from Segedunum at the mouth of the Tyne to Uxellodunum on the Solway Firth, was garrisoned by no less than twelve regiments of foot and four of horse.

Close behind the wall, all at its western end, in Cumberland and Westmoreland, were six more infantry and one more cavalry regiments, probably intended to guard against raids by the Scots from the water-side rather than to support the landward defence against the Picts. Thus, the *Dux Britanniarum* had in all one legion, twenty-eight auxiliary regiments of foot, and eight units of horse under his control, a full two-thirds of the garrison of Britain.

The third military commander in Britain was the Count of the Saxon Shore, whose sphere of office extended from Branodunum, on the eastern side of the Wash, to Portus Adurni on the Solent. Besides his fleet he had one legion, the Second Augusta—the corps which had been lodged at Isca Silurum in older days, and had been responsible for the peace of South Wales—as also two regiments of horse and six of foot. The legion lay at Rutupiae (Richborough in Kent): the two cavalry regiments were both in Norfolk, one at Branodunum (Brancaster), the second at Gariannonum on the mouth of the Yare.

The other garrisons of the count were Othona in Essex, Reculver at the mouth of the Thames Estuary, Dover and Lymne on the Straits, Anderida (Pevensey) in Sussex, and Portus Adurni, which seems to be Portchester, hard by Portsmouth.

******

That Portus Adurni is not Arundel, and that the name Adur for the river there is an eighteenth century antiquarian invention, have been conclusively shown by Professor Haverfield. (*Proceedings of Soc, of Antiquaries*, 1892).

******

Evidently all this display of force was for the benefit of the Saxons, whose beat must have extended from the Wash to Southampton Water. They habitually ran down the Frisian coast as far as the mouths of the Rhine and Scheldt, and then turned to right or left. There was another *Littus Saxonicum* in Gaul, whose defence was independent of that of South-Eastern Britain.

The notable thing about the map of military Britain furnished by the Notitia is that no provision whatever seems to be made for Wales or the South-Western regions round the Severn mouth, unless indeed the *Comes Britanniarum* was in charge of the West. But no localities are given for the garrisoning of the very modest force—three regiments of foot and six of horse under that officer—and it seems more likely that his headquarters were at London, and that his duty was to support the Northern and Eastern garrisons in time of special danger. The legion once at Isca Silurum—Second Augusta—has (as we have already seen) shifted its garrison to Richborough in Kent. The legion once at Chester (Twentieth Valeria Victrix) has disappeared entirely from the imperial muster-roll.

★★★★★★

Mr. Hodgkin's ingenious hypothesis that the Twentieth Legion had been moved to Italy to reinforce Stilicho against the Goths, but had not yet arrived there, and so escaped mention in the Notitia altogether, is not convincing. It might have gone to the Continent with Magnus Maximus and have been destroyed in one of his defeats. Or the same fate might have befallen it when Eugenius and Arbogast fell. Or it might have been destroyed by the Scots anywhere between 368 and Stilicho's reorganisation.

★★★★★★

No auxiliary regiments are found south of Lancashire or west of Portsmouth. Yet we know that the Scots had been marauding all down the Western coast of Britain, and in 405 an Irish king is recorded to have perished in the British Channel. What had become of Wales and the West Country? Is it conceivable that the Roman Government had handed over the charge of it to its own inhabitants? It will be noted in the next century that these were precisely the parts of Britain which appear as organised kingdoms at the time of the Saxon settlement, and made the longest stand against the invaders. Or had the Scottish raids bitten so deep between 383 and 400 that the West was a wreck not worth protecting? The *Historia Brittonum*, a work of the seventh century, tells us that all North Wales was in the hands of the Scots shortly before the year 400, and till they were expelled by the British chief Cunedda.

In South Wales, too, immigrants from Ireland, perhaps the already-mentioned Desse, were in possession of Gower and Kidwelly. Did Stilicho give up the reorganisation of this ravaged land as hopeless?

Yet even such a hypothesis would not account for the want of troops in the region of Gloucester and Somersetshire, which had been one of the most prosperous and thickly-peopled parts of Roman Britain. It seems impossible that Stilicho should have placed 30,000 men on Hadrian's Wall and in Yorkshire, while leaving the Midlands wholly uncovered on the Western side, where the invasions had been many and dangerous during the last generation. It is difficult to come to any safe conclusion on the fragmentary evidence that lies before us: yet, if some hypothesis must be framed, it seems quite possible that the Dumnonii and the Demetae and the Silurians may have taken arms for themselves, with the aid and approval of the provincial government, and that Western Britain was already defending itself.

If we take the legend of Cunedda as genuine history, we gather from it that British tribal levies from the North, under British leaders, had saved North Wales from the Scots before 400 B.C., *i.e.*, ten years before the formal abandonment of Britain by the imperial government. For Cunedda's exploits are placed "146 years before the reign of King Mailcun," and that prince certainly died in 547, so that his "reign" falls about the period 530-47, and Cunedda's reconquest of Wales would be somewhere about 385-401.

******

Historia Brittonum, M. H. B., 75 and 56. The phrase is "*CXLVI annis ante quam Mailcun regnaret.*": so, we must date, not from his death in 547, but from his *floruit* some years earlier.

******

Cunedda can have been no barbarian, his father and grandfather bear ordinary Roman names, Aeternus and Paternus, though he himself is said to have come from "Gododin," the land of the Otadini, just north of the Wall. Is it conceivable that the Roman defence of Britain about the year 400 had as one of its essential factors the maintenance of the West by British chiefs, heading native bands which formed no part of the imperial army? Thus, at least, some sort of an explanation for the want of troops on the side of the Severn might be made out.

The fact that the local army of Britain was steadily growing more British, through the third and fourth centuries, sufficiently explains its bitter particularism and its chronic mutinies at the end of that period. There was no desire to "cut the painter" and break loose from the empire; the province and army gloried in the name of citizens and Romans. But there was evidently a strong feeling of local self-assertion, and a wish to kick against any authority which disregarded British

170

opinion or sacrificed British interests. Usurpers who promised *"felix temporum reparatio,"* the catchword of the century, were always certain of a following. Weak or unlucky emperors, who could be accused of neglecting the defence of the province, commanded no loyalty or respect.

The end of the Roman power in Britain took place amid a very debauch of disorder and military mutiny, all the more inexcusable because it broke out at a moment of acute danger to the empire, when all citizens and soldiers should have held together with redoubled loyalty. In 402-3 began the attack of Alaric and the Visigoths upon Italy, the first serious stroke of the barbarians at the heart of the empire. To meet it Stilicho was obliged to recall one of the two British legions, no doubt accompanied by a considerable body of auxiliaries. The corps recalled was probably the Sixth Victrix, as Claudian describes it as:

> That legion which is stretched before the remoter Britons, which curbs the Scot, and gazes on the tattoo-marks on the pale face of the dying Pict.
> (Claudian, *De Bello Gallico*. But it is not certain that *legio* in Claudian need mean a definite legion. He sometimes uses it for troops in general.)

This would not suit the Second Augusta, which lay in Kent, and had the Saxons as its special care.

Stilicho beat Alaric out of Italy (402-3) after winning the tremendous Battle of Pollentia. But no troops came back to Britain, for a second, but wholly distinct, barbarian invasion, that of Radagaisus supervened. It penetrated further into Italy than the Goths had done, yet was finally defeated, with the destruction of Radagaisus and all his host, in 405. But Stilicho was holding back a flood of many waves, and one was no sooner checked than another came swelling up at a fresh point. On January 1st, 406, a new host, composed of a confederacy of Suevi, Vandals, Alans and Burgundians, crossed the Middle Rhine, sweeping the frontier guard before them. They penetrated deep into Gaul, almost cutting the line of communication between Rome and Britain. (I am taking here the sequence of Chronology in Zosimus, vi. 3, not that of Prosper Tiro.)

This moment was chosen by the British Army as a suitable one for a fierce and prolonged mutiny—as if Stilicho had not done all that was humanly possible to save the empire. But he had done nothing of late for Britain, and this was evidently resented. In the autumn of 406 the troops in Britain saluted one Marcus as emperor. But he was murdered almost as soon as he had been exalted to the purple. The mutineers then elected a certain Gratianus, who is described as "*municeps ejusdem insulae*," and was therefore certainly a Briton, to rule over them. But he reigned only four months, and was then assassinated. The third head of the insurrection was a soldier named Constantine, also a Briton, of whom we are told that he was a person of low origin, and had nothing to recommend him save his name.

At any rate he was a little more capable than his predecessors, for he succeeded in keeping alive for more than three years after his election (407-11). If Constantine had confined his energies to reorganising the defence of Britain, and keeping the island secure against Pict and Scot, we might have understood and pardoned his conduct and that of his partisans. Instead of doing so, he exactly copied the policy of Magnus Maximus. He collected as much as could be spared of the provincial army, crossed to Boulogne, and appealed to the troops in Gaul to join his standard. This they did, as their predecessors had done in 383.

Great districts of Central Gaul were in the hands of the barbarians, but both the wrecks of the Rhine Army, and the troops as far as Aquitaine on the one side, and as Lyons and Vienne on the other, acknowledged him as emperor. He promised much, and he was at hand, while Stilicho was far away and was held responsible for the late disasters on the Rhine. Again, something might be said in defence of Constantine and his friends, if they had set themselves in a whole-hearted way to the expulsion of the Vandals and Burgundians from Gaul. Instead of taking this task in hand, Constantine sent his son Constans and part of his troops to attack Spain—which for a time they subdued—while he himself bickered on the Lower Rhone with the generals of Honorius.

The war between the British usurper and the legitimate emperor went on for three years, with many rapid changes of fortune: but in the end the cause of Constantine fell: his son was murdered by one of his own generals—Gerontius, another Briton,—who wished to try Caesar-making on his own account, and nominated an obscure person, one Maximus, as emperor in Spain. Constantine, after much fighting, was besieged and captured in the city of Arles; he was taken to Ravenna and executed (411). The remains of his army were never sent back to Britain, but went to form or to reinforce a Britannic element in Gaul. Before the death of the usurper, indeed, Britain had ceased to form part of the Roman Empire. The clearest account of what happened is that given by Zosimus:

Gerontius (the traitor in Spain) stirred up against Constantine the barbarians who were in Gaul (the Vandals, Burgundians, etc.). Constantine could make no head against them, because the greater part of his army was in Spain. And the barbarians from beyond the Rhine (evidently the Saxons) ravaging everything at their pleasure, put both the Britons and some of the Gauls to the necessity of making defection from the Roman Empire, and of setting up for themselves, no longer obeying Roman laws. The Britons taking up arms and fighting for their own hand, freed their communities from the barbarians who had set upon them. And the whole of Armorica and certain other provinces of Gaul imitated the Britons, and freed themselves at the same time, expelling the Roman officials and setting up a constitution such as they pleased. This defection of Britain and certain of the Gauls took place during the usurpation of Constantine, the barbarians having attacked them because of his neglect of the empire.

The date to be assigned to this last revolt of Britain is apparently 409-10, the third and fourth years of the usurpation of Constantine, since the great incursion of the Saxons in Britain is fixed to those years by Prosper Tiro, in his annalistic notes—

In the fifteenth year of Honorius and Arcadius (409), on account of the languishing state of the Romans the strength of Britain was brought to a desperate pass. In the sixteenth year of the same emperors (410) the Vandals and Alans wasted all that part of the Gauls which had already been ravaged by the Saxons. The usurper Constantine kept up a hold on what remained.

The Britons, though they had taken up arms for themselves, did not conceive that they had thereby given up all connection with the empire. Indeed, they could plead formal justification for their conduct, since Honorius, involved in war with Constantine, and at the same time seeing Italy overrun by Alaric and his Visigoths, "sent letters to the communities of Britain bidding them defend themselves" (410 A.D.). They had done no more; and if they expelled certain officials, as would seem to be implied from Zosimus's narrative, this by no means implied a complete repudiation of the imperial authority. Possibly some new obscure Caesar may have been invested with the purple, but we have no mention of the fact.

More probably the new government theoretically acknowledged

Honorius as emperor, and the sole outward sign of the event so often miscalled "the Departure of the Romans," was the expulsion of the vicar and *praesides* whom the usurper Constantine had nominated three years before. So far as there was any "departure" at all, it was that of Constantine and his field army in 407. No doubt he took with him the sole surviving legion (Second Augusta) the picked German *numeri*, and a certain number of the best of the other auxiliaries, who, whatever the names of their corps, must have been mainly Britons by birth.

But it is quite certain that he cannot have taken off the whole garrison of Britain. He had been nominated emperor by the local army because the Britons considered themselves neglected. If he had proposed to celebrate his accession by evacuating the whole island, he would undoubtedly have perished at once, like his ephemeral predecessors in revolt, Marcus and Gratian. He left behind him in 407 most undoubtedly both a civil administration and a garrison, which subsisted till 410, when the indignation of the provincials that their nominee had failed both to conquer the whole West and also to bring better times to Britain, caused them to abandon his cause, and establish a provisional government of their own.

All our misconception of the meaning of the events of 410 may be traced back in the end to the tirades of Gildas, who wrote merely from oral tradition, and 130 years after the events which he is describing. It is from him that we derive the unhappy idea that in the fourth century the "Britons" and the "Romans" were two distinct nations, the one subject to the other, and the wholly erroneous notion that the local army was alien and non-British. His account of the events between 383 and 410 is entirely unhistorical. Magnus Maximus, he says, took away every armed man from Britain in 383, and left the province "entirely ignorant of military usages" to the tender mercy of the Pict and Scot. The Britons sent *legates* to Rome to beg for an army, and promised to be more loyal to the empire if only they were succoured.

A legion was sent, which routed the barbarians out of the land, and then, for the defence of the province, bade the Britons erect a wall from sea to sea, which they did, making it of turf. The legion then returned with great triumph to Rome: whereupon the Picts and Scots reappeared in a worse temper than before. This induced the Britons to send a second embassy to the Romans: the latter "profoundly moved by the tragic history, flew swift as eagles to the rescue," and made a great slaughter of the barbarians. But they then declared that they could not be worried any longer by having to make such laborious expeditions, and that they should return home, leaving the islanders to defend themselves.

They bade the Britons accustom their hands to the use of spear, sword and shield, and as a final legacy to them, built a stone wall from sea to sea to replace the first wall of turf, and also erected a series of castles along the sea coast " and then they said goodbye, as never intending to return." There followed a third series of Pictish and Scottish inroads, against which the Britons made as ineffective a resistance as before; these continued till the third consulship of Aetius (or Agitius as Gildas calls him), *i.e.,* till the year 446, when a third appeal to Rome was made, but this time to no effect.

It is hardly necessary to criticise this rubbish. What attention need be paid to a writer who thinks that the Walls of Hadrian and Severus and the castles of the Saxon shore were all built sometime after the rebellion of Magnus Maximus in 385? The whole narrative is nonsense: there was a continuous garrison in Britain down to 410: the Britons formed a large portion of it, and were excellent troops. It is hopeless to endeavour to find a historical basis for the "first devastation" in the years between 383 and 388, or for the "second devastation" in the years between 392 and 395. The only thing proved by the whole narrative is that by 540, even learned men in Britain (Gildas passed as such, and was called "*Sapiens*" by admiring posterity) were ignorant of all the details of the provincial history of their own country.

CHAPTER 10

Christianity in Britain During the Roman Period

There is no doubt that individual Christians, perhaps even small communities of Christians, were to be found in Britain as early as the second century after Christ, though their proportion to the whole population of the province would seem to have been very small. Even in Gaul it was not large in the age of the Antonines, and only the partly-Greek towns of the Rhone Valley contributed martyrs, nearly all with Greek names, to the roll of the victims of M. Aurelius's persecution. Among the many hundreds of religious monuments, civil and military, strewn about Britain from the second to the early fourth century, all are purely pagan.

Yet there is no reason to doubt the statements of Tertullian—writing in about 208 *A.D.*—or Origen—writing in about 230 *A.D.*—that the Christian religion had an appreciable number of converts in the remote province of the extreme north-west, although many of its wilder regions may not yet have heard the Gospel preached. The legend of King Lucius and the missionary Fagan is a blunder of the sixth century, caused originally by a confusion between the local names Britannia and Britium: for the letter of Lucius to Pope Eleutherus seems genuine, but the king ruled in Edessa, not in Britain, and Birtha (Britium) was his citadel.

******

This seems to have been clearly proved by Dr. Harnack. The earliest trace of the Lucius-letter in connection with Britain, is in the original form (drawn up about 530 *A.D.*) of the *Liber Pontificalis*, in which a sentence about Eleutherus and the letter appears. The first British mention is in Nennius.

******

It is hardly necessary to allude to the later and wilder legend, which made "Bran the Blessed," the father of Caratacus, a Christian convert long before the first century of our era had run out. This was a pious imagining of some patriotic Celt of the later Dark Ages.

It is clear that Gaul as a whole was hardly permeated by Christianity till the beginning of the third century, and that Britain was far behind Gaul. But in the long peace for the Christian community which followed the persecution of Severus and lasted practically unbroken till that of Decius and Valerian—a period of forty years—the new religion pushed northward and westward with greater power. There seems no reason to doubt the existence of the small number of British martyrs whose names appear in the earliest martyrologies, all the more so because these documents are purely continental in character, and show none of the vast array of Celtic saints whose dates belong to the time after 409, when connection between this island and the surviving Roman dominions on the continent ceased.

The very early martyrology which is wrongly known by the name of St. Jerome, but which was apparently constructed on a fifth century foundation, (its latest possible date seems to be 630, but the bulk seems to be sixth century notes on fifth century foundations), gives precisely three names which are drawn from Britain—besides one or two more wrongly ascribed to Britain, such as Faustinus and Juventia (really of Brixia), Timotheus (really a Mauretanian), and Socrates and Stephanus—the latest is that of Saint Patrick (*obiit circ.* 461) the other two are given as martyrs of the old pre-Christian time. (They are Augulus, Bishop of Augusta (London) and Alban, the saint who was long after to give his name to Verulamium, the place where he suffered.

It is strange that we know nothing of Augulus, whose name is repeated in many later martyrologies, but the fact that his see is called Augusta shows that the name was taken down somewhere between 340 and 410, for London was officially styled Londinium down to the later part of Constantine's reign, (as is proved by his large coinage at the London mint, all signed P. Lon, The only coins giving P. Avg are those of Magnus Maximus and Theodosius), and was only known as Augusta in the second half of the fourth century—perhaps the honorary title was bestowed by Constans during his visit to Britain in 343. When the city next emerges from the darkness that follows the year 410 it is London once more. The legend of Augulus and his martyrdom is one of the many things that perished in the Saxon invasion.

Of Alban's existence our knowledge is decidedly more certain, since Saint German us is recorded to have visited and honoured his grave in 429, (the visit is recorded in Constantius's *Life of Germanus,* a work written apparently within thirty years of Germanus's death); his cult, therefore, was well established at Verulamium in the early fifth century, when men were still alive who might have spoken with those who remembered the Diocletian persecution. It hardly needs the evidence of Gildas, (*Hist.*, § viii.), writing in the middle of the sixth century, to establish his name and fame. Unfortunately, the details of his life, how he served as a soldier, contrived the escape of a Christian missionary, converted one of his guards, and dried up a stream on his way to execution, are late additions to the mere fact of his martyrdom, to which no attention can be paid.

★★★★★★

This Amphibalus, whom Alban is said to have set free, is believed by many to be a stupid invention by a scribe who took "*dimisso amphibalo*" to mean "having sent off Amphibalus" instead of "having laid down his cloak".

★★★★★★

But there must have been something special and striking in his fate to account for the fact that he was honoured above all Romano-British saints in the early fifth century. Julius and Aaron of Caerleon do not appear in the earlier martyrologies, and, if they are found in later ones, probably owe their place to Gildas, who records their fate in a few words. If the *Book of Llandaff* can be trusted for its own day, we might believe that there was an estate near Caerleon which served as an endowment for a church dedicated to them. But this *territorium Julii et Aaronis* may conceivably be an invention of a ninth century forger,

177

bent on proving ancient ecclesiastical property to have existed, where land was in dispute in his own generation. There are many doubtful passages in the compilation.

✶✶✶✶✶✶

Statements in the *Anglo-Saxon Chronicle* and elsewhere, which put the British martyrdoms down to the year 286 *A.D.* are erroneous; this is merely the first year of Diocletian. The persecution did not begin till 303, and from 287 to 293 Britain, under Carausius and Allectus, was not under Diocletian's control.

✶✶✶✶✶✶

An attempt has been made to discredit the tradition of these martyrs, one and all, on the ground that Constantius Chlorus, into whose section of the empire Britain fell, along with Gaul and Spain, is declared by Eusebius (*Hist. Eccl., VIII. xiii. §12*), to have shrunk from carrying out the persecution ordered by Diocletian. Lactantius, too, definitely states that the Caesar only so far complied with the orders given by his seniors as to order the destruction of churches, while declining to authorise bloodshed. (*De Mortibus Persecutorum.*)

But we have definite proof that the proconsul Dacianus, who ruled in Spain under Constantius's authority, sought out and put to death many Christians, whether his immediate superior approved or no. If this was so, the same may have been the case in Britain, and the only effect of the tolerant mildness of Constantius may have been that the victims were few instead of many—as indeed we should judge to have been the case from the shortness of the list of names preserved.

It must be remembered also that Diocletian's edict was only issued in February, 303, and that persecution in the West ceased with his abdication in 305. (Cf. Stubbs and Haddan, *Councils*, vol. i.) The statement in the pseudo-Hieronymian Martyrology and many other later documents of the same kind, that Alban was only one of 890 British martyrs—the rest, save Augulus, being anonymous—may be disregarded.

Whatever was the strength of the British Church in the time of Diocletian, we find it as a well organised and rapidly growing body in the early years of Constantine the Great. As early as 314 three bishops from Britain appeared at the Council of Arles and signed its decrees—Eborius of York, Restitutus of London, and Adelphius, probably of Lincoln.

✶✶✶✶✶✶

He appears as "*Episcopus de civitate Colonia Londinensium*" in the list in the Corbie Codex, as "*ex civitate Colonia*" in the Toulouse Codex. Colonia by itself would probably mean Colchester; but

178

Londinensium looks like an error for Lindumensium. But it *might* stand for Legionensium (Caerleon), or be merely a careless repetition.

✶✶✶✶✶✶

The West was scantily represented at Nicaea (325), and certainly no British prelates were present at that greatest of Councils. But we are distinctly informed that Britain, along with Spain and Gaul, accepted its decisions respecting the condemnation of Arianism and the celebration of Easter. The same would seem to have been the case with regard to the Council of Sardica (343): though not represented there, the insular Church hastened to accept the decision which acquitted Athanasius, and the saint gratefully records the fact. (*Hist. Arian., op., i.*) Sixteen years later, however, at least three British bishops were counted among the four hundred fathers who sat at the Council of Ariminum, which was burned by Constantius into decisions of doubtful orthodoxy. The way in which they are mentioned shows that some at least of their Sees were very poor. Sulpicius Severus says:

> Three bishops alone, all Britons, had no private means, and drew an allowance from the public funds, refusing to live on a collection made for them by their colleagues; for they thought it more proper to draw on the exchequer rather than on the charity of individuals. I have heard Bishop Gavidius making invidious reference to this choice of theirs; but I differ from him, and think it was creditable to those bishops to be so poor that they had no private means. (*Hist. Sac.*, ii.)

There may, of course, have been many more bishops from Britain at Ariminum besides these three indigent persons. But internal evidence would lead us to conjecture that the whole British Church was probably very poor in the middle of the fourth century. There seems every reason to believe that the main bulk of the population in this remote province of the West remained pagan till a much later date than was the case elsewhere. Nothing else can explain the total lack of large churches and fine sepulchral monuments which we find in Britain; there is nothing on this side of the Channel to compare with the magnificent Christian *sarcophagi* which stand in rows in the Museum of Arles, or with the fourth century basilicas that are to be found all around the Mediterranean.

The few churches whose ruins have survived from Roman Britain are all small and plain. If the Christians of Calleva found the diminu-

179

tive church lately discovered there sufficient for their needs, they must have been but a few hundreds in a population that would seem to have numbered perhaps 2,000 souls.

In that same town a temple of Mars, (some odd local British form of the god, as the broken attributes are abnormal), was found, which must have been used down to the end of the existence of the place, for the remains of the god's statue and of a dedicatory inscription were found beneath the fragments of the roof, if Calleva had become completely Christian before the days of its evacuation, the image of Mars would not have been left on his pedestal to meet the incoming Saxon.

It is, of course, quite possible that the greater towns, such as York, London or Colchester, had more splendid buildings, but no trace of them has been discovered. (That ruins of Roman churches, capable of restoration, existed above the surface in the end of the sixth century is shown by Bede, i. 26.) The small number of Christian sepulchral inscriptions is equally notable, though such have been found at Carlisle and Lincoln and elsewhere. It is very strange that a religion which was first publicly tolerated and later encouraged by the government for nearly a hundred years before the fatal year 410 *A.D.* should have left so few records in stone behind it. It may perhaps be suggested that Christianity, as elsewhere in the empire, was strongest in the great towns during the fourth century, and that the sites of the great towns remain the most unexplored portion of Roman Britain, because they are still covered with buildings which it is impossible to remove in a systematic way for regular exploration.

The places which have been well excavated, such as Calleva, Viroconium, Venta Silurum, or Corstopitum, were small towns which perished entirely, or where the modern representative of the old Roman town was so small that it never covered any large portion of the old area, or even grew up outside it. In such localities the churches might either be small stone structures, since nothing larger was wanted, or even wooden edifices, of which no trace would remain.

A hint as to the prevalence of wood is given by Bede's mention of St. Ninian, the apostle of Galloway, which states that the saint (*circiter* 400-410) attracted some notice by building his church "*de lapide, insolito Brittonibus more,*" but Bede lived far too long after the break-up of the Roman Empire to enable us to draw a sure inference as to what methods of building were common in Britain when Honorius reigned. His words can only be taken as clear evidence that the Celts of his own century seldom or never reared stone churches.

The existence of a vigorous British Christendom in the fourth century is sufficiently proved by literary evidence which it would be absurd to attempt to minimise. But without that literary evidence we should have gathered little information about it from archaeological research. It must be borne in mind that secular inscriptions and secular buildings of fourth century date are singularly rare in Britain, no less than ecclesiastical ones. Probably the hand of the invader at the moment, and of the thrifty stone-appropriator in the Middle Ages, fell heaviest upon the most recent buildings of Roman Britain, simply because they were upon the surface, while the remains of the third and second centuries were to a great extent buried beneath them, and so escaped notice and destruction. But even this fact does not wholly account for the extraordinary lack of fourth century archaeological material.

Probably the most interesting inscribed relic of the days when Britain was ceasing to be pagan and becoming Christian, is the little pedestal of a statue of Jupiter at Cirencester, on which Septimius the *Praeses* of Britannia Prima proclaims in execrable verse that he has renewed and replaced the column and image of the God, which had been reared by the piety of the ancients.

★★★★★★

As Britannia Prima was a creation of Diocletian, who only got possession of Britain in 297, the inscription must be fourth century. And it must belong either to its very earliest years or to Julian's time. The character favours the later date.

★★★★★★

This must surely date from the reign of Julian, the only period in the century, after Constantine had turned away from the old faith, when a governor could have dared to make his boast of restoring a pagan monument. It is unfortunately quite unique in character. Roman governors of the fourth century seem to have been as chary of erecting or inscribing anything as their predecessors of the second century were lavish in so doing.

It has been observed, somewhat cynically, that schisms and heresies are proofs rather of the vigour than of the weakness of a Church, and that nothing bears greater testimony to a dearth of true spiritual life than a dead level of orthodoxy. The British Church clearly did not fall under this condemnation, since it produced in the very last days of the Romans a heresiarch, whose teaching not only proved powerful in his own lifetime but maintained its influences for many generations after his death. This was the celebrated Pelagius, a British monk who is first heard of in the pontificate of Anastasius (398-402), and whose personal activity falls into the first quarter of the fifth century. He was presumably, therefore, born somewhere about 370 or 380 in the time of Valens and Gratian. He taught not in his native country, but in Rome itself, his special doctrine that "original sin" is a vain invention.

It is not naturally engendered in every man of Adam's race by reason of his descent from a guilty progenitor. On the contrary, sin is a personal and not an inherited failing: men do evil and become hateful to God by their own individual fault: they "follow Adam" it is true, but of choice, not of necessity. This doctrine shocked the fathers of the fifth century mainly for two reasons. Firstly, it seemed to imply that Christ did not necessarily live and die to redeem all men: for if original sin was not universal in the human race, there may have been individuals who had no need of redemption. Secondly—and here the objection became more practical—if man is not necessarily sinful, and is capable of perfection through his own virtue, there is a danger that all self-righteous and overweening persons may claim to be impeccable.

And from this state of mind to mere antinomianism there is but a step, for saints of this description, in all ages, have been found to abuse their supposed sinlessness in the most scandalous fashion. This was not, however, the case with Pelagius himself, who is recorded to have been a monk, a man of austere life, and one who shunned controversy so far as it was possible for an innovator in doctrine to do so. He did not himself see that the assertion of Free Will was incompatible with a belief in the Atonement. But his opponents grasped the fact, and were never tired of urging it.

The rival doctrine, which St. Augustine taught in an extreme form a few years later, to the effect that man is congenitally sinful, and that God's grace alone, not any deliberate choice of his own, can secure him salvation, did not commend itself to everyone. Pelagius gained many followers, and his views spread all over the West: these were specially welcomed in Britain, where they were introduced by one Agricola the son of a Pelagian bishop named Severianus. (Prosper of Aquitaine, op., i.) The earliest recorded works written by Britons are those of the heresiarch himself, and of a British bishop—his See is unknown—named Fastidius, who is said to have been at least a semi-Pelagian. The tracts of the latter, which are mentioned by St. Jerome, have been preserved. So have fragments of Pelagius's own Commentary on the Epistles of St. Paul, the oldest book known to have been written by a Briton. (See Dr. Souter in *Proceedings of the British Acad-*

emy, 1906.)

Yet if the Christian Church of Britain was vigorous enough to make new sallies in *dogma*, and to indulge in controversies that lasted for several generations, it is at the same time almost certain that it had not yet succeeded in converting the heathen of the rural parts of the province, who may still have formed the larger half of its population at the moment when the Roman domination ceased.

We find that when in 429 *A.D.* the Gallic bishops Germanus and Lupus crossed to the now independent Britain, to confute the disciples of Pelagius, they had to baptise converts by the thousand. There is no reason to suppose that the *catechumens* were merely heretics asking for a second baptism. (To baptise such would have been contrary to the custom of the time.) It seems more likely that the same phenomenon was seen in Britain as on the Continent, that the turmoil of the barbarian invasions gave the death-blow to lingering paganism.

When the Roman State fell, the Christian Church was the only living power left in the West, and seems to have completed, in those years of chaos and misery that make up the fifth century, the conversion of the heathen remnant. Christianity was a better religion for those who had to suffer and endure than moribund polytheism. And the Church supplied the sole organisation round which the Romanised provincials could rally, when the State had been destroyed. Who could have faced the incoming Frank or Saxon with inspiration drawn from the worn-out faith of Mars and Jupiter?